D0072454

The Spur of Fame

John Adams

Benjamin Rush

THE SPUR
OF FAME

Dialogues of
John Adams and
Benjamin Rush,
1805–1813

Edited by John A. Schutz
and Douglass Adair

LIBERTY FUND
Indianapolis

This book is published by Liberty Fund, Inc., a foundation established
to encourage study of the ideal of a society of free and responsible individuals.

⌈✳⌉ ⵋⵊ ⵌⵌⵌ

The cuneiform inscription that serves as our logo and as the design motif for our
endpapers is the earliest-known written appearance of the word "freedom"
(*amagi*), or "liberty." It is taken from a clay document written about 2300 B.C.
in the Sumerian city-state of Lagash.

© 1966 by The Henry E. Huntington Library and Art Gallery. All rights reserved.
Frontispieces from the National Park Service
Printed in the United States of America

05 04 03 02 01 C 5 4 3 2 1
05 04 03 02 01 P 5 4 3 2 1

Library of Congress Cataloging-in-Publication Data
Adams, John, 1735–1826.
The spur of fame: dialogues of John Adams and Benjamin Rush,
1805–1813 / edited by John A. Schutz and Douglass Adair.
p. cm.
Originally published: San Marino, Calif.: Huntington Library, 1966.
Includes index.
ISBN 0-86597-286-9 (hc.: alk. paper)—ISBN 0-86597-287-7 (pb.: alk. paper)
1. United States—Politics and government—1775–1783. 2. United States—
Politics and government—1783–1809. 3. United States—Politics and
government—1809–1817. 4. Fame—Political aspects—United States—
History—18th century. 5. Fame—Political aspects—United States—
History—19th century. 6. Statesmen—United States—History—18th
century. 7. Statesmen—United States—History—19th century. 8. Adams,
John, 1735–1826—Correspondence. 9. Rush, Benjamin, 1746–1813—
Correspondence. I. Rush, Benjamin, 1746–1813. II. Schutz, John A., 1919–
III. Adair, Douglass. IV. Title.
E302.1 .A27 2001
973.3—dc21   99-046817

LIBERTY FUND, INC.,
8335 Allison Pointe Trail, Suite 300
Indianapolis, Indiana 46250-1684

Library Services
Austin Community College
Austin, Texas

CONTENTS

ILLUSTRATIONS

(Following page 144)

"The Temple of Liberty"

"Benjamin Rush"

"John Adams"

"To the Genius of Franklin"

"L'Amérique Indépendante"

"The Apotheosis of Washington"

"Commemoration of Washington"

"Mirabeau Arrive aux Champs Élisées"

ACKNOWLEDGMENTS

WHEN JOHN ADAMS opened his famous correspondence with Benjamin Rush in 1805, he set a leisurely pattern of dialogue that allowed both men to ramble. Though the principal topic of their correspondence was fame, their treatment by posterity, they interwove into the fabric of their discussion local politics and personal problems, with much repetition of observation. The editors of this book in preparing the correspondence realized that a publication of all the letters or a full text of some letters would have required several volumes and obscured the purpose of the letters. They have therefore eliminated some materials on politics, family, and incidental subjects not pertinent to the central theme of the correspondence.

Though this is the first time these letters have been published together in dialogue, all of them are available in print. Alexander Biddle printed the Adams papers in 1892 as *Old Family Letters,* Series A. His was a limited, almost a private, printing that makes the book a rare item, but it is available in most research libraries. Since the editing was not always perfect, the editors of the present volume have consulted the original Adams letters whenever possible. When the Biddle estate was auctioned, the Adams letters were scattered. Some are missing except for the printed copy in the *Old Family Letters* or photostats in the Library of Congress. Others are available only in letter-book copies of the Adams Manuscript Trust, Boston, which has granted us permission to quote continuous passages of 250 words. The Rush letters are taken from the *Letters of Benjamin Rush,* edited by Lyman H. Butterfield, and can be easily located in those two volumes. We appreciate the assistance of the American Philosophical Society, which gave us permission to quote from the *Letters,* and also the help of Mr. Butterfield, who has advised us on many important matters. In addition, we wish to thank the librarians of the following depositories who have permitted us to quote from their manuscripts: the Boston Public Library, the Lilly Library at Indiana University, the Historical Society of Pennsylvania, Princeton University, the Morristown National Historical Park, the Musée de Blerancourt, the Yale University Library, and the United States Naval Academy. We wish also to thank the librarians of the Library of Congress for their help in locating Adams manuscripts.

The editors have generally followed the standards of publication that were set by Mr. Butterfield in his preparation of the Rush letters. We agree with him that these letters were primarily intended to be read for the exchange of ideas and that eighteenth-century punctuation and spelling should give way to more modern usage. Where Adams and Rush have underlined for emphasis or purposely capitalized (or not capitalized) words, we have retained the original construction. For easier reading we have occasionally created new paragraphs; dates of the letters have been standardized. Where letters duplicate each other or do not materially contribute to the dialogue, we have omitted them.

The editors wish to thank the many scholars and friends who have helped them in this project. They appreciate the assistance of Gordon Marshall of Whittier College (now of Clark College), who worked with them in checking the sources, and that of Donn Nibblett and Neville Grow of Clark College. The editors are indebted to Professors George Mayhew of the California Institute of Technology, Albert H. Travis of the University of California, Los Angeles, French Fogle of the Claremont Graduate School, Wilbur Jacobs of the University of California, Santa Barbara, and Gilbert McEwen of Whittier College, who frequently advised them on literary problems. They are also indebted to Allan Nevins and Ray Billington of the research staff of the Huntington Library for help and to the Board of Trustees of the Library for making the publication of this book possible. The editors express their special appreciation to Director John E. Pomfret of the Huntington Library for his understanding and encouragement, and to the editorial staff of the publications department for their sympathetic regard for accuracy, particularly to Nancy C. English and Anne W. Kimber. To John M. Steadman, also, we are most thankful for editorial suggestions. We wish finally to express our appreciation to our colleges for the research assistance that was made available to us.

JOHN A. SCHUTZ
DOUGLASS ADAIR

July 4, 1965

LOCATION OF THE LETTERS

RUSH LETTERS:

Letters of Benjamin Rush, ed. Lyman H. Butterfield. 2 vols. Princeton, 1951. All Rush letters were taken from these volumes, though some originals were also examined. Cited in the text as *Letters.*

ADAMS LETTERS:

AMT   Adams Manuscript Trust, Boston
AW   Adams, *The Works of John Adams,* ed. Charles Francis Adams. 10 vols. Boston, 1850–56. Cited in the text as *Works.*
BPL   Boston Public Library
HSP   Historical Society of Pennsylvania
LC   Library of Congress
LCp   Library of Congress photostats. The Library of Congress was given photostatic copies of a few Adams letters. Some of the originals are now missing or in the hands of private collectors who prefer to remain anonymous. Though these photostats could not be reproduced, they were consulted when preparing letter-book or printed copies.
LL   Lilly Library, Indiana University
MHP   Morristown National Historical Park
MB   Musée de Blerancourt
OFL   *Old Family Letters,* Ser. A, ed. Alexander Biddle. Philadelphia, 1892. Cited in the text as *Old Family Letters.*
PU   Princeton University Library
USN   United States Naval Academy
YL   Yale University Library

October 12, 1755, AW
February 6, 1805, AMT
February 27, 1805, BPL
April 11, 1805, BPL
July 7, 1805, AMT, LCp
August 23, 1805, AMT, LCp

September 30, 1805, BPL
December 4, 1805, AMT, LCp
January 25, 1806, AMT
March 26, 1806, YL
June 22, 1806, AMT
July 23, 1806, HSP

September 19, 1806, YL
November 11, 1806, AMT
December 22, 1806, YL
February 2, 1807, BPL
April 12, 1807, AMT
May 1, 1807, AW, OFL
May 21, 1807, AW, LCp
May 23, 1807, AW
September 1, 1807, AMT
September, 1807, AMT, LCp
November 11, 1807, AMT, LCp
December 28, 1807, AMT
February 25, 1808, BPL
April 18, 1808, AMT, LCp
June 20, 1808, BPL
July 25, 1808, AMT, LCp
August 31, 1808, PU
September 27, 1808, BPL
October 10–December 19, 1808, OFL, LCp
December 22, 1808, OFL
January 23, 1809, PU
March 4, 1809, AMT
March 14, 1809, HSP
March 23, 1809, YL
April 12, 1809, AW, LCp
June 7, 1809, OFL
August 7, 1809, HSP
August 31, 1809, OFL
September 1, 1809, OFL
September 27, 1809, OFL
October 8, 1809, MB
October 25, 1809, YL
January 21, 1810, AW
February 11–23, 1810, OFL
May 14, 1810, OFL
September 16, 1810, YL
October 13–15, 1810, OFL, LCp
December 27, 1810 (1), BPL
December 27, 1810 (2), BPL
January 18, 1811, PU

February 13, 1811, YL
June 21, 1811, AMT
July 31, 1811, AMT
August 14, 1811, YL
August 25, 1811, YL
August 28, 1811, YL
December 4, 1811, YL
December 19, 1811, YL
December 25, 1811, AW
January 8, 1812, AMT, LCp
January 15, 1812 [13], YL
March 19, 1812, BPL
April 22, 1812, BPL
May 14, 1812 (1), AMT
May 14, 1812 (2), BPL
May 26, 1812, AMT
June 12, 1812, AMT
July 3, 1812, BPL
July 7, 1812, AMT
July 10, 1812, PU
July 19, 1812, BPL
August 1, 1812, BPL
August 17, 1812, YU
September 4, 1812, LL
September 6, 1812, USN
September 18, 1812, OFL, LCp
November 14, 1812, LC
November 29, 1812, YL
December 8, 1812, AMT
December 27, 1812, USN
December 29–30, 1812, AMT
January 4, 1813, BPL
January 29, 1813, AMT
February 21, 1813, BPL
February 23, 1813, LL
March 23, 1813, LL
April 18, 1813, AMT
April 24, 1813, AMT
April 28, 1813, AMT
September 20, 1816, MHP

The Spur of Fame

CHAPTER I

The Love of Fame, the Ruling Passion of the Noblest Minds

THE EFFORTS of Dr. Benjamin Rush to heal the breach between John Adams and Thomas Jefferson that developed in 1800 during their contest for the presidency stimulated Jefferson to record a most significant and dramatic confrontation in American history. The place: Jefferson's lodgings in Philadelphia; the time: Monday evening, April 11, 1791; the dramatis personae: John Adams, Vice-President of the United States; Alexander Hamilton, Secretary of the Treasury; and Thomas Jefferson himself, Secretary of State. The occasion for the meeting, as Jefferson recalled twenty years after the event, was a minor diplomatic crisis which required action during President Washington's absence from the seat of government. The President had left instructions that in case of any emergency the heads of departments concerned should meet with the Vice-President and settle the matter.[1]

Jefferson's words vividly recreate the scene for us—the only occasion of record when Adams, Hamilton, and Jefferson, not yet the bitter rivals competing to be Washington's successor, talked politics together. "I invited them to dine with me," Jefferson told Rush, "and after dinner, sitting at our wine, having settled our question, other conversation came on, in which a collision of opinion arose between Mr. Adams and Colonel Hamilton, on

---

1. See Washington's memorandum to his Cabinet, Apr. 4, 1791, in *The Writings of George Washington,* ed. John C. Fitzpatrick (Washington, D.C., 1931–44), XXXI, 272–273. See also Jefferson's letter to the President, Apr. 17, 1791, in *The Writings of Thomas Jefferson,* ed. Paul Leicester Ford (New York, 1892–99), V, 320–322.

the merits of the British constitution, Mr. Adams giving it as his opinion, that, if some of its defects and abuses were corrected, it would be the most perfect constitution of government ever devised by man. Hamilton, on the contrary, asserted, that with its existing vices, it was the most perfect model of government that could be formed." [2]

To Jefferson, who had returned from France in 1790 somewhat obsessively antimonarchical, and antiaristocratical, this praise of the British constitution from his colleagues smacked of heresy. Already in 1791 he was emphasizing privately the line of difference between his republicanism and Adams' apostasy from the principles of 1776.[3] His reporting to Rush this twenty-year-old anecdote was to reemphasize how different his opinions were from those of his great New England rival. But an even greater sin than admiration of the British constitution marked Hamilton in Jefferson's view. "Another incident took place on the same occasion," he continued to Rush, "which will further delineate Mr. Hamilton's political principles. The room being hung around with a collection of the portraits of remarkable men, among them were those of Bacon, Newton, and Locke, Hamilton asked me who they were. I told him they were my trinity of the three greatest men the world had ever produced, naming them. He [Hamilton] paused for some time: 'the greatest man,' said he, 'that ever lived, was Julius Caesar.'" [4] For Rush in 1811, when the figure dominating world politics was an ex-republican general named Bonaparte who had emulated Caesar in making himself Emperor of France and then had waded through blood to conquer half of Europe, the very name Caesar carried all of the sinister implications that Jefferson intended.

2. Jefferson to Rush, Jan. 16, 1811, *The Writings of Thomas Jefferson,* IX, 295.

3. See Jefferson to George Mason, Feb. 4, 1791, ibid., V, 274–276, expressing fear that the American Constitution would fall "back to that kind of Half-way house, the English constitution . . . we have among us a sect who believe that to contain whatever is perfect in human institutions; . . . the great mass of our community is untainted with these heresies, as is [Washington]." Compare, too, Jefferson's labored explanation (ibid., V, 328–329) to Washington of how an indiscreet letter of his, attacking Adams' Anglomania and apostasy to hereditary monarchy and nobility, got printed as an introduction to the first American edition of Thomas Paine's *Rights of Man.* Jefferson sponsored the printing of Paine's pamphlet as an antidote to Adams' newspaper essays entitled "Discourses on Davila."

4. Jefferson to Rush, Jan. 16, 1811, ibid., IX, 295–296.

We can be grateful to Jefferson for remembering so accurately this dramatic double dialogue and for reporting it to us so vividly; we can understand his eagerness to insist that as a statesman he was different both from the misguided "monarchist" John Adams and the dangerous would-be "Caesar," Alexander Hamilton. This insistence by Jefferson that Adams and Hamilton and their Federalist Party were linked in a conspiracy to subvert the Constitution was a justification for his successful bid for the presidency; their noxious opinions explained (so he believed) why he from the purest motives, without the least trace of personal and selfish ambition, was literally forced to seek political power. We can see that the very dialogue Jefferson recorded, thinking to underline the differences that set him apart from Adams and Hamilton, points rather to their likeness—points to a common and shared value that makes these three eighteenth-century revolutionaries blood brothers.

Ironically it is Sir Francis Bacon, the first named on Jefferson's list of the world's greatest men, who reveals the secret passion linking the Virginian to Hamilton and Adams. Bacon, in an essay entitled "Of Honour and Reputation," codified for his contemporaries a series of graded evaluations of fame and honor that he—and the Americans of 1776—believed would guarantee immortality to those men who could win it. He set down the neoclassic categories of fame in a five-level pyramid, at the top of which was the "*conditores imperiorum,* founders of states and commonwealths," naming such men as Romulus, Cyrus, Ottoman, Ishmael, and, most significantly, Julius Caesar. In second place on the scale of fame were the "*legislatores*" like Lycurgus, Solon, and Justinian, men who gave constitutions and principles to the commonwealth.[5]

Hamilton's remark, then, in the spring of 1791, that he considered Caesar the greatest of men did not carry the undertones that Jefferson would impute to the statement twenty years later. In 1791 the French Revolution was still in its honeymoon stage; Napoleon had not made his bloody march toward world empire; and the Atlantic community was still living in peace. Even Rush, who shuddered appropriately in 1811 at Jefferson's anecdote, had

5. *The Works of Francis Bacon,* ed. James Spedding et al. (London, 1857–74), VI, 505–506.

written that Caesar's deeds were "perhaps . . . unrivaled in the history of mankind."[6]

Jefferson's choice of greatest men reveals his own secret passion for fame. Again, Bacon explains the context. In his more famous essay, the *Advancement of Learning,* Bacon revises his categories of supreme honor, arguing that those scientists, philosophers, and inventors who employed the divine gift of reason to the use and benefit of mankind merited veneration as gods. In Bacon's view honor was the attribute of a great or disinterested man; fame or sovereign honor was an attribute of human immortality, which on the very highest level partook of the glory of divinity itself. This spur, which goaded the Americans of 1776 to action, was identified by Hamilton himself in Number 72 of *The Federalist Papers* as "the love of fame, the ruling passion of the noblest minds."

A particularly revealing and significant entry in his diary indicates that as John Adams pondered fame, fortune, and power and how best he could utilize his talents and opportunities to capture immortality for himself, these lines from Alexander Pope's "Essay on Man" came to his mind:

> Self-love but serves the virtuous mind to wake,
> As the small pebble stirs the peaceful lake;
> The centre mov'd, a circle straight succeeds,
> Another still, and still another spreads;
> Friend, parent, neighbour, first it will embrace;
> His country next; and next all human race.[7]

John Adams threw his pebbles into the lake, and the circles formed. Years later, between 1805 and 1813, he and Benjamin Rush, who also had been making circles, worried about the enduring character of their life's work. Sometimes bitter, disillusioned, and angry over what fate seemed to have given them, they watched posterity elevate some men into places of honor which they thought were rightfully theirs. Thefts of fame by Revolutionary heroes, aided by historians and "puffers," were plainly immoral and bestial. How could Virginians honor only Virginians, historians attribute all virtue

6. Rush to Jeremy Belknap, Apr. 5, 1791, *Letters,* I, 579.

7. Pope's lines (363–368 of Epistle IV) are quoted in prose form in the *Diary and Autobiography of John Adams,* ed. Lyman H. Butterfield et al. (Cambridge, Mass., 1961), I, 337.

and wisdom to Washington, Democrats credit Jefferson with declaring independence and saving the democracy and Tom Paine with starting the Revolution? Still more lamentable, posterity, ignorant of the "facts," was turning Washington and Franklin into gods. Artists were designing classical busts and shrines for them and wreathing them with olive branches, and the mythmakers were transforming the Revolutionary era into a saga of their great deeds. The next step, Adams opined, would be prayers to them: "Sancte Washington, ora pro nobis," etc.

For Adams and Rush this process of hero worship was setting off countercircles, sometimes creating whitecaps, and their own impressions in the nation's lake were unclear. Both men had labored too long and accomplished too much to let posterity go on uninstructed and ignorant: posterity must do them justice. With this impulse Adams wrote his friend Rush in 1805, renewing a thirty-year acquaintance that had grown cold by distance and differences of opinion and suggesting a regular correspondence. Their letters were to be written in the classical fashion with the great Cicero primarily in mind, whose letters they believed to be the most revealing documents of Roman history. They began their correspondence by advising each other repeatedly to burn their letters, but knowing full well that these letters must be saved so that posterity could have a "truthful" account of the nation's origin.

From 1805 to 1813, when Rush died unexpectedly, the men corresponded almost monthly. Their salty comments, sometimes too bold to be shared even with their families, were frequently raw, indiscreet, and personal, but they were trying to set the record right in their own minds. In 1816 when Richard Rush asked John Adams to let the Rush family read the correspondence, Adams assembled the letters, reread them, and then gave Richard his estimate of their importance to him: "There are naked Truths and, I am sure, nothing but the Truths, which were never communicated to your mother, yourself, your brothers or sisters, but which are so directly and so truly contradictory to all our histories and traditions that I dare not part with [the letters] without the most explicit request of your mother and yourself. . . . Dr. Rush's letters are of inestimable value to me."[8]

8. Adams to Richard Rush, Sept. 20, 1816, Morristown National Historical Park MS.

Adams and Rush first met in 1774 when Rush and other Pennsylvania "patriots" traveled out of Philadelphia to salute the arrival of the Massachusetts delegation to the Continental Congress and to escort it into the city. During the coach ride into Philadelphia, Rush spoke with John and Samuel Adams and noted that John was absorbed with problems of politics and seemed "cold and reserved."[9] First impressions changed, however, as he came to know Adams better; the New Englander's reserve also lessened as surroundings became familiar. Adams' forceful expressions, his poignant humor and satire, and his wide knowledge of ancient and modern literature drew feelings of friendship from Rush.

When they met in the country town of Frankford, the Pennsylvanian was one distinguished figure in a crowd of distinguished men and was not especially noticed by Adams. Even their conversation during the coach ride into Philadelphia received no formal notation in Adams' diary and letters. By 1776, however, they were good friends; Adams, writing to a Bostonian in July of that year, called Rush a "worthy Friend of mine" and described him as a man of eminence, polish, and character. To his wife, Abigail, Adams cited qualities of mind, breadth of knowledge, and varied community interests as Rush's strong points, but Adams believed him above everything else a "staunch American." In the diary, however, Adams criticized Rush for talking too much—he "is too much of a Talker to be a deep Thinker."[10]

During the years at Philadelphia, while Adams was a leading spokesman in the Congress, they met frequently and consulted regularly on matters of strategy that culminated in the Revolutionary cause.[11] When Adams left Philadelphia for duties in other parts of America and in Europe, Rush obliged his friend with reports on politics. In the first of many letters,

9. *The Autobiography of Benjamin Rush*, ed. George W. Corner (Princeton, 1948), p. 110.

10. Adams to Cotton Tufts, July 20, 1776; to Abigail Adams, July 23, 1776, *Adams Family Correspondence*, ed. Lyman H. Butterfield et al. (Cambridge, Mass., 1963), II, 54, 59; entry of Sept. 24, 1775, *Diary*, II, 182.

11. In his old age Adams constantly recounted for posterity his great deeds in the Continental Congress. As a member of committees to frame the Declaration of Independence, to confer and make treaties with foreign powers, and to concert war plans with Washington, and as chairman of the Board of War and Ordnance, Adams had a powerful hand in turning discontent into revolution.

August 8, 1777, Rush expressed the hope that the battle against Britain would last long enough to purge Americans of monarchical impurity so that their dress, habits, and thoughts would reflect the virtue essential for the creation of a republican state. In a letter of January 22, 1778, in which he congratulated Adams on his diplomatic mission to France, Rush admitted his fear of French influence upon American development when the culture was only partly purified of its British past: "A French war . . . would leave us in the puny condition of a seven-months child." Adams, replying from such distant places as Passy and Amsterdam, asked for information on politics in Philadelphia and then generously offered observations on the issues of the day. In a letter of September 19, 1779, he expressed satisfaction with the state of foreign affairs but thought Spain and France should be instructed in military tactics. "It is not by besieging Gibraltar, nor [by] invading Ireland, in my humble opinion, but by sending a clear superiority of naval power into the American seas, . . . by taking the West India Islands and destroying the British trade, and by affording convoys to commerce between Europe and America . . . that this war is to be brought to a speedy conclusion." [12] In making these recommendations, Adams could not always maintain a serious tone. "My best compliments to Mrs. Rush," he added in one letter, and please "desire her to move in the assemblies of the ladies, that their influence may be exerted to promote privateering. This and trade is the only way to lay the foundation of a navy." [13]

This theme of naval power was a favorite with Adams, but it did not provide the material for a continuing exchange of opinions with Rush. Though a dozen letters passed between them, the letters were sent at irregular intervals and never brought any sustained discussion. After 1780, the men traveled along radically different roads, and only a few messages were exchanged until Adams was proposed for the vice-presidency of the United States. The problems of the new national government gave them subject matter of mutual interest, but differing theories of republicanism in education and politics set off discussions that soon brought more heat than light. Adams had done much thinking since 1774 about the basis of republican government

12. *Old Family Letters*, p. 16.
13. Sept. 20, 1780, ibid., p. 20.

and had sided with those favoring a balanced distribution of power with elements of monarchy, aristocracy, and democracy woven into it. He admired Britain's constitution (and labeled it a republican type), felt that liberty flourished in the British Isles better than in most other countries, and considered the people better able to receive the blessings of peace and prosperity than Americans were. While he denied that he wanted to erect a monarchy of any kind in America, he was convinced nonetheless that some of the essentials of a monarchical government, like titles and honors, would ensure stability in a republican form of government. In trying to answer Rush's objections, he put his argument in this unique way: "What would you say or think or feel, if your own children, instead of calling you Sir, or Father or Papa, should accost you with the title of 'Ben'? Your servant comes in, and instead of saying, 'Master, my hat is much worn, will you please to give me a new one,' crys 'Ben! my hat is all in rags, and makes you the laughing stock of the town. Give me a new one.' What think you of this simple, manly republican style? . . . Let us consider, my friend, more reverently and therefore more truly the constitution of human nature. . . . Family titles are necessary to Family government; colonial titles we know were indispensable in Colonial government; and we shall find national titles essential to National government." [14]

Elaborate statements of these ideas were soon published by Adams in *The United States Gazette* under the title of "Discourses on Davila." The implied criticism of the French Revolution and its leveling tendencies put Adams into the center of a fierce public discussion about the nation's democratic philosophy and its support of revolutionary France. In the minds of many, Adams appeared to condemn the noble cause of revolution and as a result drew much harsh criticism. Rush was astonished at Adams' ideas. A republican purist himself, he had advocated schemes to cleanse the nation of its aristocratic past and had desired a reconstruction of the educational system to accomplish his purpose, including practical studies, public control, a national university, and education of women. These measures he sincerely believed would assure the United States less factionalism, fewer religious pas-

14. July 5, 1789, ibid., pp. 41–42.

sions, and fewer emotional diseases than Europe. When Adams objected to the elimination of the classics, Rush sent him these charged words: "I shall class them [Latin and Greek] hereafter with Negro slavery and spirituous liquors, and consider them as, though in a less degree, unfriendly to the progress of morals, knowledge, and religion in the United States." [15]

Though their relations were strained, neither man wanted any bitterness. Attempting a reconciliation, Rush invited Adams to his home. "After you have been feasted by our fashionable people, I will claim a family evening from you, and while Mrs. Adams is engaged with Mrs. Rush in enumerating the years in which they were both neglected by their husbands during the war, I will read extracts from my notebook to you and afterwards receive more materials for it from your conversation." [16] Adams replied sympathetically, admitting that the notebook already recorded too many of his follies, and "I fear I am not yet much more prudent." [17] Their correspondence, nevertheless, was ended. With the seat of the national government moved to Philadelphia, they were together again. Though they partially agreed to disagree, intense party activity in the newspapers exaggerated the differences between leaders, and the leaders became rivals for prestige and the presidency. Rush was deeply affected by the propaganda, considering Adams an apostate from republicanism. In the election of 1796 he favored Thomas Jefferson, whom he called a pure republican, a citizen of the world, and an enlightened scholar. He granted in fairness that Adams had great knowledge, a vigorous mind, and republican manners but, alas, had been corrupted by monarchism.

When Adams was chosen President of the United States, he did not permit his certain knowledge of Rush's hostility to the Federalist party to interfere with the offer of a position. He appointed Rush in November 1797 Treasurer of the Mint, a post that did not require much time in the office but augmented Rush's income. The appointment was undoubtedly made with some regard for Rush's personal finances and affairs. The doctor, now notorious for his treatment of yellow fever, was then waging a

15. July 2, 1789, *Letters,* I, 518.
16. Apr. 13, 1790, ibid., I, 547.
17. Apr. 18, 1790, *Old Family Letters,* p. 59.

battle with William Cobbett and John Ward Fenno, Federalist newspaper editors, who were viciously assailing his theories. The appointment also came when Rush was himself suffering considerable mental distress, perhaps approaching a nervous breakdown. Rush gladly accepted the post but advised Adams that he was not changing his political principles. "I told the President of the United States that I must act towards him as Dr. Ambrose did to Henry the 4th of France when he sent him to be his family physician. He stipulated with the King 'never to see a battle nor to exchange his religion.' I begged in like manner to be forever excused from taking a part in any political controversy. The President smiled and did not appear offended at the application of the anecdote to the case in point." [18] "He took me by the hand, and with great kindness said 'You have not more pleasure in receiving the office I have given you, than I had in conferring it upon an old Whig.'" [19]

After Adams left the presidency and returned to his home in Braintree, the men lost contact with each other save for newspaper references and their publications. Adams' letter of February 6, 1805, opened a new chapter in their lives.

In their mature lives Rush and Adams had many similar experiences that drew them together. In their youth, however, they lived miles apart, were brought up in different environments, were educated for different careers, and entered their professions under different circumstances. Except for the Revolution, they might easily have gone their separate ways without ever meeting each other. A descendant of Henry Adams who settled in Braintree in 1640, John Adams (1735–1826) was the eldest son of a farmer and landowner who had married well, had time for town politics, and had sent him to the local Latin school and to Harvard College (1751–1755). Those four years passed easily for John Adams, and he then accepted a position as schoolmaster at Worcester. The provincial atmosphere was good for him, allowing a personal examination of his education and plans for the future. He did not like what he discovered, put himself immediately on an in-

18. Rush to Ashton Alexander, Feb. 20, 1798, *Letters*, II, 797.
19. *The Autobiography of Benjamin Rush*, p. 103.

tensified program of reading, and decided to study law as soon as possible. A change of location was advisable, so he returned to the coast, dividing his time between Braintree and Boston, studying, reading, observing, consulting, and taking measure of men in public office. His friendships multiplied—Richard Cranch, Samuel Quincy, Jeremiah Gridley, and, of course, Abigail Smith, who became his wife in 1764, mother of his five children, and lifelong companion. His law practice grew, his reputation for sound judgment and scholarship attracted wide notice, and his willingness to be counted in public disputes put him in the leadership of the colonial protest against British legislation. Active in the Stamp Act controversy, in the defense of John Hancock as a smuggler, in the trials of the Boston Massacre soldiers, and in the House of Representatives, he was known as a staunch patriot, and his appointment in 1774 as a delegate to the Continental Congress was a natural result of his prominence.

While Adams was thus establishing himself as the leading lawyer of Boston, Benjamin Rush (1746–1813) was making a reputation as a distinguished physician of Philadelphia. Like the Adamses, the Rushes had settled early in the colonies, making their home in the area surrounding Philadelphia. John and Susanna Hall Rush had five children, some city property, and a small business when John died prematurely in 1751. Susanna stepped forcibly into the breach, operating a general merchandise business and managing the household in a spirit of "kindness, generosity, and attention to the morals and religious principles of her children."[20] She sent Benjamin and his brother Jacob (1747–1820) to a country school and in 1759 had Benjamin enrolled as a junior in the College of New Jersey at Princeton. With his interest in medicine already developing, he made careful comparisons of professions while at Princeton and then apprenticed himself in 1761 to John Redman, a leading physician of Philadelphia, and worked in laboratories and hospitals until 1766, when he left for advanced study at Edinburgh. Its medical faculty was undoubtedly the most eminent in the world, and the institution was situated in an unusually flourishing area of scholarship. During his hours outside of classroom and hospital, Rush met

20. Ibid., p. 26.

David Hume, Dugald Buchanan, William Robertson, and other worthies and had opportunities to talk with them. Before leaving for home he had a chance in London and Paris to attend medical lectures and visit with distinguished writers and philosophers. Upon his return to Philadelphia in 1769 he lived with his brother Jacob, who was then a lawyer, and their sister Rebecca, who kept house for them.

Benjamin had some difficulty in establishing himself in Philadelphia because the Quakers consulted members of their own faith and the medical profession was often hostile to his ideas. But he was fortunate in securing an appointment as professor of chemistry at the College of Philadelphia—a position he used as a platform for publicizing his various theories. His advanced ideas on inoculation for smallpox, treatment of croup and lockjaw, and the use of opium for fevers regularly made the newspapers. His humanitarian ideas on temperance and antislavery were published in pamphlets and circulated widely. Though he had some patients who could pay their bills, he had more who were charity patients. "My shop," he wrote in his autobiography, "was crowded with the poor in the morning and at meal times, and nearly every street and alley in the city was visited by me every day. There are few old huts now standing in the ancient parts of the city in which I have not attended sick people. Often have I ascended the upper story of these huts by a ladder, and many hundred times have been obliged to rest my weary limbs upon the bedside of the sick (from the want of chairs) where I was sure I risqued not only taking their disease but being infected by vermin." [21]

Though Rush was close to the poor of Philadelphia in the early 1770's, he moved even closer to the politicians as the Revolution enveloped the city's life. He opened his home to the delegates of the First Continental Congress in 1774 and boarded for a time John and Samuel Adams. He apparently discovered Thomas Paine, inspired the writing of *Common Sense,* and assisted in its publication. The controversy resulting over the pamphlet found him in the midst of the newspaper war. As a writer, organizer, and man of many tasks he grew more and more republican in his sympathies and became a revolutionary. "These principles," he modestly reported,

21. Ibid., pp. 83–84.

"were daily nourished by conversations with Samuel and John Adams, David Rittenhouse and Owen Biddle."[22]

In these intimate gatherings Benjamin Rush and John Adams developed their friendship. Adams was a delegate; he was always on hand to entertain and encourage the visitors. In 1776, when Rush also served as a delegate, their paths grew closer for a time. In committee and on the floor they often held similar positions, but it would appear from his *Thoughts on Government* (1776) that Adams feared the leveling spirit of *Common Sense* and looked to the establishment of a constitution as a guarantee of liberty. Rush was, however, more deeply committed to the purification of society and the erection of a republican government.

Their paths divided again in December 1776, when Rush volunteered for service with General John Cadwalader's forces in the defense of Philadelphia. Action around the city and later at Princeton led to his appointment as surgeon general of the middle department and his involvement in the medical policies of Washington's army. The overcrowded hospitals and the inefficiency of the director general, William Shippen, Jr., brought a blunt protest from Rush, who put the problems directly before General Washington. When Washington refused to take the drastic action that Rush had advised and Congress backed the general, Rush resigned his commission and criticized all concerned for what he felt was near-criminal neglect of the sick and wounded. Rush's bitterness toward the general lingered for years: Washington became a symbol of vested interest, ignorance, and bungling. And later Rush accused Washington of encouraging hero worship—the worst form of monarchical corruption.

After his resignation Rush lived at Princeton with his wife, having married Julia Stockton in 1776. When the British evacuated Philadelphia, he returned with his family to the city. Active again in hospital work, lecturing, and writing, he enlarged his practice and won friends. But he could not forget the inefficiencies of army medicine and the lack of purity of purpose in republican leadership. His thoughts were regularly given to correspondents, patients, and magazine readers.

22. Ibid., p. 115. Owen Biddle (1737–99) was a Philadelphia tradesman who was secretary of the American Philosophical Society, 1773–82.

Adams in the meantime had become an American envoy to France. His eager mind, like Rush's, surveyed the problems of office and, to his disgust and amazement, found inefficiency, luxurious living, and a lack of direction in policy making. Setting himself apart from these disturbing conditions, he introduced with the consent of Benjamin Franklin and Arthur Lee, his colleagues in the negotiations, an accounting system, orderly procedures for correspondence, and regular business hours. He also recommended to Congress the appointment of one instead of three envoys, a suggestion that, when it was accepted, deprived him of his position. He set standards of conduct for himself that would reflect the new American republicanism, and hoped that Franklin and Lee would do the same.

When his plan was accepted by Congress in 1779 and Franklin became the sole envoy, Adams returned to America in August. Elected immediately to the Massachusetts constitutional convention, he gave the state distinguished service by writing the major parts of the 1780 constitution.[23] Before it was adopted, however, Congress called him back into the diplomatic service and sent him to Europe to await negotiations for peace with Great Britain. In Paris during 1780 and 1781 his overzealous and suspicious temperament got him into many delicate situations with French and American officials, but his talent and reputation for honesty saved him. Instead of being recalled, he was appointed American envoy to the United Provinces and was held in readiness for the peace negotiations. His natural suspicion of France gave America some advantage in the discussions with Britain in 1781, making him willing to conduct them in secret and to arrange for a separate treaty. The resulting negotiations revealed Adams, John Jay, and Franklin to be hard bargainers, and the treaty of 1783 was a monument to their zeal.

After the peace was won, Adams had responsibilities in Holland, and in 1785 he was named envoy to Great Britain. Full diplomatic recognition proved to be impossible, but Adams continued in residence, amusing himself with the delights of London and allowing himself time to write his monumental three-volume *Defence of the Constitutions of Government of the*

23. Samuel E. Morison, "The Struggle over the Adoption of the Constitution of Massachusetts, 1780," *Proceedings of the Massachusetts Historical Society,* L (1917), 353–412.

United States of America (1787). Recalled at his request in 1788, he returned to Braintree amid the congratulations of Congress and his native state. His retirement was short, however, because he was soon chosen Vice-President of the United States. An office of honor, the vice-presidency put him in the very center of power. He presided in the Senate and used his power to break some significant legislative deadlocks; he advised the President on many matters concerned with the establishment of the national government; and he was a leading contender for the presidency when Washington retired.

During those eight years when Adams held what he called "the most insignificant office that ever the invention of man contrived," he widened his acquaintances and had time for speculation and observation. He read much, sometimes too hurriedly, of the new French revolutionary literature, eagerly sought pamphlets and the reports of travelers, and frequently condemned the excesses of Paris. Unlike Rush and Jefferson, who saw good in the French Revolution, Adams shuddered at the violence and worried about the spread of such influences in America.

Rush, too, disliked the chaos in France but hoped that men of good will would soon come into control. Peace, he believed, would soon overcome disorder because the Devil, like nobles and kings, could not reign forever. Rush was then occupied with an American kind of evil, yellow fever, which had caused an epidemic in 1793 and 1794. He had prescribed bleeding and purging, much to the disgust of some physicians in Philadelphia, and offered an explanation that the fever was locally generated from swampy areas around the city. The bitterness of the dispute forced his resignation from the College of Physicians, and many colleagues openly condemned his ideas. In 1797 when yellow fever again spread through the city, Rush prescribed his treatments, but this time the newspaper editors Cobbett and Fenno brutally attacked him, partly from political motives, and the libels continued until Rush lost most of his patients and was driven nearly to despair.

At this point John Adams came to the rescue by giving him a government appointment. This support in time of need enabled him to institute a successful damage suit against Cobbett. The unfavorable publicity deeply affected Rush, who carried mental scars through the remainder of his life. Though he had lost patients and friends in the 1790's, the years after 1800 brought a return of many to his office and home, and the relaxation of tension gave him time for thought and writing.

Peace of mind was a precious gift that Adams had also prized, but as President of the United States he inherited a divided party and grave international problems. Party politics were rife, making it impossible for him to command the services of all political leaders and difficult for him to count upon the loyalty of his own party. Though he had much popular backing, he had few devoted followers. The Federalists were loosely held together by philosophy and policy, and Adams himself was never considered their national leader. In the crises with France of 1797 to 1800 he got the army and navy increased in size several times and won massive support for his policies of preparedness, but he was also confronted with problems of military leadership that put Washington, the popular hero, into a position which threatened Adams' own initiative in office. Washington insisted upon Hamilton as second in command in the military buildup, and Hamilton, long known to Adams as a rival, exploited the crisis for selfish gain. Adams, though in favor of war as a last resort, held negotiation to be more desirable and less dangerous politically than belligerency. In sending Elbridge Gerry and John Marshall to France as envoys, he angered the Hamilton wing of his party and alienated many New England Federalists like Ames, Cabot, and Higginson, but Adams countered their opposition by pushing for speedy negotiations with France and by ousting Hamilton's sympathizers from the cabinet. Unfortunately for him, Adams had started too late to discipline his party, instead infuriating the Hamilton faction, whose help was needed if he wanted reelection. By that time, however, the Hamiltonians had other thoughts: Trumbull of Connecticut proposed Washington as Adams' successor; Oliver Wolcott urged the candidacy of General C. C. Pinckney; and Hamilton, in a letter that was published by the Republican press, injudiciously criticized Adams. The opposition, therefore, had unique opportunities to badger the Federalists. One of its number, James Callender, in a book entitled *The Prospect before Us,* accused Adams of creating disunion, promoting war, and advocating monarchy. As the campaign progressed, bitterness, factionalism, and confusion blurred Adams' record, and the election brought Adams' defeat. When the choice of electors was known in 1801, Thomas Jefferson and Aaron Burr had tied for the presidency and Adams was in third place. He was, of course, deeply shaken by the popular mandate and retreated to his home in Massachusetts: "I must be Farmer John of Stonyfield and nothing more . . . for the rest of my life."[24] Like his friend Rush, however, Adams could not stay out of public life and in 1805 began corresponding with Rush on the ways they could preserve the record of America's Revolutionary development and their part in it.

Both men were concerned about receiving justice from posterity.[25] Bacon had pronounced the founders of states to be deserving of highest respect and had praised those who gave their lives or exposed themselves to danger for the good of their country. In this spirit Adams recounted to Rush those times he spoke for independence—when he traveled the high seas on diplomatic missions and when he negotiated the peace of 1783—as worthy events in founding the state, events upon which honest men could lay down their lives. Rush also numbered his times of sacrifice—when he served in the Continental Congress, when he helped Tom Paine with *Common Sense,* when he ministered to the wounded in crucial battles. Bacon praised those who advanced learning, and said that no power on earth could touch those who had knowledge and used it. Adams, with a book ever in hand, educated himself throughout his life, built a library, wrote treatises, and joined learned societies. So it was with Rush, who read widely, promoted scientific inquiry, and virtually died with a pen in his hands.

Why was fame a ruling passion for these men? Had they lived in an earlier generation, they would have sought justice in the love of God and resigned themselves to His mercy. All would have been weighed and measured at the last judgment, when a return to the heavenly Eden would have been the goal of human life. But Adams and Rush were men of the eighteenth century, who had lost much of this earlier faith. For them the love of God gave way to love of humanity, the atonement to the perfectibility of man,

24. Page Smith, *John Adams* (Garden City, N.Y., 1962), II, 1056.
25. Adams suggested to his wife in 1774 that she should save their letters because the letters would one day "exhibit to our Posterity a kind of Picture of the Manners" of the age. See *Adams Family Correspondence,* I, 121.

immortality in heaven to prolonging human memory of great events.[26] They had participated in a great revolution that made possible unlimited human progress. The reward for their deeds as fathers of the new era was to be remembered by posterity, and they were ready to guarantee themselves immortality without waiting for the last judgment. Then, like the Christian martyrs of old, they could face death courageously.

Guaranteeing themselves immortality, however, was not very easy, because there were always men ready to steal the rewards of others. Jefferson was frequently accused of theft, for attributing to himself the policy of no entangling alliances. Washington and Hamilton, too, were thieves, for posing as educated men. Why did posterity allow these men to steal the reputations of others, indeed even reward them for doing it and punish the just and honorable man?

Adams and Rush could not help being a bit disillusioned and bitter over the success of certain wealthy men of their day. The new generation of shipping merchants and businessmen was reaping tremendous rewards from the exertions of the patriots who were dying in poverty or obscurity. Many of the wealthy were not participants in the Revolution, and some were not even active in the new nation, but all, somehow, fell upon the advantages that should have gone to the founders and builders of empire. The new generation, living in luxury and holding the reigns of power, was challenging the standards of the older generation. Its historians, mythmakers, and propagandists were turning the Revolution into a folk myth to suit its purposes. The rise of Washington as a hero, for example, a man who read little and wrote imperfectly, was deeply disturbing to Adams. Washington in spite of all his good points had not measured up to Baconian greatness. He was the creation of the "puffers," an idol of the Virginians but, nonetheless, a man who possessed ordinary talents and depended upon the abilities of others.

The feelings that Adams and Rush expressed, therefore, were the embittered feelings of unacclaimed heroes. They were crying out to posterity to do justice to their generation and to themselves and to assure them of fame before their death.

26. See Carl L. Becker, *The Heavenly City of the Eighteenth-Century Philosophers* (New Haven, 1935), pp. 129–130.

CHAPTER 2

Jefferson's Theft

ALMOST FOUR YEARS had passed since John Adams had left the presidency, and a few weeks had passed since Thomas Jefferson was reelected to his second term as President. While Adams was no longer active in seeking public office, his name, his deeds, and his opinions occasionally were mentioned in the newspapers. He was a controversial figure, and estimations of his influence upon the Revolution and the new nation were frequently being made as the historical accounts appeared one by one. Adams was particularly concerned over the weakening of his policies by the Jefferson administration and worried about the dangers of Jefferson's preparedness program now that Europe was again at war. He felt that the policies and legislation of the new administration had changed the character and direction of the nation; dangers to the peace and security of the nation were appearing everywhere; and he frankly blamed Jefferson for the trouble. "I read the public papers and documents, and I cannot and will not be indifferent to the condition and prospect of my country. I love the people of America and believe them to be incapable of ingratitude. They have been . . . deceived." In this mood of alarm he wrote Benjamin Rush.

To BENJAMIN RUSH

February 6, 1805

DEAR SIR,

It seemeth unto me that you and I ought not to die without saying good-bye or bidding each other adieu. Pray how do you do? How does that excellent lady, Mrs. Rush?[1] How are the young ladies? Where is my surgeon and lieutenant? How fares the lawyer?

Two learned and famous physicians, Sydenham[2] and Rush, have taught us that the plague and the yellow fever, and all other epidemic diseases, when they prevail in a city, convert all other disorders into plague. I cannot help thinking that Democracy is a distemper of this kind, and when it is once set in motion and obtains a majority, it converts everything good, bad, and indifferent into the dominant epidemic. Here is our good old New England, almost as far gone as the United Irishmen in Pennsylvania, as some people think and say; I am not however of that opinion yet. . . .

Let me put a few questions to your conscience, for I know you have one. Is the present state of the nation republican enough? Is virtue the principle of our government? Is honor? Or is ambition and avarice, adulation, baseness, covetousness, the thirst of riches, indifference concerning the means of rising and enriching, the contempt of principle, the spirit of party and of faction, the motive and the principle that governs? These are serious and dangerous questions; but serious men ought not to flinch from dangerous questions. My Thomas[3] and I have been reading together the impeachments in *The State Trials,* and we find that all nations are too much alike.[4]

My family unite with me in presenting respects and assurances of old regard to you and yours.

John Adams

1. Julia Stockton Rush (1759–1848), married to Benjamin on Jan. 11, 1776, was the mother of his thirteen children. Their happy marriage was doubtless due to her sensible and tactful management of an exacting husband.

2. Thomas Sydenham (1624–1689), famous English pathologist, was admired by Rush because of certain parallel experiences in their careers. Sydenham held that one epidemic disease swallows up another. One of Rush's discourses in *Six Introductory Lectures* (Philadelphia, 1801) was devoted to Sydenham's career. The autographed copy of these lectures in the Boston Public Library may have prompted Adams to begin this correspondence.

3. Adams' third son, Thomas Boylston (1772–1832), was a Philadelphia lawyer who in later life became a legislator and judge.

4. Adams had been following the impeachment trial of Samuel Chase, who had presided over the trial of James Callender. This notorious propagandist and libelist of John Adams had been roughly handled by Justice Chase, and now the Jeffersonians were seeking revenge by impeaching the justice. During the trial, events in Adams' administration were frequently recalled, and sometimes Adams' opinions on aristocracy were openly discussed.

To JOHN ADAMS

February 19, 1805

MY MUCH RESPECTED AND DEAR FRIEND,

Your letter of the 6th instant revived a great many pleasant ideas in my mind. I have not forgotten—I cannot forget you. You and your excellent Mrs. Adams often compose a subject of conversation by my fireside. We now and then meet with a traveler who has been at Quincy, from whom we hear with great pleasure not only that you enjoy good health, but that you retain your usual good spirits, and that upon some subjects you are still facetious. . . .

Many thanks to you for your kind inquiries after my family. My eldest daughter is still happy with an excellent husband at Montreal. My second daughter [Mary] visited her in 1803, where she was addressed by a captain [Thomas Manners] in the British army. Both her parents objected to a connection with him. Her sister and brother-in-law became intercessors for him, and we reluctantly submitted to his taking her from us in February 1804. He appeared to be a man of uncommon worth. We were sometimes disposed to wish he were not so, that we might have had a good excuse for refusing him our daughter.[5] . . .

My son John, whom you honored with two commissions, left the navy after its reduction in 1802 and resumed the study of medicine. He graduated in June last but soon afterwards lost his health, to recover which he went to South Carolina in October.[6] . . . My second son, Richard, is still studious. The hostility of our legislature to the bar has rendered the progress of young lawyers slow in business, but he expects soon to rise superior to the obstacles that have been thrown in their way.[7]

5. In 1799 Anne Emily Rush (1779–1850) married Ross Cuthbert, a member of the Quebec Parliament at various times from 1801 to 1820.

6. John Rush (1777–1837), after study at the College of New Jersey and in his father's office, took his medical degree at the University of Pennsylvania in 1804 and joined the United States Navy as surgeon.

7. Richard Rush (1780–1859), the famous future United States minister to Great Britain, was a lawyer in Philadelphia before entering politics.

By the second part of your letter I am reminded of the answer of Sancho in *Don Quixote* when he was asked how he liked his government. "Give me," said he, "my shoes and stockings."[8] In like manner I feel disposed to reply to your questions relative to the present state of the United States, "Give me my lancet and gallipots." My children are often the witnesses of my contrition for my sacrifices and of my shame for my zeal in the cause of our country. Among the fatherly cautions I deliver to them, none are repeated oftener than the dangers of public and the sin of party spirit.

I live like a stranger in my native state. My patients are my only acquaintances, my books my only companions, and the members of my family nearly my only friends. The odious opinions I have propagated respecting the domestic origin of our American pestilence have placed me *permanently* in the same situation in Philadelphia that your political opinions placed you for *a while* in the year 1775. Linnaeus in conversing one day with a brother naturalist at Upsala pointed suddenly to some little boys whom he saw playing before his door and said, "These are our judges." How consoling these reflections to those who have been the subjects of the injustice and cruelty of their contemporaries in their journey through life!

My dear Mrs. Rush and my son Richard unite in cordial and affectionate regards to you, Mrs. Adams, and your son Thomas. . . .

Benjn: Rush

To RUSH

February 27, 1805

DEAR SIR,

I have just now received your friendly letter of the 19th and rejoice with you sincerely in the welfare of your family. I wish you had named the captain in the British army who has been so fortunate as to marry your second daughter. . . . John, I doubt not, will do well, and Richard, with patience and perseverance indispensable in a lawyer, sometimes and indeed com-

8. See Miguel de Cervantes Saavedra, *The Visionary Gentleman Don Quijote de la Mancha,* trans. Robinson Smith (New York, 1932), II, 503 (Ch. lx).

monly through a long noviciate, will have no cause to fear. No civilized society can do without lawyers.

Now for the first part of your letter. I have enjoyed as much health for the last four years as during any part of my life; and my spirits have been as cheerful as they ever were since some sin, to me unknown, involved me in politics. It must have been my own, for my father had certainly none towards me, and as little toward God or man as any man I ever knew in my life. You hear I am still facetious upon some subjects. But my facetiousness, you know, was always awkward and seldom understood. When I was young, I had two intimate friends, Jonathan Sewall and Daniel Leonard—they both went away to England in 1775.[9] They used to tell me I had a little capillary vein of satire, meandering about in my soul, and it broke out so strangely, suddenly, and irregularly that it was impossible ever to foresee when it would come or how it would appear. I have thought of this sometimes and have had reasons enough to do so. Certainly there is none of the caustic of Juvenal in it; certainly none of the wit of Horace, and I fear little or none of his good nature or good humor. . . . I know nothing of any facetiousness in myself. If it is ever there, it comes of itself; I hunt it not. You will expect from me the garrulity of narrative old age, and here you have it.

Now for the latter part of your letter. I resemble you and Sancho. I call for my levers and iron bars, for my chisels, drills, and wedges to split rocks, and for my wagons to cart seaweed for manure upon my farm. I mount my horse and ride on the sea shore; and I walk upon Mount Wollaston and Stonyfield Hill. Notwithstanding all this, I read the public papers and documents, and I cannot and will not be indifferent to the condition and prospects of my country. I love the people of America and believe them to be incapable of ingratitude. They have been, they may be, and they are deceived. It is the duty of somebody to undeceive them. A philosopher like Linnaeus might safely appeal to the boys. But what are those to do who are to be tried by boys, on the testimony of false witnesses—boys who are to have laid be-

9. Before he left Boston in 1775 to spend the remainder of his life in exile, Jonathan Sewall (1728–1796), the famous Loyalist, was Adams' best friend. Another Loyalist, Daniel Leonard (1740–1829), was the author of the "Massachusettensis" articles to which Adams replied as "Novanglus."

fore them a dozen volumes of lying newspapers and pamphlets edited annually for twenty, thirty, or forty years together without any contradiction, and aggravated by as many more volumes of private letters at least as lying as the newspapers.

An appeal to the last day, eternal justice, and an assembled world, like Judge Chase, to be sure, is perfect safety, when it can be made.[10] Although I have no doubt that able and upright man could make it with sincerity as to his integrity and good intentions, yet I confess, for myself, I should rather say at that tribunal, "God be merciful to me a sinner." Yet if called to such a trial as his, I could do as he did, and I believe I should have done it.

My family join in friendly regards to yours. . . .

John Adams . . .

To ADAMS

March 23, 1805

MY MUCH RESPECTED AND DEAR FRIEND,

. . . you say it is the duty of every man who loves his country to step forth in defense of its institutions. To this paragraph [in your last letter], as far as it was intended to awaken me to exertion, I shall reply by giving you an account of a singular dream.

About the year 1790 I imagined I was going up Second Street in our city and was much struck by observing a great number of people assembled near Christ Church gazing at a man who was seated on the ball just below the vane of the steeple of the Church. I asked what was the matter. One of my fellow citizens came up to me and said, the man whom you see yonder has discovered a method of regulating the weather, and that he could produce rain and sunshine and cause the wind to blow from any quarter he pleased. I now joined the crowd in gazing at him. He had a trident in his hand which

10. Chase's impeachment trial got under way on Feb. 4, 1805, with a reply by Chase to the list of eight charges. Chase ended his statement with a reminder that all the participants will one day appear before the "Omnipotent Judge" where the "secrets of all hearts shall be disclosed." See *The Debates and Proceedings in the Congress of the United States,* 8th Cong., 2nd Sess. (Washington, D.C., 1852), p. 150; see also Randolph's reply, p. 165.

he waved in the air, and called at the same time to the wind, which then blew from the northeast, to blow from the northwest. I observed the vane of the steeple while he was speaking, but perceived no motion in it. He then called for rain, but the clouds passed over the city without dropping a particle of water. He now became agitated and dejected, and complained of the refractory elements in the most affecting terms. Struck with the issue of his conduct, I said to my friend who stood near to me, "The man is certainly mad." Instantly a figure dressed like a flying Mercury descended rapidly from him, with a streamer in his hand, and holding it before my eyes bid me read the inscription on it. It was: "De te fabula narratur."[11] The impression of these words was so forcible upon my mind that I instantly awoke, and from that time I determined never again to attempt to influence the opinions and passions of my fellow citizens upon political subjects. . . .

Benjn: Rush

To RUSH

April 11, 1805

DEAR SIR,

. . . I admire the brilliancy of your invention when asleep. I know not whether Aesop or Phaedrus or La Fontaine or Moore or Gay have given us a more ingenious fable than yours of the man upon the ball of the steeple of Christ Church. The structure and application of the fiction are very clever. But the moral I cannot approve. I cannot quite reconcile it to philosophy, morality, or religion. When I was almost tempted to wish I could reconcile it to all that is good, I recollected, unfortunately, a pair of couplets in Prior and began to doubt whether the devil had not mounted on the golden ball instead of an angel of light.

> The Truth is this: I cannot stay,
> Flaring in Sunshine all the Day:
> For *entre nous,* We hellish Sprites
> Love more the Fresco of the Nights;

11. "The story is told of you yourself." Horace, *Satires* I.i.69–70.

And oftener our receipts convey
In Dreams than any other Way.[12]

If, however, it were certain that no more impression can be made upon man than was made upon the wind and weather by the man upon the ball, your inference and conclusion would be logical. But when we know what impressions have been made by Freneau, Lloyd, Andrew Brown, Peter Markoe, Bache, Callender, Duane, Wood, Cheetham, Denniston, Ben Austin, Tom Paine, and others of that stamp,[13] shall we conclude that no impression can be made in favor of truth and virtue by the popular talents and scientifical attainments of Dr. Rush? If so, the cause of liberty is lost.

Mistake me not, however, my worthy friend. It was far from my intention in anything I have written to stimulate you to any exertions beyond your inclination. You have done enough and suffered enough in the cause of liberty and humanity, and unless your encouragements and rewards had been greater, and unless your prospects of success were better, you may fairly be excused.

But "The Stirrs" in Pennsylvania indicate the return of Zubly's government, or rather the Franklinian system of a government in one center, which will be followed by other states. If I were a painter, I would sketch it. A splendid coach drawn by six fiery coursers, like those of Achilles, in full gallop, constantly lashed by a drunken coachman, should start from the top of the Peak of Tenerife down the steepest pitch of the mountain. The gentlemen, ladies, and children, of whom the coach should be full, should thrust their heads out of the windows before, behind, and on each side, expressing in their countenances the passions of their hearts and especially their desire of leaping out, checked by the horror of the precipice. Remember! there must be no horses hitched on behind the coach to draw up hill,

12. Matthew Prior, "Hans Carvel," lines 89–94.

13. These men were newspaper editors and political pamphleteers who had steadily attacked Adams, both as Vice-President and as President. His sense of grievance and bitterness is understandable if it is remembered (1) that the focus of resentment could not be directed as easily against Washington, (2) that Adams had written a book giving the traditional arguments against pure democracy, and (3) that his indiscreet directness (which makes Adams so delightful to us) made him easy to characterize by contemporaries.

to check the progress to destruction.[14] This would be too aristocratical. Perhaps it would be thought to give some privilege to virtue, talents, courage, industry, frugality, or even to services, suffering, sacrifices, or, what is more horrible still, to property, birth or genius, or learning!

Believe me, my friend, a government in one center is as hostile to law, physic, and divinity, and even to pen, ink, paper, inkhorns, standishes, and even to reading and ciphering, as it is to stars and garters, to crowns and scepters, or any other exclusive privileges. It is content with no state of society that ever existed. Negroes, Indians, and Kaffrarians cannot bear democracy any more than Bonaparte and Talleyrand. . . .

My letter is shockingly written because it was written in a hurry. You will excuse it. . . .

John Adams . . .

To ADAMS

June 29, 1805

MY DEAR OLD FRIEND,

. . . I seldom see any of the persons who now ride in the whirlwind and direct the storm of politics in Pennsylvania, but my son Richard, who mixes with the parties, says it is impossible from all he can collect of their relative strength and intentions to tell who will be the successful candidate for the chair of our state next October. The friends of Mr. McKean and Mr. Snyder are alike sanguine, but the latter are far the most industrious.[15] The leading Federalists will be passive in the controversy. T. Paine has said

14. This description reminds one of Edward Bellamy's coach ride in his *Looking Backward 2000–1887* (Boston, 1888), pp. 11–15. Adams may have gotten inspiration for the idea from Joseph Addison, "Visions of Mirzah," in *The Spectator,* No. 159.

15. Thomas McKean (1734–1817), governor of Pennsylvania from 1799 to 1808, was a turncoat Federalist. Though he remained conservative in temperament, he joined the Jeffersonians and experienced unhappy relations with subordinates. Simon Snyder (1759–1819) was a Philadelphia aristocrat and well-known legislator who succeeded McKean as governor. The complex politics of Pennsylvania are analyzed by James Hedley Peeling, "Governor McKean and the Pennsylvania Jacobins (1799–1808)," *Pennsylvania Magazine of History and Biography,* LIV (1930), 320–354.

in one of his publications that it is "impossible to unknow a truth that has
been once believed." Sad experience has refuted this assertion in Pennsylvania, for alas! all the errors upon the subjects of government . . . that were
written down in the year 1789 have revived and are now in full operation in
every part of our state.

Do you remember a speech you made to me at Mrs. Yard's[16] door in
September 1776, the evening after Congress passed a resolve to hold an
intercourse by means of commissioners on Staten Island with Lord Howe?
It was: "It would seem as if mankind were made to be slaves, and the
sooner they fulfill their destiny the better." I will hope that if the liberties
of Pennsylvania should expire in the present struggle, our sister states will
not follow our example. Many things will contribute to our ruin that cannot operate in other states. We are divided by local, national, and religious
prejudices, each of which by a constant repulsive agency prevents union in
public and general enterprises. A large portion of our citizens are ignorant,
and an equal portion are idle and intemperate. We have at present no *native*
Pennsylvanians preeminent for genius or patriotism among us, and if we
had, they would have no natural or American allies, for a majority of the old
and wealthy *native* citizens of our state are still Englishmen in their hearts
and would afford them no support. This was exemplified in Peters, Clymer,
Hopkinson, and some others who were deserted by that class of people
as soon as the repeal of the test law restored them to the right of suffrage
and a participation in the power of the state. It was in part from this view
of things in 1790 that I ceased to labor for the several interests of my country, nor do I repent of it. My family and my profession afford me pleasures
and pursuits so adequate to my wishes that I often look back upon the
hours I spent in serving my country (so unproductive of the objects to
which they were devoted) with deep regret. A chair in my study is now to
me what Dr. Johnson used to say a chair in a tavern was to him, "the throne
of human felicity."[17]

16. Mrs. Sara Yard was Adams' landlady between 1774 and 1776 when he attended the
Continental Congress in Philadelphia.

17. The description was undoubtedly taken from Sir John Hawkins' *The Life of Samuel
Johnson* (London, 1787), p. 87.

Do you ever see our Philadelphia papers which contain the publications of the two contending parties in our state? . . .

Benjn: Rush

P.S. I need hardly suggest that certain parts of this letter must not be read out of your own family.

To RUSH

July 7, 1805

[MY DEAR FRIEND,]

. . . I have not seen an *Aurora* a long time, but last night I was told that in the late papers of Mr. Duane he or his writers are elaborately answering my *Defence* and recommending a government in one assembly.[18] This coincides with your account that the old errors on the subject of government, learning, and lawyers are revived. There is a body of people in every state in the union who are both in heart and head of this sect. This tribe will always be courted by the seekers of popularity and opposers of a good systematic government. They are properly the sans-culottes of this country. Whoever courts them and builds upon them will find himself in the situation of Danton, who made two speeches on the subject which reveal the whole mystery. "They now cry Danton and Robespierre," said he, "but the moment they change the order and cry *vive* Robespierre and Danton, off goes my head."[19] . . . Danton, however, was not the first nor the last demagogue who has gone down into the pit with his eyes open.

It would indeed seem as if mankind were destined to be slaves, as you tell me I said 30 years ago. All history and all experience seem to evince such a tendency. There is liberty, however, and there has been in some ages and

18. The Philadelphia *Aurora*, 1790–1835, was the chief Jeffersonian Republican newspaper in the city—a violent and abusive journal that opposed Governor McKean in 1805.

19. Adams may have read this statement in some contemporary writings by Jacques Necker and then confused the order of the names. See Jacques Necker, *Oeuvres complètes de M. Necker, publiées par M. le Baron de Stael, son petit-fils* (Paris, 1820–1821), X, 39: "Tout ira bien tant qu'on dira Robespierre et Danton. Malheur a moi si l'on disait jamais Danton et Robespierre."

countries; and if this fact is admitted, wise men should never despair, but always remember that no effort will be lost. When I said, "the sooner they fulfill their destiny the better," I said as peevish and extravagant a thing as Brutus did when he said he found virtue but a shadow, though he had worshipped her all his days as a goddess. Such foolish escapes of ill humor ought not to be remembered; or if not forgotten, they ought to be reprobated.

Pennsylvania is not alone. Every state in the union is in her case in a larger or smaller degree. Patriotism in this country must be tinctured with English or French devotion or be without support and almost without friends. Independent, unadulterated, impartial Americanism is like Hayley's old maid, a decayed tree in a vast desert plain of sand, or like Burke's old oak, torn up by the roots and laid prostrate by the late hurricane.[20]

Every state in the union has a party . . . who are still Englishmen in their hearts and will afford a mere American no support. These factions . . . have made it a fixed principle all along to hunt down every true American and every revolutionary character as soon as they possibly could and get them out of their way. They were all, in one of these parties, taught to turn their eyes for this purpose upon that Scottish Creole, Alexander Hamilton, as their head, and what he was to do with them or what they were to do with him I will not at present conjecture; but I have an opinion which may one day be developed. Probably it went no further than an alliance with England and an alienation from France, without well considering what must have been the necessary effect of such a plan.

In this they fundamentally departed from my system and my maxim, which you know I have preached and inculcated for thirty years and which Jefferson has been mean enough to steal from me and display as his own, "friendship and commerce with all nations, alliances with none."[21] Wash-

20. "The Old Maid is like a blasted tree in the middle of a wide common." [William Hayley], *A Philosophical, Historical, and Moral Essay on Old Maids* (London, 1785), I, 15. Burke's old oak is in his "Letter to a Noble Lord," *The Works of the Right Honorable Edmund Burke* (Boston, 1866–1867), V, 208: "The storm has gone over me; and I lie like one of those old oaks which the late hurricane has scattered about me. I am stripped of all my honors, I am torn up by the roots."

21. According to Professor Felix Gilbert, Adams must be "considered as the chief architect of the Model Treaty and its accompanying instructions." Adams in 1776 interpreted the word "alliance" differently than later in life—it meant a commercial agreement, not political or

ington learned it from me, too, as you very well know, and practiced upon it, as far as he could, to my certain knowledge and by my constant advice at a time when he consulted me in everything, to the infinite jealousy of Hamilton. Your lady's father, Judge Stockton, knew very well that this was my maxim on the day of the vote of independence. . . .

I am always mortified when I see my administration supported by the name, opinion, or authority of that man [Washington], great and good as he certainly was. If my conduct cannot be justified by reason, justice, and the public good, without the smallest aid from the prejudices or caprices of the people, or from the judgment of any single individual on earth, I pray that it may be condemned.

The human understanding is very well in the ordinary affairs of life. In architecture, men consider the elements about them, the earth, the air, the water, and the fire, and construct their houses very well to guard against the dangers and inconveniences of each. In dress, in furniture, in equipage, they consult nature tolerably well and provide for their comfort and decency. But in government they seem to be destitute of common sense. The nature of men and things is laid out of the question. Experiment, which is admitted in all other arts and sciences, is wholly unheeded in this. A strange disposition prevails throughout all stages of civilization to live in hollow trees and log houses without chimneys or windows, without any division of the parlor from the kitchen or the garret from the cellar. . . .

John Adams

To ADAMS

August 14, 1805

MY DEAR OLD FRIEND,

Your letters are full of aphorisms. Every paragraph in them suggests new ideas or revives old ones. You have given a true picture of parties in our

---

military relations. Adams was not completely successful in 1776 in limiting American foreign involvements only to commercial affairs. See Gilbert, *To the Farewell Address: Ideas of Early American Foreign Policy* (Princeton, 1961), pp. 44–53.

country. We have indeed no national character, and however much we boast of it, there are very few true Americans in the United States. . . .

Ever since the Revolution, our state has been like a large inn. It has accommodated strangers at the expense of the landlord and his children, who have been driven by them from the bar and their bedrooms and compelled at times to seek a retreat in their garret and cellar. In consequence of this state of things, everything not connected with individual exertions languishes in our state, particularly our commerce, which is tending fast to annihilation from the operation of a most absurd quarantine law, the result of Boeotian ignorance and disbelief. I am kept from feeling the anger and contempt which such conduct is calculated to create by considering our citizens as *deranged* upon the subject of their political and physical happiness.

I well remember your early cautions to your country upon the subject of treaties. In Baltimore you advised Congress to be careful how they threw themselves into the arms and power of France when they applied to her for aid, for "the time might come," you said, "when we should be obliged to call upon Britain to defend us against France." In being deprived of the credit of that just opinion as well as the honor of your accumulated services to your country, you share the fate of most of the patriots and benefactors of mankind that ever lived. . . .

The French and American Revolutions differed from each other in many things, but they were alike in one particular—the former gave all its *power* to a single man, the latter all its *fame*. The only credit which the other servants of the public in the successful contest for American independence possess with the world and will possess with posterity is and will be wholly derived from their imitating the example and carrying into effect the counsels of General Washington in the cabinet and the field. In reviewing the numerous instances of ingratitude of governments and nations to their benefactors, I am often struck with the perfection of that divine government in which "a cup of cold water" (the cheapest thing in the world), given under the influence of proper principles, "shall not lose its reward." [22]

I once intended to have published a work to be entitled "Memoirs of the

22. Matthew 10:42.

American Revolution," and for that purpose collected many documents and pamphlets. But perceiving how widely I should differ from the historians of that event, and how much I should offend by telling the truth, I threw my documents into the fire and gave my pamphlets to my son Richard. Of the former I have preserved only a short account of the members of Congress who subscribed the Declaration of Independence, part of which I once read to you while you were President of the United States. From the immense difference between what I saw and heard of men and things during our Revolution and the histories that have been given of them, I am disposed to believe with Sir Robert Walpole that all history (that which is contained in the Bible excepted) is a romance, and romance the only true history.[23]

You remark in your last letter that the tories have hunted down all the Revolutionary characters of our country. To this General Washington and Colonel Hamilton are exceptions. They are both idolized by them, and to their influence is owing the almost exclusive honor those gentlemen possess of having begun, carried on, and completed the American Revolution. Colonel Hamilton is indebted for much of his fame to his funding system, the emoluments of which centered chiefly in the hands of the tories. They may say of him what Leo the X impiously said of the Christian religion, *mutatis mutandis:* "Quantas divitias peperit nobis hoc nomen Hamiltoni."[24] . . .

Mr. Madison and his lady are now in our city. It gave me great pleasure to hear him mention your name in the most respectful terms a few days ago. He dwelt largely upon your "genius and integrity," and acquitted you of ever having had the least unfriendly designs in your administration upon the present forms of our American governments. He gave you credit likewise for your correct opinion of banks and standing armies in our country. Colonel Burr also in his visit to my family last spring spoke of your character to me with respect and affection. Your integrity was mentioned by him

23. "Anything but history, for history must be false." [Horace Walpole], *Walpoliana* (London, 2nd edn., n.d.), I, 60, No. 79.

24. "What riches the name of Hamilton has brought us"—a paraphrase of a saying referring to the favors Pope Leo X (1513–21) gave his hungry followers.

in the highest terms of commendation. For what virtue above all others would a good man wish to be generally known by the world and by posterity? I should suppose integrity. . . .

Benjn: Rush

P.S. You see I think *aloud* in my letters to you as I did in those written near 30 years ago, and as I have often done in your company. I beg again they may be read only in your own family. I live in an enemy's country.

To RUSH

August 23, 1805

MY DEAR OLD FRIEND,

. . . I am extremely sorry you relinquished your design of writing memoirs of the American Revolution. The burning of your documents was, let me tell you, a very rash action, and by no means justifiable upon good principles. Truth, justice, and humanity are of eternal obligation, and we ought to preserve the evidence which can alone support them. I do not intend to let every lie impose upon posterity.

You rank Colonel Hamilton among the Revolutionary characters. But why? The Revolution had its beginning, its middle, and its end before he had anything to do in public affairs.[25] Col. Reed, Col. Harrison, and Mr. Edmund Randolph were secretaries to General Washington before Hamilton was in his family.[26] . . . I never knew that such a man or boy was in his suite, nor did I ever hear the name of Hamilton till after the evacuation of New York; this boy came forward a bawling advocate for the Tories.[27]

25. Adams refers to his idea that the American Revolution was completed before hostilities broke out in 1775. If this was true, Hamilton played little part in the Revolution. But if the Revolution continued to 1783, then Hamilton's part in the liberation of the colonies was almost as important as that of Washington or Adams.

26. Benjamin Harrison (ca. 1726–91) was Washington's political supporter in the Continental Congress; Edmund Randolph (1753–1813), an aide-de-camp; Joseph Reed (1741–85), a military secretary.

27. An allusion to Phocion, the Greek military leader, and the resemblance to Hamilton. Phocion's parentage was mysterious, but there was sufficient money to give him an education. As a boy he attached himself to General Chabrias, a sluggish leader out of battle, but a man

Then Smith, Humphreys,[28] and Hamilton were first talked of as aides. They were all advocates for the Tories, and honorably and justly so because the Tories had clear right to the stipulations of the Treaty of Peace. Hamilton's zeal in their favor procured him their votes and interest not only in the city of New York but all over the continent as long as he lived. He quitted the army for a long time, as I have heard, in a pet and a miff with Washington. Great art has been used to propagate an opinion that Hamilton was the writer of Washington's best letters . . . , especially that to the governors of the states on his resignation of his command of the army. This I know to be false. It was the joint production of Col. Humphreys and another gentleman, a better writer and more judicious politician, whom I will not name at present.

The Revolution began in strict exactness from the surrender of Montreal in 1759.[29] It took a gloomy and dreadful form in 1761, so as to convince me at least that it would be inevitable.[30] It continued till 1776, when on the fourth of July it was completed. The parts we acted from 1761 to 1776 were more difficult, more dangerous, and more disagreeable than all that happened afterwards, till the Peace of 1783. I know, therefore, of no fair title that Hamilton has to a revolutionary character.

You say that Washington and Hamilton are idolized by the tories. Hamilton is; Washington is not. To speak the truth, they puffed Washington like an air balloon to raise Hamilton into the air. Their preachers, their orators, their pamphlets and newspapers have spoken out and avowed publicly since Hamilton's death what I very well knew to be in their hearts for many years before, viz: that Hamilton was everything and Washington but a name. . . .

---

afire in conflict. Chabrias gave Phocion commands and honors and made him an important man. In 1784 Hamilton authored two pamphlets using the signature of Phocion.

28. As aide and long-time friend, David Humphreys (1752–1818) was a close associate of Washington. The Smith is undoubtedly William Stephens Smith, Adams' son-in-law.

29. Adams felt that the capture of Montreal from the French in 1759 gave Britain an opportunity to turn from problems of defense to problems of empire, resulting in the imposition of policies that eventually aroused America to rebellion.

30. Probably a reference to the contest waged by James Otis, Jr., over the Writs of Assistance.

The "quantum profuisti de fabulâ Christi" of Leo the Tenth,[31] which you apply to the funding system with so much ingenuity, I cannot think applicable with strict justice. I know not how Hamilton could have done otherwise. To be sure, it was a very lucrative turn of affairs to some people. Hamilton's talents have been greatly exaggerated. His knowledge of the great subjects of coin and commerce and their intimate connections with all departments of every government, especially such as are so elective as ours, was very superficial and imperfect. He had derived most of his information from Duer, who was a brother-in-law of Mr. Rose, the deputy secretary of the treasury under Mr. Pitt.[32] Duer had long been secretary to the board of treasury. Lee, Osgood, and Livingston were all men of abilities and kept the books of the treasury in good order. . . .[33] Wolcott's indefatigable industry with a seven year's experience at the Connecticut pay table came in aid of Hamilton and Duer, so that I see no extraordinary reason for so much exclusive glory to Hamilton.[34] I have never had but one opinion of banks. One national bank with a branch for each state, the whole inexorably limited to ten or fifteen millions of dollars, is the utmost length to which my judgment can go.[35]

The army was none of my work. I only advised a few companies of artillery to garrison our most exposed forts, that a single frigate or picaroon privateer might not to take them at the first assault. Hamilton's project of

31. "How much you have profited from the fable of Christ." See William Roscoe, *The Life and Pontificate of Leo the Tenth* (London, 1846), II, 388 ("It is well known to all ages how profitable this fable of Christ has been to us") and 508, n. 327. Adams may have seen the Liverpool edition of 1805.

32. William Duer (1747–99) held an office in the American treasury from 1786 to 1789, and then served for six months as assistant secretary of the treasury in the Washington administration. Duer's sister, Theodora, married George Rose (1744–1818). A friend and supporter of William Pitt the Younger, Rose was appointed a joint secretary in the British treasury in 1783.

33. The three treasury officials were Arthur Lee, Samuel Osgood, and Walter Livingston.

34. Oliver Wolcott (1760–1833) was first charged with setting up routine procedures in the United States Treasury Department and was then appointed comptroller and later Secretary of the Treasury. He had Adams' friendship until his departure from office in 1800.

35. Here Adams is trying hard to express a moderate opinion on banking institutions. Elsewhere he was more radical, considering them "swindling" institutions because they issued paper money in excess of gold and silver on deposit.

an army of fifty thousand men, ten thousand of them to be horse, appeared to me to be proper only for Bedlam. His friends, however, in [the] Senate and the House embarrassed me with a bill for more troops than I wanted.

When I first took the chair, I was extremely desirous of availing myself of Mr. Madison's abilities, experience, reputation, and amiable qualities.[36] But the violent party spirit of Hamilton's friends, jealous of every man who possessed qualifications to eclipse him, prevented it. I could not do it without quarreling outright with my ministers, whom Washington's appointment had made my masters, and I gave it up. Yet Hamilton himself intrigued in a curious manner, which I may perhaps explain hereafter, if you desire it. . . .

John Adams

To ADAMS

September 21, 1805

MY VENERABLE AND DEAR FRIEND,

The hurry always connected with the prevalence of a yellow fever in our city has prevented my answering your letter of August 25th at an earlier day.

The opinion relative to too close an alliance with France in the year 1776 was communicated to me by you, I think for the first time, in Baltimore. I was led from this circumstance to believe you had delivered it on the floor of Congress in *that* place. I well recollect to have heard you repeat it during our intercourse in Philadelphia and have often since been struck with the propriety of it. . . . I well remember your once saying, "The conduct of France would determine the fate of the world, for that she was at the head of human affairs." One day, sitting with you and Mrs. Adams in your garden while you were President of the United States, you said to me, "Expect, Doctor, no changes in the condition of the human race for the better from the present convulsions in Europe. Things will wind up as they began, and

36. Adams had considered naming Madison an envoy to France. See Adams, *Works,* IX, 285–286, and Irving Brant, *James Madison, Father of the Constitution 1787–1800* (Indianapolis, 1950), pp. 449–450.

the affairs of the world will go on for two or three centuries to come as they have done for centuries past." Upon the same subject you said to me in your front room upstairs, "Don't deceive yourself, Doctor, in a belief that a republic can exist in France. The present revolution will certainly end in the restoration of the Bourbon family or in a military despotism." . . .

There is quackery in everything as well as in medicine, and it is because politicians neglect to form principles from facts that so many mistakes are committed in calculations upon the issue of commotions in human affairs. Louis the 14th lamented that we were only fit to live in the world when we were called to leave it. I feel the truth of this remark daily in myself as well as see it in others. *Learned* men, I now find, know what *was; weak* men know what *is;* but men made *wise* by reflection only know *what is to come.* . . .

Your political anecdotes are very interesting, particularly to my son Richard. Did you ever hear who wrote General W.'s farewell address to the citizens of the United States? Major [Pierce] Butler says it was Mr. Jay. It is a masterly performance.[37] I think, however, I have seen many of the General's letters (certainly written by himself) not much inferior to it. He possessed a talent for letter writing, and so anxious was he to appear neat and correct in his letters that General Mifflin informed me he had known him when at Boston copy a letter of 2 or [3?] sheets of paper because there were a few erasures in it.[38] . . .

Benjn: Rush

P.S. My wife and daughter are gone to Princeton to attend a commencement at which my third son is to graduate. The subject of his oration is on the future prospects of America. It was composed by his brother Richard.

---

37. Alexander Hamilton was Washington's principal aide in shaping the Farewell Address. See Victor Hugo Paltsits, *Washington's Farewell Address* (New York, 1935), p. 53. Butler (1744–1822) was a South Carolina planter and in 1805 a United States senator. John Jay (1745–1829) was the first Chief Justice of the United States Supreme Court. A New York lawyer before the Revolution, he was a member of the Continental Congress from 1774 to 1776 and again between 1778 and 1779. He and Adams served as members of the peace delegation that wrote the 1783 treaty with Great Britain.

38. Thomas Mifflin (1744–1800) was Washington's aide-de-camp and later critic. As governor of Pennsylvania in the 1790's, he sympathized with the Jeffersonians.

In the close of it he describes the great council of our country legislating in great pomp on the banks of one of our western rivers a hundred years hence. In that council he hears peals of eloquence from the descendants of the Washingtons, Adamses, &c., of the Revolution. Among them he hears one of the posterity of Moreau rejoicing in his father's exile and in his own birth in a land of liberty. Above them he sees Columbus and hears him exulting in his toils and suffering, and declaring that the everflowing stream of time never fails of doing justice to the benefactors of mankind.

To RUSH

September 30, 1805

DEAR SIR,

Although it is a gratification to my feelings to write to you and a much greater pleasure to receive a letter from you, yet I have no desire to give you any trouble or the least anxiety on my account when your answer is delayed. I know your avocations and respect them. No apology is ever necessary for any pause in our correspondence.

The Journals of Congress afford little light in developing the real history of the years 1774, 1775, 1776, and 1777. By the contrivance of a secret journal, and another refinement of a third more select and sublimated still, the most important motions and their movers are still concealed from the public, and some of them will never be known. In a letter I wrote to Judge Chase dated Philadelphia, July 9, 1776, I find these words: "Your motion last fall for sending ambassadors to France with conditional instructions was murdered, terminating in a Committee of Secret Correspondence which came to nothing." [39]

The truth is that in consequence of many conversations and consultations between Mr. Chase and me he made a motion in Congress in the fall of the year 1775 for sending ambassadors to France. I seconded his motion. . . . It was a measure which I had long contemplated, and as I then thought and have confidently believed, from that time to this, well digested.

39. Adams to Samuel Chase, July 9, 1776, *Letters of Members of the Continental Congress,* ed. Edmund Cody Burnett (Washington, D.C., 1921–36), II, 7–8 and n. 5.

The principle of foreign affairs which I then advocated has been the invariable guide of my conduct in all situations as ambassador in France, Holland, and England, and as Vice-President and President of the United States, from that hour to this.[40] It was indeed my unchangeable adherence to this principle that turned those whom you call tories and which the Bostonians call Essex Junto against me in the election of 1800.[41] This principle was that we should make no treaties of alliance with any European power; that we should consent to none but treaties of commerce; that we should separate ourselves as far as possible and as long as possible from all European politics and wars.

In discussing the variety of motions which were made as substitutes for Mr. Chase's, I was remarkably cool and, for me, unusually eloquent.[42] On no occasion before or after did I ever make a greater impression on Congress. Caesar Rodney told me I had opened an entire new field to his view and removed all his difficulties concerning foreign connections. Mr. Duane said to me, "We all give you great credit for that speech, and we all agree that you have more fully considered and better digested the subject of foreign connections than any man we have ever heard speak upon the subject."[43] . . .

All this you will call vanity and egotism. Such indeed it is. But Jefferson and Hamilton ought not to steal from me my good name and rob me of the reputation of a system which I was born to introduce, "refin'd it first and show'd its use," as really as Dean Swift did irony.[44]

40. Adams told James Warren, Oct. 7, 1775, that the best principle for the new country was based on the old saying that "God helps those who help themselves," ibid., I, 220.

41. The "Essex Junto" was a general term given by many people, including Adams and Jefferson, to the leading Federalist politicians of Massachusetts, like Fisher Ames, George Cabot, Stephen Higginson, John Lowell, Sr., and Timothy Pickering, who came primarily from Essex County. Most gained their wealth in the Revolution, developed marital and business connections, and moved into Boston in the wake of the fleeing Tories. Most were conservative in politics—like the Tories that they had supplanted in Boston society—and reluctantly supported John Adams in 1796 and 1800 in preference to a "French" President.

42. Adams is trying to establish the point that he was the first member of the Congress to mention the need for declaring America independent. His concern in the speech of October 18, 1775, was over the legality of laws and court decisions because of colonial resistance to British authority.

43. Both Caesar Rodney (1728–84) of Delaware and James Duane (1733–97) of New York were members of the Continental Congress and influential in their states' politics.

44. Jonathan Swift, "Verses on the Death of Dr. Swift," line 58.

After all our argumentation, however, we could not carry our motion; but after twenty subtle projects to get rid of it, the whole terminated in a Committee of Secret Correspondence. When the ballots were taken, not one of the committee was from the eastern states. Franklin, Dickinson, Jay, &c., were elected.[45] . . .

Long after this came the motion for a committee to prepare a plan of a treaty to be offered to France. I was of this committee and drew up the plan.[46] I carefully excluded every idea of alliance and reported a mere treaty of commerce. . . . I constantly asserted that anything like a treaty of alliance would make us forever the sport of the politics of the cabinets of Europe, whereas our duty and interest both would exact from us a perfect neutrality in all European wars at least as long as the European powers would permit it. If any one of them should force a war upon us, we must meet it like men; but we should avoid it with the utmost caution and anxiety.[47]

My opinion of the French Revolution has never varied from the first assembly of the notables to this hour. I always dreaded it, and never had any faith in its success or utility. . . . My friend Brissot has recorded a conversation he held with me at my house in Grosvenor Square which I esteem as a trophy.[48] He says, and says truly, that I told him the French nation were not capable of a free government, and that they had no right or cause to engage in a revolution. By this I did not mean that a nation has not a right to alter the government, to change a dynasty or institute a new constitution in the place of an old one, for no man is clearer in these points than I am; but I know that the nation was not disposed to a revolution and that it never

45. Later Robert Morris was added to the Committee for Foreign Affairs. See Edmund Cody Burnett, *The Continental Congress* (New York, 1941), pp. 118–119.

46. Besides Adams the committee had as members Franklin, John Dickinson, Benjamin Harrison, and Robert Morris. The report brought in what became the "Plan of 1776," which established the general principles of United States trade overseas—free ships make free goods, etc. See Edmund Cody Burnett, "Notes on American Negotiations for Commercial Treaties, 1776–1786," *American Historical Review*, XVI (1911), 579–587.

47. Typical of Adams' attitude is his remark to James Warren, May 3, 1777, "I don't love to be intangled in the Quarrels of Europe. I don't wish to be under Obligations to any of them." Burnett, *Letters of Members of the Continental Congress*, II, 354.

48. Jean Pierre Brissot de Warville (1754–93), guillotined Girondist of the French Revolution, visited the United States in 1788 and published *Considerations on the Relative Situation of France, and the United States of America* (London, 1788).

could be made a national act, as indeed it never was. I knew the men and the families who were at the bottom of it: the Rochefaucaulds, the Noailles, the Lemoines, and Orleans with their satellites, not one man of whom knew what he was about.[49]

I rejoice that you do not despair. A pendulum that vibrates seconds must vibrate half a second one way before it can return to vibrate the other. I will not give any opinion whether it is advisable to stop the watch or let it run on. . . .

I am fully convinced that the yellow fever sometimes, and indeed often, is generated in many places in America, especially in our great cities, by natural causes of putrefaction; but [I am] not yet quite clear that it is not contagious and frequently imported.[50] I, therefore, as David Hume said of himself in Paris, dine with the dinnerites and sup with the supperites.[51] I am for cleansing the cities with all possible industry and, at the same time, for maintaining the quarantine laws to keep it out from abroad. At the same time I must confess my total incapacity to judge in this case, for want of experience and theory too, and therefore that my opinion is not worth anything. I would say not worth a Rush if it were not a most detestable pun.

The class of people in your state who oppose you have always adopted a principle to oppose to the utmost of their power every man who had any conspicuous share in the Revolution. The similar class in every state acts on the same principle. Hence the universal agreement and strenuous exertions of that class to ascribe the whole Revolution to Washington and the whole federal government to Hamilton.

If my little political anecdotes are interesting to your son Richard, of whom I have conceived high hopes, he shall have as many more as he pleases.

49. Adams believed the French Revolution was started by aristocratic groups. He predicted that the unnatural revolution would end in the restoration of the Bourbons.
50. Rush theorized that yellow fever originated locally, out of decaying vegetable matter; he wanted stricter sanitation laws. *The Autobiography of Benjamin Rush,* ed. George W. Corner (Princeton, 1948), p. 98n.
51. The exact quotation has not been found. See *Life and Correspondence of David Hume,* ed. John Hill Burton (Edinburgh, 1846), II, 224—"Hume . . . was always willing to conform to established regulations."

When the office of Treasurer of the Mint was vacant, I had, as nearly as I recollect, about forty applications for it. I never had more difficulty in examining and comparing testimonies, qualifications, merits, &c., in order to determine conscientiously in my own mind whom to nominate. After the most serious deliberation and weighing every man's pretensions, I concluded to give the office to Dr. Rush, who had not applied for it. Among the solicitors for this twelve hundred dollars a year was the Honorable Frederick Augustus Muhlenberg, who wrote me a letter with his own hand, signed with his name, beseeching me to give it to him. . . . I was desirous of obliging him, I pitied his situation, and I was very sensible of the policy of attaching the Germans to the national government.[52]

During the half war with France, General Peter Muhlenberg applied to me directly for a commission in the army and expressly said he would make no conditions or difficulties about rank. I concluded from this that General Muhlenberg was convinced of the justice and necessity of the war, and I should have been very happy to have appointed him notwithstanding his party in politics. Accordingly, I proposed him to General Washington, who allowed him to be a good officer. But I was only viceroy under Washington, and he was only viceroy under Hamilton, and Hamilton was viceroy under the tories, as you call them, and Peter Muhlenberg was not appointed.[53] . . .

Now let me propose to your son Richard a political theorem or two for his solution.

1. If Washington had seen as I did and consented to the appointment of Col. Burr as a brigadier in the army, a rank and command he would have eagerly accepted, for he was then in great humiliation and near despair, what would at this hour [have] been the situation of the United States? . . . Would the momentary union of the Livingstons and Clintons have ever been formed? Would the state of New York have been democrified?[54] . . .

---

52. Frederick Muhlenberg (1750–1801), first Speaker of the House of Representatives, sacrificed his popularity in Pennsylvania by supporting the Jay Treaty.

53. Washington struck the names of Aaron Burr and Peter Muhlenberg off Adams' list of general officers. See Page Smith, *John Adams* (Garden City, N.Y., 1962), II, 978.

54. Adams repeated these observations to James Lloyd, Feb. 17, 1815. *Works*, X, 123–124.

2. If I had appointed Augustus Muhlenberg Treasurer of the Mint, or Peter a brigadier in the army, would Augustus have united with Tench Coxe at Lancaster in that impudent and insolent address to the public, with their names, in which I was so basely slandered and belied? If the Germans had been gratified with appointments of these their leaders, would not the electors of Pennsylvania have been all Federal? and, consequently, the Federal cause triumphant?[55] . . .

With usual good will . . . ,

John Adams

P.S. I admire Bonaparte's expression "The Scenery of the Business."[56] The scenery has often if not commonly in all the business of human life, at least of public life, more effect than the characters of the dramatis personae or the ingenuity of the plot. Recollect within your own times. What but the scenery did this? or that? or the other? Was there ever a *coup de théâtre* that had so great an effect as Jefferson's penmanship of the Declaration of Independence? Or as Gage's exception from pardon of Mr. J. Adams and Mr. Hancock? Or Hamilton's demand, upon pain of a pamphlet, of the command in the attack of the redoubt of Yorktown? . . . I have a great mind to write a book on "The Scenery of the Business." You could write another much sooner and much better.

I know not Major Butler's evidence of his opinion, but it is new to me, and the most probable I have ever heard.

To ADAMS

November 21, 1805

MY VERY DEAR FRIEND,

I am pleased in reflecting that I destroyed all the documents and anecdotes I had collected for private memoirs of the American Revolution. I

55. An edited version of the manifesto of April 9, 1799, is printed in Paul A. W. Wallace, *The Muhlenbergs of Pennsylvania* (Philadelphia, 1950), pp. 292–293.

56. Rush was quoting Jean Victor Moreau (1763–1813), who lived in Morrisville, Pa., after his banishment from France in 1804.

discovered from your letter that I have now nothing but the "scenery of the business," and know but little more than what servants who wait upon table know of the secrets of their masters' families, of the springs of the events of the war and of the administration of the general government since the year 1791. I am, however, satisfied that the whole business was a drama and that some persons who acted a conspicuous part in it never composed a single act nor scene in the play. There is, as the logicians say, a "non causa, pro causa" in everything. . . .

I always believed that General W. relied chiefly upon the understanding and knowledge of General H., but I did not know that his influence extended over his very passions until I read your last letter. That he governed his judgment after he left the Treasury, I believe from several circumstances that came to my knowledge. I shall mention one of them. In the interval between the application to General W. by Congress for the documents of the British treaty, two letters were put into the post office, one to A. H——and another to J. Jay franked G. W., and *two* were sent to him from New York a few days afterwards and the day before his answer and refusal were sent to Congress. . . .

Adieu! my dear friend. Your son and his lady are now in our city. They are to do us the favor of spending a day with us before they set off for Washington. . . .

Benjn: Rush

P.S. What do you allude to in the hint of what passed between G. W. and General H. at Yorktown?

To RUSH

December 4, 1805

DEAR SIR,

I am half inclined to be very angry with you for destroying the anecdotes and documents you had collected for private memoirs of the American Revolution. From the memoirs of individuals the true springs of events and the real motives of actions are to be made known to posterity.

The period in the history of the world the best understood is that of Rome from the time of Marius to the death of Cicero, and this distinction is entirely owing to Cicero's letters and orations. There we see the true character of the times and the passions of all the actors on the stage. Cicero, Cato, and Brutus were the only three in whom I can discern any real patriotism. . . . Cicero had the most capacity and the most constant as well as the wisest and most persevering attachment to the republic. Almost fifty years ago I read Middleton's *Life* of this man, with great pleasure and some advantage. Since that time I have been more conversant in his writings as well as in the other writers and general history of that period. Within a month past I have read Middleton's *Life* of him again, and with more pleasure because with more understanding than before.[57] I seem to read the history of all ages and nations in every page, and especially the history of our own country for forty years past. Change the names and every anecdote will be applicable to us. I said I read with pleasure; but it was a melancholy pleasure. I know of no more melancholy books than Sully's *Memoirs* and Cicero's *Life*.[58]

The triumvirates of Caesar, Pompey, and Crassus, and the other of Octavius, Anthony, and Lepidus, the first formed by Caesar and the last by Octavius for the purpose of worming themselves into the empire, . . . their intrigues and cabals have analogy enough with Hamilton's schemes to get rid of Washington, Adams, Jay, and Jefferson and monopolize all power to himself. You may introduce Burr and McKean and Clinton into the speculation if you please, and even Mr. Madison. You may pursue the subject if you think fit—I have not patience for it.

You inquire what passed between W. and Hamilton at Yorktown? Washington had ordered, or was about to order, another officer to take the command of the attack upon the redoubt. Hamilton flew into a violent passion and demanded the command of the party for himself and declared if he had

---

57. Conyers Middleton, *The History of the Life of Marcus Tullius Cicero* (London, 1741).
58. Rush liked to quote from the *Memoirs* of Maximilien de Béthune, Duc de Sully (1559–1641). These histories, though translated into English by Charlotte Lennox in 1778, were already popularized by such writers as Bolingbroke.

it not he would expose General Washington's conduct in a pamphlet. Thus you see

> Its proper power to hurt, each Creature feels,
> Bulls aim their horns, and asses lift their heels.[59]

Hamilton's instruments of offense were libels, not true libels according to the New York doctrine, but lying libels.

The storming of a redoubt by a boy was to be the *coup de théâtre,* or the scenery of the business, to make him afterwards commander in chief of the army and president of Congress, though there is no more qualification for either in storming a redoubt than there would have been in killing a deer in the woods. The one proved him a good partisan; the other would have gained him the reputation of a good shot; but neither would fit him to command armies or govern states. . . .

There is a concurrence, if not a combination, of events that strikes me. Col. Burr at Washington, General Dayton at Washington,[60] General Miranda at Washington,[61] General Hull returning from his government,[62] General Wilkinson commanding in Louisiana, &c., &c. Enterprises of great pith may be in a state of coction. You may say, perhaps, that I am jealous. But there is a long history in my memory attached to several of those names, which suggest the possibility of profound councils and great results, whether good or not I will not conjecture. If our government should risk the giving offense to France by a war with Spain, I should be surprised. . . .

John Adams

59. Alexander Pope, "Imitations of Horace," Satire I, lines 85–86.

60. Jonathan Dayton (1760–1824), a friend of Aaron Burr, was involved in the famous conspiracy and indicted for treason, but later the charges were dropped because of a lack of judicial evidence.

61. Francisco de Miranda (1756–1816), Spanish American adventurer, served in American and French revolutionary armies. His later life was spent in planning the liberation of Latin America.

62. A former officer in the American revolutionary army, William Hull (1753–1825) was then serving as governor of the Michigan territory.

To ADAMS

January 6, 1806

MY VENERABLE AND DEAR FRIEND,

. . . General Miranda, whose name you have mentioned in your last letter, called upon me on his way to and from Washington. He appeared to be as animated as he was two and twenty years ago, but much better informed. He reminded me, in his anecdotes of the great characters that have moved the European world for the last twenty or thirty years, of *The Adventures of a Guinea,*[63] but with this difference—he has passed through not the purses but the heads and hearts of all the persons whom he described. Of Catherine of Russia he spoke with admiration; of Frederick the IInd with some respect; of the late King of Poland with contempt; and of Napoleon with horror. . . . Mr. Pitt, he thinks, is restrained from destroying the remains of liberty in Britain only by the asylum which the United States offer to the people of that country. . . . He mentioned his intimacy with General Hamilton in his former visit to this country and surprised me very much by informing me that the General spoke with great contempt of the person whom he threatened with a pamphlet at Yorktown. Miranda told him his fame in Europe with posterity was placed beyond the reach of his hostility to him. "No, it is not," said H. "I have written a history of his battles, campaigns, &c., and I will undeceive them." This history I presume was destroyed after he became secretary of the treasury. . . .

In return for your anecdote of the redoubt at Yorktown, I will give one which would have made a part of my memoirs of the Revolution. Thirteen members of Congress voted against the funding system. One of these members assured me that while that business was depending, a gentleman came to him and offered him 200,000 dollars at 4/6 in the pound for his note payable a year afterwards. The offer was promptly and decidedly refused. Within the year the funded debt sold for 23/ in the pound.

---

63. *Chrysal or, The Adventures of a Guinea* (London, 1760) was a popular novel written by Charles Johnstone.

Ah! Why did I ever suffer myself to be withdrawn a moment from the noise of pestle and mortar to be thus distressed and disgusted with the imposture and frauds of public life? . . .

Benjn: Rush

To RUSH

January 25, 1806

DEAR SIR,

I never had the good fortune to meet General Miranda nor the pleasure to see him. I have heard much of his abilities and the politeness of his manners. But who is he? What is he? Whence does he come? And whither does he go? What are his motives, views, and objects?[64] Secrecy, mystery, and intrigue have a mighty effect on the world. You and I have seen it in Franklin, Washington, Burr, Hamilton, and Jefferson, and many others. The judgment of mankind in general is like that of Father Bouhours, who says, "For myself, I regard secret persons, like the great rivers, whose bottoms we cannot see, and which make no noise; or like those vast forests, whose silence fills the soul, with I know not what religious horror. I have for them the same admiration as men had for the oracles, which never suffered themselves to be understood, till after the event of things; or for the providence of God, whose conduct is impenetrable to the human mind."[65] . . .

Miranda's anecdote of Hamilton's scorn of Washington is no surprise to me. Those who trumpeted Washington in the highest strains at some times spoke of him at others in the strongest terms of contempt. Indeed, I know of no character to which so much hypocritical adulation has been offered. Hamilton, Pickering, and many others have been known to indulge them-

---

64. The Philadelphia *Aurora,* Mar. 10, 1806, asked these same questions: "Who is Miranda? A man undoubtedly of distinguished talents, but 'a bird of passage,' perhaps of prey; one who, having no local habitation, has no local attachments."

65. Dominique Bouhours (1628–1702), a French Jesuit and scholar, was the author of biographies of Ignatius Loyola and Francis Xavier. The quotation has not been located, but similar imagery may be found in his *Pensées ingénieuses des anciens et des módernes* (The Hague, 1721), pp. 41, 316.

selves in very contemptuous expressions, but very unjustly and ungratefully. His character as an able general, a wise statesman, and an honest man is justly established. . . . The history with which Hamilton threatened to destroy the character of Washington might diminish some of that enthusiastic exaggeration which represents him as the greatest general, the greatest legislator, and the most perfect character that ever lived but could never take from him the praise of talents and virtues, labors and exertions, which will command the esteem of the wisest and best men in all ages.

Although I read with tranquility and suffered to pass without animadversion in silent contempt the base insinuations of vanity and a hundred lies besides published in a pamphlet against me[66] by an insolent coxcomb who rarely dined in good company, where there was good wine, without getting silly and vaporing about his administration like a young girl about her brilliants and trinkets, yet I lose all patience when I think of a bastard brat of a Scotch pedlar daring to threaten to undeceive the world in their judgment of Washington by writing an history of his battles and campaigns. This creature was in a delirium of ambition; he had been blown up with vanity by the tories, had fixed his eyes on the highest station in America, and he hated every man, young or old, who stood in his way or could in any manner eclipse his laurels or rival his pretensions. . . .

The sudden rise of the public securities after the establishment of the funding system was no misfortune to the public, but an advantage. The necessity of that system arose from the inconsistency of the people in contracting debts and then refusing to pay them. The states would not adopt the five per cent impost, and there were not means of paying the interest or principal of the public debt. That obstinate and willful ignorance of the nature of money and of public credit, which suffered the depreciation of the continental currency, effected a similar depreciation of the public certificates and is now inforcing a depreciation of the only currency we have, the bank bills; and when or how this element of confusion will stop, I know not. Experience is lost upon our people. The injustice occasioned by these

66. A reference to Hamilton's *Letter . . . concerning the Public Conduct and Character of John Adams, Esq., President of the United States* (New York, 1800).

bills will be as great, for anything I can see, as that which arose from paper money or the public certificates. The government of the nation and of individual states will have their hands full of business to prevent greater evils from this than arose from the other two causes. . . .

I am, dear Sir, as usual, with usual regards from my family to yours, your friend . . .

John Adams

CHAPTER 3

The Empire of Death

RUSH WAS VERY BUSY practicing medicine, writing, and lecturing. In his consciousness was always his reputation and how posterity would treat it. He had burned his notes for a history of his own time, but he revised and republished his essays and counseled his students to look for principles of lasting value in his medical works, especially those which would lessen the "empire of death." Rush worried about the future and asked Adams about his thoughts on the subject: Would the world be any better? Would civilization progress? Would the people build upon what had been done? Adams offered his friend some encouragement, but he feared the historical record was often inadequate. Public opinion is never right about the present or future, he felt; events are too complex, men too secretive, yet progress has been made. Principles are important—a living man is better than a dead one—and supporting good principles will have an influence upon humanity.

To ADAMS

March 15, 1806

MY DEAR AND EXCELLENT FRIEND,

I avail myself of the first leisure hour I have had since the conclusion of my lectures to acknowledge your last favor.[1] . . .

From the interest you have kindly taken in my principles and fate in medicine, I shall take the liberty of transcribing a part of the farewell lecture with which I concluded my labors in our University a few days ago.

1. Rush is replying to Adams' letter of Jan. 25, 1806.

"I am aware, gentlemen," said your friend, "of the import of the declaration that I have taught a new system of medicine. The declaration has been forced upon me by its enemies, from whom it first received that odious and unpopular name. It has since been given to it by its friends in different and remote parts of the world. . . .

"Among the many painful circumstances that have attended the propagation of the new system of medicine I have taught you, my being obliged to oppose the system of Dr. Cullen was not the least. He was very dear to me as a master, and I shared largely in his friendship. I am reconciled to my conduct *only* by reflecting that our objects were the same, and were it possible for his departed spirit to meet me in my study or in an evening walk, he would say to me, '*Go on, my son. Continue to exercise the freedom of inquiry with which it was my pride and pleasure to inspire my pupils. If the empire of death has been lessened in a single instance by your rejection of any part of my principles of medicine, I shall rejoice in the successful issue of your labors.*' Yes! venerable Shade! I am sure you do, for your whole life was animated not less by the love of our science than by the most sublime and disinterested benevolence to your fellow creatures. . . .

"Perhaps I am now addressing the gentleman who shall, from the chair I now occupy, or from the press, expose the errors of my system of medicine. Did I know who was to be that person, I would take him by the hand and cordially wish him success in his noble undertaking. Perish my name and the memory of my labors from the records of time, provided that the science I have loved and cherished be advanced and perfected in the world."

The length of this extract from my lecture has, I am afraid, so far tired you that you will hardly have patience with me when I add that our governor has lately promoted my brother to be judge of the first district in the state, by which means he will be restored to his official rank and situation in Philadelphia from which Governor Mifflin had removed him.[2] This appointment was unsolicited and unexpected. It has added much to my happiness.

2. Governor McKean appointed Jacob Rush judge of the Court of Common Pleas for the city and county of Philadelphia.

What is to be the fate of our country, of Europe, of the globe, from the operation of the events which have lately taken place in every part of them? The calculations of the philosopher, the wisdom of the statesman, and the energies of the patriot are all prostrated by the aims and ambition of the new Emperor of France. Our only refuge now seems to be in the prayer of the Church—"Save us, good Lord! for there is no other fighteth for us, but only thou, O Lord!" . . .

Benjn: Rush

To RUSH

March 26, 1806

DEAR SIR,

. . . Thanks for the pathetic extract from your closing lecture. It must have made a deep impression on the minds of the young gentlemen, your pupils and hearers.

I sincerely rejoice in the promotion of your brother, whose talents, virtues, and experience have well merited this distinction. But I cannot help laughing at McKean, *entre nous, sub rosa, tace, taisez-vous.*[3] I cannot convey the injunction in too many languages. I suppose McKean promoted Jacob because he is a brother monarchist. You and I remember the time when we heard your brother say that, in his opinion, "the executive and senate ought to be hereditary." You replied that you was "of a different opinion." I have heard McKean say the same thing in the same words, and I know other substantial witnesses who can depose that he freely expressed this opinion in many companies for several years. I never thought McKean or your brother less friendly to our Constitution for these speculative opinions. I never in my life went to such a length as this; although wrap'd into future times, when numbers, wealth, luxury, and corruption shall have rendered this constitution insufficient to restrain the passions of men, I may have thought

---

3. Note his caution to Rush that their opinions should not be made public—at least not until after their deaths.

that the only way to preserve liberty from an emperor would be to make the executive and senate more permanent than they are now.[4] . . .

You ask me a question of great importance, far beyond my capacity to answer. "What is to be the fate of Europe and of the globe?" In Europe, according to present appearances, "the Devil's own government" is to prevail till it changes all the dynasties of kings and nobles and levels all distinctions and privileges under emperors and their minions. Commerce, manufactures, and science will languish under this gloomy tyranny and Europe grow up into a forest inhabited only by wild beasts and a few hunters who shall have fled into the wilderness from the tyranny of pen and ink.

You ask also what will be the fate of our country? If the philosophers had not undermined the Christian religion and the morals of the people as much in America as they have in Europe, I should think civilization would take its flight over the Atlantic. But as it is, I see nothing but we must, or rather that we shall, follow the fate of Europe. Voltaire, Buffon, D'Alembert, Diderot, Raynal, Rousseau, Dr. Priestley, Dr. Franklin, Mr. Helvetius, and that miserable dupe of his own vanity and their intrigues, Frederick the Great,[5] have made all Europe so discontented with themselves, their government, and religion that to abolish the title of king they are compelled to assume that of emperor, and instead of the whips of monarchy they are obliged to have recourse to the scorpions of despotism.[6]

Democracy is always so horribly bloody that it is always short-lived, and its atrocious cruelties are never checked but by extinguishing all popular elections to the great offices of state. I hope Americans will reflect

---

4. Adams believed that executive power should be independent of the popular and aristocratic and have qualities of monarchy in it. An executive of this kind could then maintain a proper balance in government and protect the people from the encroachments of the nobility.

5. Except for Frederick the Great, these men were leaders of revolutionary thought in Europe. Noah Webster, in his *The Revolution in France* (New York, 1794), p. 18, observed that the "philosophical researches of Voltaire, Rousseau and the Abbé Raynal, had long before unchained the minds of that part of the French nation who read; a respectable class of men." Frederick, "the first servant of Prussia," was a devoted administrator who developed agriculture and state power to unbelievable levels during his forty-six-year reign.

6. I Chronicles 10:11.

upon these things before it is too late. But a war will bring them to a severe trial. To me, who must soon travel into another country to return no more, these things are of little consequence; yet I cannot throw off the habits of this world so entirely as to be indifferent to the future fate of my friends, country, and species. I love them all and would cheerfully sacrifice myself to promote their happiness; but nothing I have done, or can do, availeth anything. . . .

You, my friend, I see, are a greater proficient in this philosophy than I am. You are grown as wise as a serpent and as harmless as a dove. I cannot force a word of politics out of you; for this discretion I blame you not. Yet I will not adopt it yet. Johnson said when he sat upon his throne in a tavern, there he dogmatized and was contradicted, and in this he found delight.[7] My throne is not in a tavern but at my fireside. There I dogmatize, there I laugh, and there the newspapers sometimes make me scold; and in dogmatizing, laughing, and scolding I find delight, and why should not I enjoy it, since no one is the worse for it, and I am the better. Regards from and to the family as usual from your friend

John Adams

To ADAMS

June 10, 1806

MY MUCH RESPECTED AND DEAR FRIEND,

. . . I perfectly accord with you in your opinions respecting the tendency and issue of the present state of things in the world. Never, perhaps, was there a time in which there was more to fear from the wickedness and folly, and less to hope from the virtue and wisdom, of man. A newspaper, once the vehicle of pleasing and useful intelligence, is now the sad record only of misery and crimes. All systems of political order and happiness seem of late years to have disappointed their founders and advocates. Civilization, science, and commerce have long ago failed in their attempts to improve the condition of mankind, and even liberty itself, from which more was ex-

---

7. Sir John Hawkins, *The Life of Samuel Johnson* (London, 1787), p. 87.

pected than from all other human means, has lately appeared to be insufficient for that purpose. If we fly from the lion of despotism, the bear of anarchy meets us, or if we retire from both and lean our hand upon the wall of our domestic sanctuary, the recollection of past or the dread of future evils bites us like a serpent.

> "Oh! for a lodge in some vast wilderness!
> Some boundless contiguity of shade,
> Where rumor of oppression and deceit,
> Of unsuccessful and successful war,
> Might never reach me more."[8]

My only hope for suffering and depressed humanity is derived from a belief in a new and divine order of things which we are told will be introduced into our world by the influence of the gospel upon individuals and nations. It was predicted of the Messiah that he would be "the desire of *all* nations."[9] Should the present system of violence and subjugation of the nations continue, that prophecy must soon be fulfilled, for I believe there is at this time scarcely a nation upon the face of the earth that is satisfied with its government or its rulers and that would not exchange both for others, though probably, in their present state of ignorance, not for the government of the future King of Saints and Nations. A few more years of suffering will probably bring about the fulfillment of the prophecy and render him indeed the "desire of *all* nations."

You complain of my reserve upon political subjects. This you know is not natural to me. My silence upon those subjects arises wholly from ignorance and perhaps a criminal indifference to the affairs of our country. You may easily conceive the extent of both when I add no praises or censures pronounced upon J. Randolph's famous speeches could induce me to read them, and that at a time when little else was spoken of in all the fashionable circles in Philadelphia.[10] . . .

8. William Cowper, "The Task," lines 1–5.
9. Haggai 2:7.
10. John Randolph managed the impeachment proceedings against Samuel Chase and supported many of the legislative proposals of the first Jefferson administration. In 1805,

I have lately been favored with a visit from a Polish gentleman who spent six weeks in Paris on his way to America. He described the present miserable state of his native country in the most pathetic terms. He dined with Talleyrand while in Paris, who spoke with great contempt at his table of the American character. He saw but one man in the United States (he said) who was unwilling to sell everything he possessed. The property held by that man so very dear was "a favorite dog."

I lament that my letters are such feeble echoes of yours. Continue to honor me with your matured reflections upon men and things. . . .

Benjn: Rush

To RUSH

June 22, 1806

DEAR SIR,

. . . I must confess to you that the data upon which we reason from the prophecies concerning the future amelioration of the condition of mankind are too obscure and uncertain to authorize us to build any system upon them for the conduct of nations. It is well to understand as much of them as we can; but the rulers of men would presume too much if they neglected history, experience, and philosophy and depended upon the theological interpretations of mysterious predictions which were not intended to be perfectly understood until the time of their accomplishment. Our friend Priestley believed that France would establish a free government because the king of France was the first of the ten horns which were to fall off.[11]

I rather approve than censure your reserve upon political subjects. It would certainly have been better for me, and probably for the public, if I had been wise enough to have adopted some of it.

---

however, he broke with Jefferson on various issues of foreign policy, like the acquisition of Florida and the Embargo, and in 1806 he attracted much attention by his violent denunciations of party compromises and concessions to those favoring more democracy.

11. Joseph Priestley uses symbols from Daniel and Haggai frequently. See his *The Present State of Europe Compared with Antient Prophecies; A Sermon, Preached at the Gravel Pit Meeting in Hackney, February 28, 1794* (London, 1794), pp. 6–10, 42. The sermon may be found in *The Theological and Miscellaneous Works of Joseph Priestley,* ed. John Towill Rutt (London, 1817–32), XV, 532–552.

I have read the last winter and spring the debates in Congress with more regularity and attention than I ever did before and have derived more information of the motives, principles, and designs of the present majorities than I could ever before penetrate. I must give to Mr. Macon, Mr. Early, and many others the praise of system and consistency.[12] Their fundamental principle is that the moment you raise a public force, you give up your liberties; and therefore there must be neither an army, navy, fortifications, a select militia, or even a revenue because if any of these exist, they must be entrusted to the executive authority, establish a system of patronage, and overthrow the Constitution. All this is very fine. But it will fly like chaff before the wind as soon as any nation by a series of insults and depredations shall excite a serious national resentment. Mr. Randolph is an unusual phenomenon.[13] I have read all his speeches. He has formed himself on the great models of Wilkes,[14] Junius, Cobbett, Tom Paine, and Callender.

He has introduced their modes into the legislature, where I should have expected it would have produced from the duelling moralists and Christians as many bullet holes through his body as there are cells in a honeycomb. . . . If his constitution endures till he has sown all his wild oats, and he begins to reason and exercise his judgment, I am not without hopes he will come to something solid and useful.

Talleyrand's observation on the character of Americans is somewhat enigmatical, or rather equivocal. If he meant that Americans are not attached to their houses, lands, and memorials of their ancestors like the European nobility and landholders in general, this is true and not very disgraceful. But

---

12. Peter Early (1773–1817) of Virginia served in the House of Representatives from 1803 to 1807. He supported the impeachment of Samuel Chase and restrictions on slave trade. Nathaniel Macon (1757–1837) of North Carolina was speaker of the House from 1801 to 1807. He was known for his hatred of Alexander Hamilton.

13. Randolph lost his case against Chase because of his ineffective offense. He was also opposed by five of the most eminent Federalists: Luther Martin, Robert G. Harper, Philip B. Key, Joseph Hopkinson, and Charles Lee. In defeat Randolph followed up his attack on the courts by proposing a constitutional amendment that would have permitted the President upon a joint address of Congress to remove a justice.

14. John Wilkes (1727–97), founder with John Churchill of *The North Briton* and notorious critic of ministerial policies, suffered expulsions from the House of Commons for his boldness. Backed by the city of London, he was reelected and seated finally without opposition in 1774.

if he meant that Americans would universally sell their consciences and their honor, he lied. Although to my grief and indignation, I believe he found some whom he bought or hired and keeps still in his pay. . . .

I never saw Miranda. He came to London when I was there and was very intimate with Smith, but never visited me. I have ever disliked the character of the man, though I have always heard him spoken of in terms of admiration.[15]

If our government knew or suspected the design, I wonder they did not prevent it. Have they considered the consequences to this country, to France, Spain, Portugal, or England, of the independence of South America? Is it an event to be desired by us? I think not. It would increase and multiply the distractions of the world, already too numerous. The elements of confusion are already too many to be soon exhausted. To augment them with this additional source of them would be to make them interminable. If the headlong, dashing fellow Miranda could take a province, he could not hold it without England, and England, unless she is crazy, will neither promote nor consent to the independence of that country. It would be the means of their losing their possessions in the West Indies, and the East Indies, too, and breaking up their empire. The consequences of our independence have been so much more sudden, extensive, and astonishing than we expected, sanguine as we were, that I am by no means disposed to assist in hastening on events which we know must come of themselves in the natural course of things. The independence of South America must occasion convulsions and revulsions over the whole globe, and ultimately pit Europe against America. It is an abyss into which I dare not look. We stand well; let us stand still.[16]

15. William Stephens Smith (1755–1816), secretary of the United States legation in London, married Adams' daughter Abigail Amelia in 1786. Before his marriage he toured the continent with Miranda. During the war crisis with France in 1798 Adams received Miranda's plans for an attack by Britain and the United States upon Spain's territories in Latin America. Adams put aside such ideas when he finally resolved the crisis in the negotiated peace with France. Adams considered Miranda an opportunist and a visionary, and his plans like "a Quixotic attack of a windmill." See William Spence Robertson, *The Life of Miranda* (Chapel Hill, 1929), II, 245.

16. Adams believed that the American Revolution set off unrest around the world. The revolutionary settlement and the United States Constitution of 1787 determined the principles of the new order, at least for the United States. Since people are weak, not wicked, con-

Our Massachusetts resembles at present the monster of Horace, a hand-some human head upon the body of a squalid fish.[17] "Sic volo, sic jubeo," says the people; "Stet pro ratione voluntas."[18] Absolute power in a majority is as drunk as it is in one.

Family salutes family, and blessings on it are supplicated by

John Adams

To ADAMS

July 11, 1806

MY VENERABLE AND DEAR FRIEND,

At the request of my wife I called upon a friend of mine a few days ago to borrow *The Secret Memoirs of the Court of St. Cloud.*[19] He said he had not a copy of it, but politely put into my hands Cumberland's *Memoirs of His Own Life,*[20] which I have since filled up the leisure minutes of the day in reading. . . . He moved in subordinate situations and often saw the events and characters he describes through the medium of other people's glasses. How much more interesting would a work of the same kind be, written by a man who was the principal actor in the events which he describes and who lived in those times which laid the foundation for the present convulsions among the nations of the earth!

I once suggested in a whisper to Mrs. Adams at Mr. Boudinot's[21] table that the history of your political life drawn up by yourself would be an in-valuable legacy to the public, or to your family if you should forbid its publication. I am the more anxious for such a record of opinions and facts

stitutional order is necessary for human happiness, Adams asserted, and the United States should appreciate the gains in liberty she has obtained.

17. Horace, *Ars poetica,* lines 1–5.

18. "Thus I wish [and] thus I command; let wish stand for reason." Cf. Juvenal, *Satires* VI.223.

19. *The Secret History of the Court and Cabinet of St. Cloud* (Philadelphia, 1806). It was a book full of scandal that attracted wide attention.

20. Richard Cumberland, *Memoirs of Richard Cumberland* (London, 1806).

21. Elias Boudinot (1740–1821) married Hannah Stockton, the aunt of Mrs. Rush. He was a member of Congress for three terms, a director of the mint in Philadelphia, and a promoter of various religious and social causes.

from the gross ignorance and errors which we daily hear and read from men who were children or not born in the memorable and eventful years which *preceded* the American Revolution.

The *Life of Washington*[22] has not lessened the number of those errors. Two military men of high rank have complained loudly of being overlooked in the details of the battles that are included in that history. One of them assured me that the account of one of those battles was so different from what he observed to take place in it that he did not believe for a while that it was the same event. The historian of that work should not be blamed. He is candid and upright. His documents have deceived him. I know the execution of such a work as I have recommended will be attended with difficulties if it should be written so as to meet the public eye before the present tide in favor of error has spent itself. But it may be withheld some years and resorted to only by your family for faithful statements of facts, till time shall remove the persons or lessen the influence of the families that might be offended by it. . . .

I once heard a pious minister of the gospel say that "God *threw away* kingdoms and empires upon the most worthless part of mankind." May not the same thing be said in many instances of fame? There is a disease known among physicians by the name of "error loci." If fame is not thrown away upon the worthless part of mankind, it is certainly often given to those to whom it does not belong, thereby constituting an historical "error loci."

But why this solicitude to establish historical or political truth in our world? In what single instance have mankind been the better for it? We not only repeat the errors of other people though warned by their confessions to avoid them, but we repeat errors in spite of our *own* experience and even of our *own* sufferings from them. . . .

To resume the subject of the memoirs of your life. Frederick the 2nd asks in his *Seven Years War*,[23] "What did human reason ever do *great* in human affairs?" Where great events are brought about apparently by human reason, men are often, I believe, prompted to accomplish them by motives that are

22. John Marshall, *Life of George Washington*, 5 vols. (Philadelphia, 1804–07).

23. *Posthumous Works of Frederic II, King of Prussia*, 13 vols. (London, 1789). The first three volumes contain *The History of My Own Times* and *The History of the Seven Years' War*.

contrary to *right* reason. I am led to make this remark by recollecting the absurd and frivolous reasons which were given by many of our patriots in 1776 for concurring in the separation of our country from Great Britain. One of these men said to me, "I am now for independence, since the King of Great Britain has employed Hessian mercenaries to assist in subjugating us." Foolish man! As if there was any difference between being killed by a Hessian and a British bayonet! Hundreds advocated the measure only because the Indians were let loose upon our western settlements, as if the British decrees and attempts to enslave us were rendered more absolute by that link in the chain that was contrived to bind us. Few, very few, consented to our becoming an independent nation from the influence of causes and motives that rendered our reunion with Great Britain as impracticable after what had passed on both sides in 1774 and 1775 as the reunion of a body dissevered from its head by the stroke of an ax. Still fewer were actuated by a prospect of the future and permanent safety, happiness, and prosperity of our country. Indeed we were conducted with our eyes obliquely directed, and backwards, in spite of ourselves, to the haven of peace and independence. We are the causes of our own misery in most cases, but our happiness came to be forced upon us by the kind and invisible hand of heaven.

With respects and love as usual, I am, my ever dear friend, ever yours,

Benjn: Rush

To RUSH

July 23, 1806

DEAR SIR,

I have two of your letters to acknowledge at once. . . .

The appointment of my son to a professorship founded by one of his relations I hope will do no harm to the public, although I dread the consequences of it to his health.[24] Aristotle, Dionysius Halicarnassensis, Longinus, Quintilian, Demosthenes, and Cicero, with twenty others, are not

---

24. In 1806 John Quincy Adams was appointed to the chair of rhetoric and oratory in Harvard College.

easily read and studied by a man of the world and a senator of the United States. And after all *cui bono?* Oratory in this age? Secrecy! Cunning! Silence! *voila les grands sciences des temps modernes.* Washington! Franklin! Jefferson! Eternal silence! impenetrable secrecy! deep cunning! These are the talents and virtues which are triumphant in these days. And in ancient days was it much otherwise? Demosthenes and Cicero, the two consummate masters, died martyrs to their excellence. When I group Washington with Franklin and Jefferson, I mean only in the article of silence. He had integrity and public virtue, as I seriously believe. . . .

Is there in the world at this day a Thuanus?[25] There may be, but I fear there is not. An historian who could look through Europe and America and detail the events and characters of the world from 1760 to 1806 and then solemnly and truly say at the end of his work "Pro veritate historiarum mearum Deum ipsum obtestor"[26] would, as slightly as you and I think of history in general, be a great blessing to mankind. To such an historian even the *Secret Memoirs of the Court of St. Cloud* and Cumberland's *Memoirs of His Own Life* might be of some use. I have the most curiosity to see the last. . . .

You are not the only one of my friends who has very seriously urged me to write an history of my own times or of my own life. I have very serious ideas of the duties of an historian. I think that no history should be written but under the oath of Thuanus. I know not whether his oath ought not to be extended farther and administered and taken in the words of the oath of a witness in our courts of justice to tell the truth, the whole truth, and nothing but the truth.

Of all men who have acted a part in the great affairs of the world, I am afraid I have been the most careless and negligent in preserving papers. I must write too many things from memory, and oftentimes facts to which there is no other witness left alive. The task, besides, is so extensive that I

25. Jacques Auguste de Thou (1553–1617) wanted to produce a strictly scientific history but failed to convince his colleagues that the use of Latin composition helped him escape error. See his *Historiarum sui temporis,* ed. Samuel Buckley, 7 vols. (London, 1733).

26. "For the truth of my history I invoke God himself as a witness." Apparently Adams loosely quoted De Thou's statement in his "Testamento et Morte," ibid., VII: *Sylloge scriptorum varii generis et argumente,* Sec. VII, p. 2.

have not time left to execute it. To rummage trunks, letter books, bits of journals, and great heaps and bundles of old papers is a dreadful bondage to old age and an extinguisher of old eyes. The few letters of which I made copies are preserved, but so many accidents happened to such things that they may be lost; and, indeed, they were all written in so much haste and so carelessly put upon paper that they are not fit for the public eye.

What must I say of my own vanity and levity? Crimes, I thank God, I have none to record. Follies, indiscretions, and trifles, enough and too many. What of the jealousy and envy of those who have been my most intimate friends, colleagues, and coadjutors? What of the malice and vengeance of unprovoked enemies? It would be an easier employment to publish a collection of my political works; but I cannot afford to print them at my own expense, and I don't believe a subscription could be obtained for the purpose, and no bookseller would undertake it at his own expense and risk. These would be a tolerable account of my own life and contain some materials for public history.

Cobbett once said to Sam Malcolm,[27] "There never was a greater difference between two men than between Washington and Adams in one point, the desire of fame. Washington had an enormous, an insatiable thirst for it; but Adams was as excessively careless of it." He did not, I presume, intend it, and I certainly did not consider it, as a compliment. I am very sensible that I have been negligent of it to a fault, and a very great fault, too. There have been very many times in my life when I have been so agitated in my own mind as to have no consideration at all of the light in which my words, actions, and even writings would be considered by others. Indeed, I never could bring myself seriously to consider that I was a great man or of much importance or consideration in the world. The few traces that remain of me must, I believe, go down to posterity in much confusion and distraction, as my life has been passed. Enough surely of Egotism! . . .

I have no idea that the Spaniards in South America are capable of a free government; and a military despotism under Miranda, or even a simple monarchy, would not be better, that I can see, than their present subjection to the Court of Spain. . . .

27. Samuel Malcolm was Adams' private secretary during part of the presidency.

Your reflections on human affairs, and particularly on the progress of the public opinion in the case of our Revolution, are as profound as they are just and true. I have sometimes thought that the public opinion is never right concerning present measures or future events. The secret of affairs is never known to the public till after the event, and often not then. Even in the freest and most popular governments, events are preparing by causes that are at work in secret, known only to a very few, partially communicated in confidence to a few others, but never fully made known to the people till long after all is past. And very often the real springs, motives, and causes remain secrets in the breasts of a few, and perhaps of one, and perish with their keepers like the secret of Junius' *Letters*.[28]

Your divine was more satirical than theological. God throws empires and kingdoms, as he does rains, plagues, earthquakes, storms, sunshine, good and evil, in a manner that we cannot comprehend and, as far as we can see, very often without that regard to morality which we think should govern the world. But although we see not as He sees, we have reasons enough to establish a rational belief that all these things are disposed by unerring wisdom, justice, and benevolence. Nor do I see any reason to distinguish emperors, kings, consuls, or presidents from the rest of mankind. They are as good, in general, in proportion to their numbers as their subjects, and if worthless men are sometimes at the head of affairs, it is, I believe, because worthless men are at the tail and in the middle. The most exalted talents, too, are thrown upon the most worthless and wicked of men as exorbitant wealth was given to Chartres, as it were to show in how small estimation are talents, wealth, and power in the sight of heaven, according to Arbuthnot's Epitaph.[29]

28. The *Junius Letters* were published in the London *Public Advertiser* from 1769 to 1772. Forcibly written, using satire, metaphor, and personal characterization, they created a near sensation because they revealed the intimate details of government policy which only an insider could tell. Their authorship has been disputed for years. Many authorities feel, however, that Sir Philip Francis is the author. There were many editions of the *Junius Letters* at this time, but Adams may have been thinking of Cumberland's comments in the *Memoirs,* p. 506: "The thing to wonder at is, that a secret, to which several must have been privy, has been so strictly kept. . . . The man, who wrote it, had a savage heart, for some of his attacks are execrable."

29. Francis Chartres, a man of meanness, low talent, and unworthiness, possessed an enormous income and estate at death—a proof, according to Dr. Arbuthnot, that God has

These things would go far towards seducing men to the opinions of *Jacques le Fataliste,*[30] if they did not take into their consideration a future state of retribution. I should never be weary of writing to you, but I am sure you must be weary of reading as much as this from your assured friend.

John Adams

I send you my son's oration.

To ADAMS

August 22, 1806

MY DEAR FRIEND,

You ascribe wonders to the influence of silence and secrecy in public men. I agree with you in their effects upon characters and human affairs. Dr. South says the "world was made for the bold."[31] But they possess only half of it—the other half was made for the "artful," among whom I include nearly all silent men. . . .

The silence of one of the persons named in your letter [i.e., Washington] has been generally ascribed to modesty. Mr. Liston once remarked to me that he was taciturn beyond any man he had ever known in his life,[32] so much so as not even to give an indirect or evasive reply to questions when it was improper for him to answer. I said, "He had derived great reputation from this line of conduct." "Yes," said Mr. L., "He has, but it has cost him

---

little regard for wealth in rewarding the deeds of men. See *The Works of Alexander Pope,* ed. Whitwell Elwin and William John Courthope (London, 1871–86), III, 128–129n. See also Pope's "Moral Essays," Epistle III, lines 20–86, and his "Imitations of Horace," Satire I, lines 1–90.

30. An English edition of Denis Diderot's *Jacques le fataliste et son maître* appeared in 1797 as *James the Fatalist and His Master.*

31. Robert South (1634–1716) was an Anglican minister whose sermons were very popular in the eighteenth century. See his *Sermons Preached upon Several Occasions* (Oxford, 1842), V, 399, 401.

32. James Madison gave Jefferson, Feb. 1798, a remarkable contrast of the temperaments of Washington and Adams. Washington, "cool, considerate, and cautious; the other, headlong, and kindled into flame by every spark that lights on his passions: the one, ever scrutinizing into the public opinion, and ready to follow, where he could not lead it; the other, insulting it by the most adverse sentiments and pursuits." *Letters and Other Writings of James Madison* (Philadelphia, 1867), II, 127. Robert Liston was British minister to the United States.

very dear," meaning constant restraint and self-denial, for that this was the case I infer from his frank and open conversation and conduct in making bargains and doing his private business. . . .

From what models human or divine was taciturnity in company derived? Caesar charmed by his conversation even his enemies as well as his friends. Alexander opened his soul over a convivial glass with his generals. If we turn our eyes from these two men (the greatest probably that have lived) to the Saviour of the world, we shall find him affable, sociable, and instructing by his parables and questions or by his allusions to present circumstances, such as a harvest field, a bed of lilies, or a flight of birds, in all companies. I conclude therefore that taciturnity is neither a pagan or a Christian virtue, and certainly not essential to true greatness. On the contrary, I believe (cases of invincible modesty and absence or depression of mind from a morbid state of the nerves excepted) it is always the effect of pride, ill breeding, or stupidity, or dictated by unfair designs to obtain wealth, power, or fame. Where it is not a mental or bodily disease, it is of course at all times a downright vice. . . .

Dr. Priestley's *Life*, written partly by himself and partly by his son, Thomas Cooper, and a Unitarian clergyman of the name of Christie, has just made its appearance.[33] I have read it with pleasure. It contains a list of all his publications on political, metaphysical, theological, philosophical, and *chemical* subjects. Upon the last he discovers great original genius. Chemistry owes more to him than any other science. . . . In politics Mr. Cooper ascribes to him the original idea of the perfectibility of man commonly ascribed to Dr. Price and the Marquis of Condorcet.[34] . . .

I write for a chimney corner. None of my letters I hope will be preserved or read to anybody but your other self, to whom my dear Mrs. Rush sends much love with ever yours,

Benjn: Rush . . .

33. *Memoirs of Dr. Joseph Priestley, to the Year 1795, Written by Himself: With a Continuation, to the Time of His Decease, by His Son, Joseph Priestley: and Observations on His Writings, by Thomas Cooper . . . and the Rev. William Christie* (London, 1806–07).
34. Ibid., I, 344–348. The Marquis de Condorcet (1743–94) was famous for his *Outlines of an Historical View of the Progress of the Human Mind.* An English edition was published in Baltimore in 1802.

To RUSH

September 19, 1806

DEAR SIR,

. . . My experience is perfectly conformable to yours respecting silent men. Silence is most commonly design and intrigue. In Franklin it was very remarkable, because he was naturally a great talker. I have conversed with him frequently in his garrulous humors, and his grandson, or son, Billy, has told me that he never knew a greater talker than his grandfather. But at other times he was as silent as midnight, and often upon occasions and in relation to subjects on which it was his duty to speak. Arthur Lee told me he had known him [to] sit whole evenings in London, without uttering a word, in company with the first men for science and literature, when the conversation had turned upon subjects on which he was supposed to be well informed.

Whether the age of oratory will ever return I know not. At present it seems to be of little use, for every man in our public assemblies will vote with his party, and his nose is counted before he takes his seat. Dialectics are as unavailing as rhetoric. The man is determined and his vote is decided, let reason, justice, policy, or humanity say what they will. The theory [of rhetoric], however, ought not to be neglected in our seats of education. Better times may arrive. . . .

Dr. Priestley's *Life* I should be very glad to see and hope that some of them will be sent to Boston for sale. He was a man of very extraordinary talent and incredible application. If he had written but a tenth part of his works, he would have left a ten times greater reputation. If he had written nothing but his *Chemistry,* he would have been thought a prodigy.

Suppose a grave controversy should arise among the friends of Dr. Rush, Dr. Franklin, and Dr. Rittenhouse,[35] which of the three had the best pretensions to the honor of the discovery of the demonstration that the 3 angles

---

35. David Rittenhouse (1732–96), a well-known Pennsylvania mathematician, was Rush's friend. He was a contributor to the American Philosophical Society's *Transactions* and served as the society's president from 1791 to 1796.

of a triangle are equal to two right angles! You will say this would be ridiculous, for the discovery was made some thousands of years before either of those philosophers was born. Very true, and equally absurd is the dispute whether the original idea of the perfectibility of man is to be ascribed to Dr. Price, Dr. Priestley, or Mr. Condorcet. It is more ancient than either by thousands of years.

Plato had it when he talked of imitating God. The Stoics had it when they described their wise man. Epicurus had it when he described his man of pleasure. The human mind is made capable of conceiving something more perfect than any created being that exists. Artists, painters, poets, statesmen, musicians are all capable of conceiving and imagining something in their arts superior to anything they have done or has been done by others. It is a precept in all these arts as well as in ethics to aim at greater perfection than has ever been attained and, perhaps, than ever can be attained.

The Christian religion has adopted and sanctioned this theory in stronger terms than any modern philosophers have employed. Be ye perfect, even as your Father in heaven is perfect. The eternal, omniscient, omnipotent, and all-benevolent model of perfection is placed before men for their perpetual meditation and imitation. By this, however, it is not intended that every man can ever become eternal, almighty, and all-wise. It is an idea of the Christian religion, and ever has been of all believers in the immortality of the soul, that the intellectual part of man is capable of progressive improvement for ever.[36] Where then is the sense of calling the perfectibility of man an original idea or a modern discovery? What is their meaning under these words, perfectibility of man? Do they mean that the human body can be made immortal on earth and incorruptible, free from pains and diseases, by human reason? . . . Do they mean that the human intellect can be enlarged, here in the body, to comprehend the whole

---

36. Adams was a bit confused about the meaning of progress as interpreted by Condorcet. He was right in saying that progress was a concept well known before Condorcet's famous book, but Condorcet looked to a day when man would master his environment and create heaven on earth. Adams himself was influenced by Condorcet to the degree that he wanted to ensure his fame and earthly immortality.

constitution and course of nature? This is not less incredible and extravagant than the rest. In short, I consider the perfectibility of man as used by modern philosophers to be mere words without a meaning, that is, mere nonsense.

The continual amelioration of the condition of man in this world, moral, physical, political, civil, and economical, is a very intelligible idea and no doubt is to be desired, meditated, labored, and promoted by all men, and those who do most for it ought to be most esteemed. But in this there is nothing but simplicity and common sense. Nothing to excite the gaping wonder of a vicious mob, nor the ignorant admiration of superficial philosophers. . . . Condorcet is welcome to as much of this honor as he pleases, and to all the mischievous nonsense, impudence, and cruelty that he instigated and promoted. Poor Price was once left gravely to publish in print that the progress of knowledge might discover a method of rendering men immortal on earth.

Kant, the German philosopher, has advanced, as I understand, though I never could find any intelligible account of his reveries, something like this notion of perfectibility, and I believe before Priestley, Price, or Condorcet.[37] His system is antagonism. And what is antagonism? Why, all government is to be abolished, as well as all religion, and men are to be left to their natural jealousies and competitions, till they beat and bruise and murder one another sufficiently to convince and compel each other to practice perfect justice, humanity, and benevolence. . . .

We in this commonwealth are making great advances, if not in the perfectibility of human nature, yet in the great arts of lying and libeling and the other arts which grow out of them, such as wielding the cudgel and the pistol. When democratical governments begin to produce such fruits as these in such great abundance, what are we to expect? A conviction in favor of mixed governments? Or a Caesar, or Bonaparte? To be sure, it is safest in such cases to be on the side of the populace because men are safer from proscriptions and denunciations, confiscations, and guillotines. There is little for me to lose in the worst times or cases that can happen. My prop-

37. Immanuel Kant (1724–1804) supported tendencies toward moral rationalism.

erty is small and the remainder of my life is short. But Oh my Country, how I mourn over thy follies and vices.[38] . . .

I once thought our Constitution was quasi or mixed government, but they have now made it, to all intents and purposes, in virtue, spirit, and effect, a democracy.[39] We are left without resources but in our prayers and tears, and have nothing that we can do or say but the Lord have mercy upon us. . . .

If Mr. Jefferson was a warrior, I should suspect that his administration was contrived to give employment to the people and turn their minds from faction and politics by involving himself and them in a war with Spain, France, or England, or with all three. The Romans were obliged to practice this policy for seven hundred years. But Jefferson is not a Roman. If peace should be concluded between France and England, we shall be in a perilous situation. . . .

John Adams

To ADAMS

October 24, 1806

DEAR SIR,

Ever since the receipt of your last letter I have passed my days like an arrow shot from a bow. . . . Even my studies (the times for which are taken from family society or sleep) are laborious, for they consist chiefly of difficult and long-controverted subjects in physiology. I mention these

38. See Matthew 23:37 and Luke 23:28.

39. Adams observed in 1787: "If there is one certain truth to be collected from the history of all ages, it is this; that the people's rights and liberties, and the democratical mixture in a constitution, can never be preserved without a strong executive, or, in other words, without separating the executive from the legislative power. If the executive power, or any considerable part of it, is left in the hands either of an aristocratical or democratical assembly, it will corrupt the legislature as necessarily as rust corrupts iron, or as arsenic poisons the human body; and when the legislature is corrupted, the people are undone." *A Defence of the Constitutions of Government of the United States of America,* in *Works,* IV, 290.

things not as matters of complaint but to apologize for my apparent neglect of your invaluable letters. . . .

Two pamphlets are now in circulation in our city—one called the *Quid Mirror,* which contains a most virulent attack upon the characters of the leading members of the Quid party.[40] It has produced several challenges and one assault and battery. . . . I have seen neither of these publications. By preserving my beloved ignorance of the contents of such performances, I am kept from imbibing their spirit and from giving offense by deciding upon their respective merits. Indeed I now consider the disputes of our parties as Hume considered the wars during the heptarchy in England, as "the battles of kites and crows in the air."[41] . . .

Excuse this short and hasty scrawl. . . .

Benjn: Rush

To RUSH

November 11, 1806

DEAR SIR,

When I received your favor of the 24 Octr., I soberly expected a grave dissertation on the perfectibility of man. Although I thank you for the political information you give me, which is amusing, and although I doubt not your physiological researches will result in something useful to the public, yet, as I have ever considered all arts, sciences, and literature as of small importance in comparison of morals, I was disappointed in finding nothing upon the great subject of the perfectibility of human nature, which I suppose is to be ranged under the head of ethics.

I really wish you would tell me what you understand by this mighty discovery of Price, Priestley, or Condorcet. Perfectibility I should suppose to mean capability of perfection, or susceptibility of perfection. But what is

40. *The Quid Mirror. The First Part* (New York, 1806). William Dickson of Lancaster, Pa., is probably its author.
41. David Hume, *The History of England* (London, 1806), I, 28.

perfection? It is self-evident there cannot be more than one perfect being in the universe. . . . These great philosophers . . . cannot be supposed to mean that every man, woman, and child is capable of becoming a supreme and all-perfect being. What then do they mean? Do they mean perfection in this world or in a future state? Do they mean perfection of mind or body or both? . . .

Do they mean that chemical processes may be invented by which the human body may be rendered immortal and incapable of disease upon earth? This, in a fit of enthusiasm, resembling instances which I shall enumerate before I finish this letter, Dr. Price advanced in a printed note to one of his publications.[42] Surely the good doctor had forgot his Bible, which pronounces an irrevocable decree of death on every human being, almost in every page of it. Price and Priestley were honest enthusiasts carried away by the popular contagion of the times . . . but the greater part of politicians and philosophers who prated about the perfectibility of man mean nothing but to seize, occupy, and confound the attention of the public, while they were amusing and cheating the populace with promises of equality and levelism, which they know impracticable and never intended to promote any further than for the purposes of present plunder.

It is really humiliating to the pride of human nature that so frivolous a piece of pedantry should have made so much noise in the world and been productive of such melancholy and tragical effects; especially as another discovery had been made long before, of much more importance. . . . The discovery I mean is this. If we take a survey of the greatest actions that have been performed in the world, which are the establishment of new empires by conquest and the advance and progress of new schemes in philosophy,[43] we shall find the authors of them all to have been persons whose brains had been shaken out of their natural position. For the upper region of man is furnished like the middle region of the air. Mists arise from the earth, steam

42. Richard Price, *The Evidence for a Future Period of Improvement in the State of Mankind* (London, 1787), pp. 12–16, 21–25, 51–53.

43. Adams at this point is borrowing heavily from the opening paragraph of Sec. 9 of Swift's *A Tale of a Tub*.

from dunghills, exhalations from the sea, and smoke from fire; yet all clouds are the same in composition as well as consequences; and fumes issuing from a jakes will furnish as comely and useful a vapor as incense from an altar. As the face of nature never produces rain but when it is overcast and disturbed, so human understanding seated in the brain must be troubled and overspread by vapors ascending from the lower faculties to water the invention and render it fruitful. . . .

The philosopher from whose works I have borrowed this ingenious theory is Dr. Swift, who in that great philosophical effort, the *Tale of the Tub,* has in the ninth section given the world a profound discourse on the original use and improvement of madness in a commonwealth, which whole section I earnestly recommend to your serious meditations as one of the profoundest and most important systems of philosophy which the last century produced. . . .

John Adams . . .

To ADAMS

November 25, 1806

DEAR SIR,

. . . I thank you for your excellent strictures upon the visionary ideas of the perfectionists in morals, physic, and government. It was from hearing and reading their nonsense in 1792 that I first despaired of the happy issue of the French Revolution. Perhaps Lord Bacon laid the foundation, in part, of their madness by the well-known aphorism that "knowledge is power."[44] One of the zealots of this opinion supposed it would extend over matter as well as mind, that it would suspend and invert the laws of nature, and thus destroy the inductions from miracles. I well remember one of his sayings was "that the time would soon come when a man should thrust his head into the fire without burning it."

44. "Nam et ipsa scientia potestas est." *Meditationes Sacra,* No. 11, "De Haeresibus," *The Works of Francis Bacon,* ed. James Spedding et al. (London, 1857–74), VII, 241.

Where are all the vagaries of that eventful year now? The conventions, Directories, and Emperor of France have dissipated them all, and the foundations of that religion which can alone make men and nations happy have acquired by their destruction a firmness in our world they never had before. Thus not only the wrath but all the follies and crimes of man have, in the language of Scripture, combined indirectly to praise God. . . .

Benjn: Rush

To RUSH

December 22, 1806

DEAR SIR,

I thank you for yours of the twenty-fifth of November. I was in hopes you would have explained to me the system of human perfectibility which is claimed as the invention of Dr. Priestley. The system of the French economists I took some pains, more than five and twenty years ago, to understand, but could not find one gentleman among the statesmen, philosophers, and men of letters who pretended to understand it. . . .

The perfectibility of man was, as I think, one of the dogmas of this sect. And one great branch of this perfectibility was a universal and perpetual peace among all nations and all men. This idea was not invented by Dr. Priestley, for the Abbé de Saint-Pierre had written two volumes upon universal and perpetual peace an hundred years before him.[45]

Some who pretend to believe in these pacific systems advance that it is only necessary to convince all nations and peoples and individuals that war is never in any case advantageous to them. This, to be sure, does not at first blush appear to be very easily done. But let us never cease to din in the ears of the people this great truth and others connected with it. Let us fatigue them with perpetual exclamations on the enormous increase of taxes, imposts, excises, and duties for the maintenance of armies and navies always

45. The work of Charles Irénée Castel, Abbé de Saint-Pierre (1658–1743), was popularized by Jean Jacques Rousseau, who edited some of his writings: *Extrait du projet de paix perpetuelle de Monsieur l'abbé de Saint-Pierre* (Amsterdam, 1761).

on foot. . . . On the impossibility of preserving internal liberty, with the system of permanent troops or standing armies. . . . On the immense destruction of lives (for a dead man is good for nothing, but a living man as long as he can work and consume the fruits of the earth or the manufactures of industry is useful to the whole society of the human race). On the inconceivable barbarity of cutting one another's throats. Our philosophers add that no other being but man is guilty of this crime, although he is the only one whose interest is connected with the life of his fellow. But in this they assert facts diametrically contrary to the truth; for the whole animal creation, as far as we are acquainted with it, are daily destroying and feeding on their fellow creatures. And those of the same species fight and kill as often as men. . . . In sum, on the evils, absurdities, inconsistencies, and horrors of war.

On the other hand, we must challenge all mankind to produce one single advantage which results from war.

Anciently, the people sometimes appeared to derive some advantage by the spoils which were placed in the public treasuries, to defray the expenses and exempt them from taxes. This benefit, however, was only in appearance. But now the fruits of victory are so far from compensating the expenses of it that we must support our taxes even in time of peace.

Now the people arm themselves against each other, only to support the mad pretensions and to cherish the stupid pride of an handful of despots, nobles, and priests. Now commerce, the instrument of an universal alliance, establishing a channel of communication between man and man, from the North Pole to the South, renders it visible to the grossest eyesight that we are made for one another, that our destination is to be useful reciprocally, that we are members of the same body and children of the same family. Now the art of printing, that gift of heaven, applying the reason of the present and all past generations to the benefit of all nations, carries with the rapidity of lightning these benevolent, salutary, and beneficent sentiments over all parts of the globe.

These are the arms with which we are to excite the holy insurrection of nature against the despots who would stifle her voice. . . .

Differences may arise between nations as well as individuals, but as the

latter discuss their rights before tribunals, there is no difficulty, moral or political, to prevent the former from following a similar procedure. The time
will come when the whole world will cover with benedictions the generous
nation which, by being the first to pronounce that she renounced the right
of conquest, has displayed the standard of universal peace. . . .

Give me leave now to turn your attention to a set of philosophers much
more ancient than these. I shall confine myself to one of them at present,
and to save you the trouble of consulting concordances, will quote chapter
and verse. Turn then, if you please, to the eleventh chapter of Isaiah and the
sixth verse, "The wolf [also] shall dwell with the lamb, and the leopard shall
lie down with the kid, and the calf and the young lion and the fatling together; and a little child shall lead them."[46] . . . And again in chapter sixty-
fifth, verse 25, "The wolf and the lamb shall feed together." . . . There are
other prophecies which speak of a time to come when men shall beat their
swords into ploughshares and their spears into pruning hooks and learn war
no more. What may be the meaning of these highly figurative expressions,
I shall not at present inquire. But they seem to intimate an happier and
more pacific state of human life than reason or experience would justify us
in expecting. . . . Price and Priestley believed these prophecies to be inspired. How then can they pretend to have invented the same thing? I say
Priestley believed these prophecies, for they seemed to be the only parts of
the Bible that he thought inspired.[47]

Forty-five years ago when I wore my barrister's gown, band, and tie wig, a
French barber in Boston was in the habit of shaving and dressing me. His
name, I think, was Dehon. One morning he told me he had lived some years
in London and dressed several of the nobility, of one of whom he related a
long story of some very extravagant conduct which I have forgot. Dehon
concluded his story by observing that his lordship "was a little crack." "All
the nobility in England, Mr. Adams," added Dehon, "are crack." He meant

46. This quotation and those that follow were used by Price in *The Evidence for a Future
Period of Improvement in the State of Mankind*, pp. 6–11, 24. Adams seems to be using Price's
arguments.

47. Priestley had great respect for the Scriptures and particularly for the prophecies. See
his *Works*, XVI, 13, 166, and XXI, 167–169.

cracked. I have long thought the philosophers of the eighteenth century and almost all the men of science and letters crack. In my youth I was much amused with the idea that this globe of earth was the Bedlam of the universe. If I were now to judge of it by the conduct and writings of the men of science, I should be more disposed than ever to believe that the sun, moon, and stars send all their lunatics here for confinement as they used to send them from Paris to Bicétre. I must tell you that my wife, who took a fancy to read this letter as it lay upon my table, bids me tell you that she "thinks my head, too, a little crack," and I am half of that mind myself. . . .

My paper allows me room to subscribe myself your affectionate friend

John Adams

CHAPTER 4

Prudence—
A Rascally Virtue

CONSIDERING THE MISERABLE STATE of the nation today, would Adams still want to be a politician if he had his life to live over? Dr. Rush's query touched the sensitive Adams hard, and he replied spiritedly: "I do not curse the day when I engaged in public affairs. I do not say when I became a politician, for that I never was." Though Adams admitted that public service had brought its moments of grief, some the result of mistakes of judgment and some due to the inconstancy of the people, yet he believed he had held to the Republican virtues of patience, temperance, and disinterestedness and the nation had benefited from his sacrifices. If only the people had appreciated his services, they would be in better hands now. Their lack of judgment had unsettled the nation; signs of trouble were appearing in all its parts. In the West the conspiracy of Burr and Eaton meant revolution; in the East politicians like Ames and Mc-Kean were unsteady in their principles. The fate of the nation was indeed precarious.

These signs of moral decay worried Rush, too. Living in a town disturbed by rumors and reacting to the opinions of visitors, Rush had information constantly at his command which the more secluded Adams wanted to know, and Rush could not help thinking, as he passed the news along, that Philadelphia (like the rest of the nation) needed guidance in this hour of crisis.

To ADAMS

January 23, 1807

MY DEAR FRIEND,

I have been waiting like Horace's clown till the stream of my business should so far lessen that I could pass over it,[1] in order to acknowledge the receipt of your interesting letter upon the subject of the perfectibility of human nature, but as that stream, from adventitious currents pouring into it, rather increases than lessens, I have seized a few moments merely to testify my gratitude for that letter and to assure you that I subscribe to every sentiment contained in it. By renouncing the Bible, philosophers swing from their moorings upon all moral subjects. . . .

Our citizens are now gazing at the storm that has lately risen in the western states. General [William] Eaton, who lately passed through this city on his way to Washington, has mentioned several details of Colonel Burr's propositions to him not published in any of the newspapers. Among others, he said in a large dining company that he asked Burr what he intended to do after establishing the independence of the western states. "Turn Congress out of doors," replied the Colonel, "and hang Tom Jefferson."[2]. . .

Benjn: Rush

To RUSH

February 2, 1807

MY DEAR DOCTOR,

You make me very happy when you say that you agree with me upon the subject of the perfectibility of man. Let every man endeavor to amend and improve one[self], and we shall find ourselves in the right road to all the

---

1. Horace, *Epistles* I.ii.41–43.

2. For an analysis and bibliography of the Burr insurrection see Thomas P. Abernethy, *The Burr Conspiracy* (New York, 1954).

perfection we are capable of. But this rule should by no means exclude our utmost exertions to amend and improve others and in every way and by all means in our power to ameliorate the lot of humanity. . . . You have done a great deal, and I very little, in this way. I sometimes wish that I had never been concerned in any public business. I might then have been sure that I had done no harm. One of the popes ordered an inscription upon his monument which would suit me very well. *Hic situs est Adrian, qui nihil sibi in vita infelicius duxit, quam quod imperaret.*³. . .

The Bible contains the most profound philosophy, the most perfect morality, and the most refined policy, that ever was conceived upon earth. It is the most republican book in the world, and therefore I will still revere it. The curses against fornication and adultery, and the prohibition of every wanton glance or libidinous ogle at a woman, I believe to be the only system that ever did or ever will preserve a republic in the world. There is a paradox for you. But if I don't make it out, you may say if you please that I am an enthusiast. I say then that national morality never was and never can be preserved without the utmost purity and chastity in women; and without national morality a republican government cannot be maintained.⁴ Therefore, my dear Fellow Citizens of America, you must ask leave of your wives and daughters to preserve your republic. I believe I shall write a book upon this topic before I die, and if I could articulate a word, I don't know but I would go into the pulpit and preach upon it. I should be very learned: ransack Greece and Rome and Judea and France and England and Holland, &c.

What shall I say of the Democratical Vice-President and the Federal would-be President, Burr? Although I never thought so highly of his natural talents or his acquired attainments as many of both parties have represented them, I never believed him to be a fool. But he must be an idiot or a lunatic if he has really planned and attempted to execute such a project as is im-

3. Adrian IV (1154–59), Nicholas Breakspear (ca. 1100–59), is said to have written the following epitaph for himself: "Adrianus hic situs est qui nihil sibi infelicius in vita, quam quod imperaret, duxit." ("Here lies Adrian, who regarded nothing in life more unfortunate to himself than that he ruled.") See Alfred H. Tarleton, *Nicholas Breakspear* (London, 1896), p. 255.

4. Rush had published in 1787 an essay on women's education, considering it an essential element in the nation's prosperity.

puted to him. It is even more senseless and extravagant than Miranda's. It is utterly incredible that any foreign power should have instigated him. It is utterly incredible that without foreign aid he should have thought that the trans-Alleghenian people would revolt with him; or even if they should revolt, that he and they could maintain themselves against the United States, who could so easily block up the Mississippi. Any man who has read the circular letters to their constituents from members of the House of Representatives in Congress from some of the southern states, while I was President, must be convinced that there were many among them who had no more regard to truth than the Devil. At present I suspect that this lying spirit has been at work concerning Burr and that Mr. Jefferson has been too hasty in his message in which he has denounced him by name and pronounced him guilty.[5] But if his guilt is as clear as the noonday sun, the first magistrate ought not to have pronounced it so before a jury had tried him.

Wilkinson's conduct, as it is represented, is equally unjustifiable.[6] But we shall hear more about it. The whole thing is a kind of waterspout, a terrible whirlpool, threatening to engulf everything. But it may be, as the fable says, that single bullet shot through it will quell it all at once to the level of the sea. . . .

John Adams

To ADAMS

April 3, 1807

MY VENERABLE AND DEAR FRIEND,

. . . I concur with you in your reflections upon the western insurrection, but not altogether in your opinion of Colonel Burr's objects. "Prudence in enterprises and even common business and a guilty conscience," Sully long ago remarked in his character of Count Biron, "are generally in-

5. Message to Congress, Jan. 22, 1807, *The Writings of Thomas Jefferson,* ed. Paul Leicester Ford (New York, 1892–99), IX, 14–20.

6. James Wilkinson (1757–1825) had a reputation as a turncoat and was then involved with Aaron Burr in the western conspiracy.

compatible."[7] Burr's plans have been directed like doctors' prescriptions by *pro re nata* circumstances.[8] I will give you a specimen of them. He applied indirectly to Governor McKean for the chief-justiceship of Pennsylvania just before he set off for Kentucky last year. Success here was as improbable as revolutionizing the western states. "To be unfortunate," says Richelieu, "is to be imprudent."[9] The history of Colonel Burr's pursuits verifies this remark. He failed, 1st, in obtaining a foreign embassy the first year he took his seat in the Senate; 2, in supplanting Mr. Jefferson; 3, in obtaining the government of New York; 4, in his western enterprises; and 5, in being chief justice of Pennsylvania. There is often something said or done by men in their youth that marks their destiny in life. I attended the commencement at Princeton at which Mr. Burr took his degree. He was then between 16 and 17 years of age. He spoke an elegant oration and with great spirit upon "Building Castles in the Air," in which he exposed its folly in literary, political, and military pursuits. These anecdotes are between ourselves.

Poor Pennsylvania is still upon her broadside. Our governor, who is now the only anchor of our state, is in bad health and upon the eve of being impeached. . . .

Benjn: Rush

To RUSH

April 12, 1807

DEAR SIR,

. . . I am willing to allow you philosophers your opinion of the universal gravitation of matter, if you will allow mine that there is in some souls a principle of absolute levity that buoys them irresistibly into the clouds.

---

7. Charles de Gontault, Duc de Biron (1562–1602), a peer of France, was executed for treachery when Sully discovered Biron's correspondence with agents of Spain and Savoy. The parallel careers of Biron and Burr are suggestive; both lacked prudence and sacrificed country to ambition. See Sully, *Memoirs,* trans. Charlotte Lennox (London, 1778), III, 110–112.

8. That is, according to the appearance of affairs.

9. "One of the Cardinal's maxims was, 'That an unfortunate and an imprudent person were synonymous terms.'" See [William Seward], *Anecdotes of Distinguished Persons* (London, 1804), IV, 185.

Whether you call it ethereal spirit or inflammable air, it has an uncontrollable tendency to ascend and has no capacity to ascertain the height at which it aims or the means by which it is to rise. This I take to be precisely the genius of Burr, Miranda, and Hamilton, among a thousand others of less or more note. These creatures have no prudence. If a man is once so disarranged in his intellect as to deliberate upon a project of ascending to the seven stars, it is natural enough that he should first attempt to seize the two horns of the new moon and make her his first stage.

Burr's project of making himself Vice-President of the United States to a reasonable man would have appeared an high degree of extravagance. . . . Yet in this he succeeded. Buoyed up by the flattery of the Presbyterians in Connecticut, New York, New Jersey, Pennsylvania, and all the southern states from the veneration in which they held his father and grandfather, the factions of Clintons and Livingstons alternately employed him as their instrument, till the Virginians conceived the project of engaging him to corrupt the state of New York from the Federal interest. In this they and he succeeded; but all the rest of his projects have been chimerical and without success. What could have inspired Burr with hopes of being an ambassador, a chief justice of Pennsylvania, or a governor of New York, or Vice-President of the United States?

Omnia Numina absunt si absit Prudentia.[10] Prudence is the first of virtues and the root of all others. Without prudence there may be abstinence but not temperance; there may be rashness but not fortitude; there may be insensibility or obstinacy but not patience. . . .

Pennsylvania can fall down on one broadside and then roll over to the other broadside, and then turn keel upwards, and then right herself up again. She is a ship, however, so violently addicted to pitching and rolling that I should not wonder if she dismasted herself.

To quit the figure and speak plain English, I have long thought that the first serious civil war in America will commence in Pennsylvania. The two nations of Irish and Germans who compose the principal part of the people are so entirely governed by their passions that it will be impossible to keep

---

10. "All Divinities are absent if Prudence is absent." Cf. Juvenal, *Satires* X.365.

them steady in any just system of policy. They will one day repent in sack-cloth the ascendency they have given to the trans-Alleghenian and southern Atlantic states, and so will New York. . . .

John Adams

To ADAMS

April 22, 1807

DEAR SIR,

. . . Your remarks upon the characters of three gentlemen mentioned in your last letter I believe to be just. They were all visionary in their principles and projects. The two Americans attempted to rise in the same kind of vehicle but by different kinds of gas—the one was the result of Federal, the other of Democratic, putrefaction. They both looked forward to a civil war to place them in the situation to which they aspired. One of them ac-knowledged it the evening before he fell—the other certainly attempted it. . . . His [Burr's] object was not Mexico but Louisiana, where my son in-forms us two-thirds of the inhabitants were in favor of his revolutionary en-terprise. You have mentioned in your letter the true cause of his success when he became Vice-President of the United States. . . .

In looking back upon the years of our Revolution, I often wish for those ten thousand hours that I wasted in public pursuits and that I now see did no *permanent* work for my family nor my country. Such is the delight I now take in my professional studies that I daily regret that ever I was seduced from them for a moment to assist in an enterprise such as the late Catherine of Russia accomplished at Petersburg, I mean building "a palace of ice.". . .

Benjn: Rush . . .

To RUSH

May 1, 1807

[MY DEAR FRIEND,]

You ask me if I do not sometimes imprecate evils on the day on which I became a politician. I have endeavored to recollect that day. It is a remote

one. A mighty impression was made upon my little head at the time of the
expedition against Cape Breton under General Pepperrell in 1745,[11] and on
the approach of the Duke d'Anville's armament against Boston.[12] But I have
only my memory to testify so early. An odd accident has within a month
brought to light the enclosed letter [to Nathan Webb], which has lain fifty-
one years and a half in darkness and silence, in dust and oblivion.

October 12, 1755

. . . All that part of creation which lies within our observation is liable
to change. Even mighty states and kingdoms are not exempted.

If we look into history, we shall find some nations rising from contemptible beginnings and spreading their influence till the whole globe is
subjected to their sway. When they have reached the summit of grandeur,
some minute and unsuspected cause commonly effects their ruin, and the
empire of the world is transferred to some other place. Immortal Rome
was at first but an insignificant village, inhabited only by a few abandoned
ruffians; but by degrees it rose to a stupendous height and excelled in arts
and arms all the nations that preceded it. But the demolition of Carthage
(what one should think would have established it in supreme dominion)
by removing all danger, suffered it to sink into a debauchery and made it
at length an easy prey to barbarians.

England, immediately upon this, began to increase (the particular and
minute causes of which I am not historian enough to trace) in power and
magnificence and is now the greatest nation upon the globe. Soon after
the Reformation, a few people came over into this new world for conscience' sake. Perhaps this apparently trivial incident may transfer the
great seat of empire into America. It looks likely to me; for if we can remove the turbulent Gallics, our people, according to the exactest compu-
tations, will in another century become more numerous than England itself. Should this be the case, since we have, I may say, all the naval stores

11. William Pepperrell (1696–1759), merchant and landholder of Massachusetts-Bay,
commanded the expeditionary forces in the siege of Louisburg in 1745.

12. Jean Baptiste de La Rochefoucauld, the Duc d'Anville, commanded a fleet in American waters in 1746. Bostonians feared for a time that their city might be attacked, but the
force went to Nova Scotia instead. See John A. Schutz, *William Shirley: King's Governor of
Massachusetts* (Chapel Hill, 1961), pp. 115–117.

of the nation in our hands, it will be easy to obtain the mastery of the seas; and then the united force of all Europe will not be able to subdue us. The only way to keep us from setting up for ourselves is to disunite us. *Divide et impera.* Keep us in distinct colonies, and then, some great men in each colony desiring the monarchy of the whole, they will destroy each others' influence and keep the country *in equilibrio.*

Be not surprised that I am turned politician. This whole town is immersed in politics. The interests of nations, and all the *dira* of war, make the subject of every conversation. I sit and hear, and after having been led through a maze of sage observations, I sometimes retire and, by laying things together, form some reflections pleasing to myself. The produce of one of these reveries you have read above. Different employments and different objects may have drawn your thoughts other ways. I shall think myself happy if in your turn you communicate your lucubrations to me.[13]. . .

Pray tell me your reflections on the sight of this droll phenomenon. I fancy they will be, first, what would our tories and Quakers and proprietors have said of this letter had it been published in 1774, '5, or '6? But I will not guess at any more of your observations. You shall make them yourself and relate them to me. But I will make my own remarks first and submit them to you.

1. Paine in *Common Sense* says that nobody in America ever thought, till he revealed to them the mighty truth, that America would ever be independent. I remember not the words, but this is the sense as I remember it. This I have always, at all times and in all places, contradicted and have affirmed that the idea of American independence, sooner or later, and of the necessity of it sometime or other was always familiar to gentlemen of reflection in all parts of America, and I spoke of my own knowledge in this province.

13. The original letter, dated Oct. 12, 1755, was included in Charles Francis Adams' biographical study of his grandfather (*Works,* I, 23–24). John Adams had been reading in 1755 Dr. William Clarke's *Observations on the . . . Conduct of the French* (Boston, 1755), which had published as an appendix Benjamin Franklin's "Observations concerning the Increase of Mankind and the Peopling of Countries." The essays had been published at the suggestion of Governor William Shirley, who was interested in colonial union and wanted these papers available to support his case for union, then before the Massachusetts General Court and the British ministry.

2. I very distinctly remember that in the war of 1755 a union of the colonies to defend themselves against the encroachments of the French was the general wish of the gentlemen with whom I conversed, and it was the opinion of some that we could defend ourselves and even conquer Canada better without England than with her, if she would but allow us to unite and exert our strength, courage, and skill, diffident as we were of the last.

3. It was the fear of this union of the colonies, which was indeed commenced in a congress at Albany,[14] which induced the English to take the war into their own hands.

4. The war was so ill conducted by Shirley, Lord Loudoun, Braddock, and all other British commanders till Wolfe and Amherst came forward that the utmost anxiety prevailed, and a thousand panics were spread lest the French should overrun us all.[15] All this time I was not alone in wishing that we were unshackled by Britain and left to defend ourselves.

5. The treatment of the provincial officers and soldiers by the British officers during that war made the blood boil in my veins.

6. Notwithstanding all this, I had no desire of independence as long as Britain would do us justice. I knew it must be an obstinate struggle and saw no advantage in it as long as Britain should leave our liberties inviolate.

7. Jefferson has acquired such glory by his declaration of independence in 1776 that I think I may boast of my declaration of independence in 1755, twenty-one years older than his.[16]

8. Our governor-elect, in his biographical sketch of Samuel Adams, ascribes to him the honor of the first idea and project of independence.[17] In 1755, when my letter to Dr. Webb was written, I had never seen the face of Samuel Adams.

14. The Albany Congress met in the summer of 1754 to settle problems of Indian trade and frontier defense. At the conference Franklin and others presented plans for colonial union.

15. The war was not so ill conducted under these generals as it was poorly managed from London. See Schutz, *William Shirley,* Ch. xii.

16. Time had corrupted Adams' memory. This letter hardly was intended to support American independence. It was rather an argument for empire, the enlarged position of America in the future British empire.

17. A few days after Samuel Adams' death on Oct. 2, 1803, Sullivan published a lengthy memoir. See Thomas C. Amory, *Life of James Sullivan* (Boston, 1859), II, 111–112.

9. The English, the Scotch, the tories, and hyperfederalists will rebellow their execrations against me as a rebel from my infancy, and a plotter of independence more than half a hundred years ago.

10. The present ruling party in the United States will repeat, renew, and redouble their curses and sarcasms against me for having meditated the ruin of this country from a boy, from a mere chicken in the eggshell, by building a navy under pretense of protecting our commerce and seaports but in reality only as a hobby-horse for myself to ride and to increase my patronage. For there can be no doubt but the boy, though not yet twenty years old and though pinched and starved in a stingy country school, fully expected to be king of North America and to marry his daughter to the Prince of Wales and his son, John Quincy, to the Princess Royal of England.

11. There can be no doubt but this letter, puerile and childish as it is, will make a distinguished figure in the memoirs of my life.[18] A grave and important question arises on a point of chronology, whether it should be inserted in the month of October, 1755, the time of its birth, or in the month of April, 1807, the time of its resurrection. As you have advised me to write my own life, you must resolve this question for me, for it is too perplexed for my judgment to determine. . . .

Now, Sir, to be serious, I do not curse the day when I engaged in public affairs. I do not say when I became a politician, for that I never was. I cannot repent of anything I ever did conscientiously from a sense of duty. I never engaged in public affairs for my own interest, pleasure, envy, jealousy, avarice, or ambition, or even the desire of fame. If any of these had been my motive, my conduct would have been very different. In every considerable transaction of my public life, I have invariably acted according to my best judgment for the public good, and I can look up to God for the sincerity of my intentions. How, then, is it possible I can repent? Notwithstanding this,

18. As Adams had predicted, his letter became important in accounts of his life. William Wirt referred to it in the eulogy to him and Jefferson, Oct. 19, 1826, before the United States House of Representatives: "Considering the age of the writer, and the point of time at which it was written, that letter may be pronounced, without hyperbole, a mental phenomenon." See *Eloquence of the United States,* comp. Ebenezer B. Williston (Middletown, Conn., 1827), V, 461–464.

I have an immense load of errors, weaknesses, follies, and sins to mourn over and repent of, and these are the only afflictions of my present life. . . .

Your "Palace of Ice" is a most admirable image. I agree that you and I have been employed in building a palace of ice. . . .

John Adams

To ADAMS

May 12, 1807

MY VENERATED AND DEAR FRIEND,

In one of your former letters you say as an excuse for your not assuming the reserve of certain public men, that you never believed yourself to be a "great man" and of course did not expect that anything you said and did and wrote would be the subject of public observation and scrutiny. I consider your not preserving a copy of your letter to your youthful friend Mr. Webb as proof of the truth of that assertion. I rejoice in its fortuitous discovery. It does great honor to your head and heart. Even the style of it did not escape commendation by my son Richard. He remarked that it contained the same *nerve* that characterizes your present compositions. What would not the biographers of Franklin and Washington give for such an early specimen of reflection and foresight? It would have served to elevate them above the rank of prophets. It would have made them little———; I must not apply the epithet that would have been given to them by mortal men. Your letter shall not perish.

I recollect, in dining with Dr. Franklin when he was president of the executive council of Pennsylvania, he said that Lord Camden[19] first suggested to him the idea of American independence at a gentleman's table in Paris some years before it took place. The Doctor revolted at the proposition, for at that time he never (he said) had once conceived of the glory or happiness of America as unconnected with the glory and happiness of

19. Charles Pratt, 1st Earl of Camden (1714–94), was a well-known supporter of the American cause during the Revolution.

Great Britain. Samuel Adams once told me that the independence of British America had been the *first* wish of his heart *seven* years before the commencement of the American Revolutionary War in 1774. An intimate friend of General Montgomery's[20] told me in 1776 that when he returned from America after the peace of 1763 he spoke in raptures of our country and often said, "What might not that country be, were it independent of Great Britain?" but neither of the two last-named gentlemen can date their wishes or views of that event in the year 1755, nor did they hint at the resources of our country for a navy which would one day deprive Great Britain of her empire upon the ocean. . . .

I thank you for the flattering notice you have taken of my present from the Queen of Etruria.[21] I have had reason to regret that an account of it found its way into our newspapers. An indiscreet friend has thereby done me more harm in one day than ten enemies could have done me in a year. I live in Philadelphia (though the country of ancestors who accompanied William Penn in 1683 to his wilderness on the Delaware) in an *enemy's* country. . . . My account of the yellow fever of the year 1793 was translated a few years ago into the Spanish language by order by the King of Spain.[22] His minister lately called upon me for my subsequent publications on that disease. He sent them to his court, since which he has conveyed to me in a polite letter the thanks of his royal master for them.[23] From several literary and philosophical societies in different parts of Europe I have received diplomas, an account of which I have likewise never mentioned to more than three persons out of my own family.

These attentions to my professional labors have consoled me under domestic charges of insanity upon medical subjects, and this has been the

20. Richard Montgomery (1738–75), a British soldier who was stationed in New York from 1763 to 1765 and returned as a civilian in 1772, joined the colonial expedition against Canada in 1775 and was killed in service.

21. Rush was proud of the international recognition that the gold medal from Queen Marie Louise gave his work on yellow fever.

22. *Relación de la calentura biliosa, remitente amarilla, que se manifesto en Filadelfia en el año de 1793* (Madrid, 1804).

23. Don Carlos Martinez, Marqués de Casa Yrujo (1763–1824), was minister to the United States from 1796 to 1806.

principal source of the gratification they have afforded me. If it has pleased God to grant me any degree of favor among men, I can truly say it has orig-inated in his goodness. I have not sought fame; on the contrary, my friends have often told me I must throw sixes (to use an allusion from the dice board) to eclipse the ruin of my reputation from the total repugnance of my opinions to the common sense and general practice of physicians in every part of the world. In reviewing my medical life I can find nothing in it that gives me pain except too much ardor in propagating my principles and too little forbearance of the ignorance, dullness, and malice that opposed them. Would to God that I had always said of my enemies, "Father, forgive them, they know not what they do." Their hostility to me was indeed the offspring of ignorance. Had they known that by the publications they dictated to Cobbett and Fenno against my opinions in medicine they would have stim-ulated me to further inquiries to defend them, and that they would spread my name far beyond the notice it would have otherwise attracted, they never would have acted towards me as they have done. But where has my pen carried me? I have written to you as I used to converse with you in your chamber at Mrs. Yard's in 2nd Street in the years 1774, 1775, and 1776. Let me beg of you to destroy this letter as soon as you have read it, in order to prevent one of your grandsons sending it *fifty-two* years hence to one of my grandsons, not as a mark of the reflection and foresight but of the folly and vanity of his grandfather. . . .

Poor Pennsylvania continues her wayward course. "I am not of this vile country," said Dean Swift when he was offended at the conduct of the people of Ireland.[24] But I am a native and citizen of Pennsylvania. Our gov-ernor has returned from Lancaster to Philadelphia in tolerable health, but with such a lameness in his hand as still to prevent his using his pen.

All my family join in love to you and yours. . . .

Benjn: Rush

24. The quotation has not been found, but it reflects accurately Swift's sentiments. Swift called Ireland in 1737 a "wretched kingdom, to which I was almost a stranger, . . . though I happened to be dropped . . . [there], and was a year old before I left it, and to my sor-row, did not die before I came back to it again." See *The Correspondence of Jonathan Swift*, ed. F. Elrington Ball (London, 1910–14), VI, 21–22.

To RUSH

May 21, 1807

DEAR SIR,

. . . My not preserving a copy of my letter to Doctor Nathan Webb (for he was a physician) is no wonder; for I never kept a copy of any letter till I became a member of Congress, in 1774. . . .

I have always laughed at the affectation of representing American independence as a novel idea, as a modern discovery, as a late invention. The idea of it as a possible thing, as a probable event, nay, as a necessary and unavoidable measure, in case Great Britain should assume an unconstitutional authority over us, has been familiar to Americans from the first settlement of the country and was as well understood by Governor Winthrop in 1675 as by Governor Sam Adams when he told you that independence had been the first wish of his heart for seven years. I suppose he dated from 1768, when the Board of Commissioners arrived and landed in Boston under the protection of nine ships of war and four thousand regular troops.[25]

A couplet has been repeated with rapture as long as I can remember, which was imputed to Dean Berkeley. The first line I have forgot, but the last was, "And empire rises where the sun descends."[26] This was public many years before my letter of Oct. 1755 to Doctor Webb. In 1760, Col. Josiah Quincy, the grandfather of Josiah Quincy, now a member of Congress from Boston, read to me a letter he had then just received from a Mr. Turner, I believe, one of the first mercantile houses in London, con-

25. Unlike many of his colleagues, Samuel Adams was an early advocate of revolution and was already giving Governor Francis Bernard much trouble by 1768. See John C. Miller, *Sam Adams: Pioneer in Propaganda* (Boston, 1936), pp. 153–154. John Adams' estimate of the original detachment of troops is high. Gage sent the 14th, 29th, 64th, and 65th regiments, but none was complete. See John Richard Alden, *General Gage in America* (Baton Rouge, 1948), pp. 163–164.

26. George Berkeley's famous poem "Verses on the Prospect of Planting Arts and Learning in America," 1726, does not contain the line as quoted. See *The Works of George Berkeley*, ed. Alexander Campbell Fraser (Oxford, 1901), IV, 365–366. A variation ("Westward the Star of empire takes its way") was quoted and attributed to Berkeley by John Quincy Adams in *An Oration, Delivered at Plymouth, December 22, 1802* (Boston, 1802), p. 31.

gratulating him on the surrender of Montreal to General [Jeffrey] Amherst, and the final conquest of Canada, "as a great event for America, not only by insuring her tranquility and repose, but as facilitating and advancing your (Col. Quincy's) country's rise to independence and empire."

Within the course of the year before the meeting of Congress in 1774, on a journey to some of our circuit courts in Massachusetts, I stopped one night at a tavern in Shrewsbury, about forty miles from Boston; and as I was cold and wet, I sat down at a good fire in the barroom to dry my greatcoat and saddlebags till a fire could be made in my chamber. There presently came in, one after another, half a dozen or half a score substantial yeomen of the neighborhood, who, sitting down to the fire after lighting their pipes, began a lively conversation upon politics. As I believe I was unknown to all of them, I sat in total silence to hear them. One said, "The people of Boston are distracted." Another answered, "No wonder the people of Boston are distracted. Oppression will make wise men mad." A third said, "What would you say, if a fellow should come to your house and tell you he was come to take a list of your cattle, that Parliament might tax you for them at so much a head? And how should you feel, if he should go out and break open your barn, to take down your oxen, cows, horses, and sheep?" "What would I say?" replied the first, "I would knock him in the head." "Well," said a fourth, "if Parliament can take away Mr. Hancock's wharf and Mr. Rowe's wharf, they can take away your barn and my house." After much more reasoning in this style, a fifth, who had as yet been silent, broke out. "Well, it is high time for us to rebel. We must rebel sometime or other, and we had better rebel now than at any time to come. If we put it off for ten or twenty years and let them go on as they have begun, they will get a strong party among us and plague us a great deal more than they can now. As yet they have but a small party on their side." I was disgusted with his word "rebel," because I was determined never to rebel, as much as I was to resist rebellion against the fundamental privileges of the Constitution, whenever British generals or governors should begin it. I mention this anecdote to show that the idea of independence was familiar, even among the common people, much earlier than some persons pretend. I have heard some gentlemen of education say that the first idea of independence was suggested to them by the pamphlet "Common Sense," and others, that they were first converted by it to that doctrine; but these were men of very little conversation with the world and men of very narrow views and very little reflection.

Your enemies are only your would-be rivals; they can never hurt you. Envy is a foul fiend that is only to be defied. You read Sully. His *Memoirs* are a pretty specimen. Every honest, virtuous, and able man that ever existed from Abel down to Doctor Rush has had this enemy to combat through life. "Envy does merit as its shade pursue."[27] You need not fear the charge of vanity. Vanity is really what the French call it, *amour-propre,* self-love, and it is an universal passion. All men have it in an equal degree. Honest men do not always disguise it. Knaves often do, if not always. When you see or hear a man pique himself on his modesty, you may depend upon it he is as vain a fellow as lives and very probably a great villain. I would advise you to communicate freely all the compliments you have had or may receive from Europe. Defy the foul fiend. . . .

The ominous dissolution of morality, both in theory and practice throughout the civilized world, threatens dangers and calamities of a novel species beyond all calculations, because there is no precedent or example in history which can show us the consequences of it. Perhaps you may say Tyre and Sidon, Sodom and Gomorrah are examples in point. But we have no relations of their rise, progress, or decline. You may say the old world, when it repented God that he had made man, when it grieved him in his heart that he had made so vile a creature, is a case in point. I know not what to say in answer to this, only that the same authority we have for the fact assures us that the world shall never be again drowned. . . .

May 23, 1807

I have mentioned my brother Cranch, a gentleman of four-score, whose memory is better than mine; I will relate to you a conversation with him last evening.[28] I asked him if he recollected the first line of a couplet whose second line was "And empire rises where the sun descends." He paused a moment and said,

27. Alexander Pope, "An Essay on Criticism," Pt. II, line 266.
28. Richard Cranch (1726–1811) was Abigail's brother-in-law.

The eastern nations sink, their glory ends,
And empire rises where the sun descends.

I asked him if Dean Berkeley was the author of them. He answered no. The tradition was, as he had heard it for sixty years, that these lines were inscribed, or rather drilled, into a rock on the shore of Monument Bay in our old colony of Plymouth and were supposed to have been written and engraved there by some of the first emigrants from Leyden, who landed at Plymouth. However this may be, I may add my testimony to Mr. Cranch's that I have heard these verses for more than sixty years. I conjecture that Berkeley became connected with them, in my head, by some report that the bishop had copied them into some publication. There is nothing, in my little reading, more ancient in my memory than the observation that arts, sciences, and empire had travelled westward; and in conversation it was always added, since I was a child, that their next leap would be over the Atlantic into America.[29]

The claim of the 1776 men to the honor of first conceiving the idea of American independence, or of first inventing the project of it, is as ridiculous as that of Dr. Priestley to the discovery of the perfectibility of man. I hereby disclaim all pretensions to it, because it was much more ancient than my nativity. . . .

John Adams

To ADAMS

July 9, 1807

MY DEAR FRIEND,

. . . In one of your former letters you spoke in high terms of *prudence*. I neglected to reply to your encomiums upon it. General Lee used to call it a

29. New Englanders were much concerned about their western boundary during Adams' youth, and the expedition against Louisburg in 1745 was followed by plans for expeditions against Canada in 1746 and 1747. They also related biblical prophecies such as Genesis 28: 14 to their own dreams of westward expansion.

"rascally virtue." [30] It certainly has more counterfeits than any other virtue, and when *real* it partakes very much of a selfish nature. It was this virtue that protected the property and lives of most of the Tories during the American Revolution. It never achieved anything great in human affairs. Luther, Harvey, and many other authors of new opinions and discoveries were devoid of it; so were the Adamses and Hancock, who gave the signals for war in the year 1775. In private life what is commonly called prudence is little else than a system of self-love. A patient of mine once named me (without my knowledge) with two other persons, one of whom was his brother, as executors of his will. Knowing this brother to be a notorious rogue, and wishing not to act as an executor myself, I called upon my third colleague and urged him instantly to take charge in a legal way of all the property of our deceased friend. He said he could not do this without offending our friend's brother. I asked him if he did not believe he would apply all our friend's property to his own use? He said yes, but that he could not act as I advised without a quarrel with him and "that he never had a dispute with any man in his life." Foreseeing the loss of our friend's property, I qualified as an executor and thereby rescued all his estate from the hands of his brother except 300 dollars which he collected and appropriated to his own use. By acting in this manner, I paid my friend's debts and saved a handsome sum for his only child, and that I might not incur even a suspicion of acting from interested motives, I gave all my commissions on the cash I received or expended to my brother executor who refused to concur with me in offending our friend's brother. The result of this conduct was not a quarrel with the fellow (for he was below a resentful reply), but the most intemperate abuse from him and a threat to expose me in the newspapers for an attack upon his honor and character. My colleague in the meanwhile kept up a friendly intercourse with him and thereby retained the character of a *prudent,* peaceable man. . . .

Colonel Burr retains in his confinement his usual good spirits. He is a

30. Charles Lee (1731–82) was court-martialed for disobeying Washington's orders at the battle of Monmouth in 1778. He spent his remaining years writing abusive letters about Washington's character and addressing Congress regarding his grievances. Rush first quotes Lee on June 12, 1781; see *Letters,* I, 264.

nondescript in the history of human nature. Should he be acquitted, you say he may yet be President of the United States. It is possible. Some worse men hold high appointments in every part of our country. . . .

Benjn: Rush . . .

To RUSH

September 1, 1807

DEAR FRIEND,

. . . When General Lee called prudence "a rascally virtue," his meaning was good. He meant the spirit which evades danger when duty requires us to face it. This is cowardice, not prudence; or he meant that subtilty which consults private interest, ease, or safety by the sacrifice or the neglect of our friends or our country. This may be cunning, but is more properly called knavery than prudence. . . .

By prudence I mean that deliberation and caution which aims at no ends but good ones, and good ones by none but fair means, and then carefully adjusts and proportions its good means to its good ends. Without this virtue there can be no other. Justice itself cannot exist without it. A disposition to render to everyone his right is of no use without prudence to judge of what is his right and skill to perform it.

When in 1797, '8, and '9, I promoted the fortification of our seaports, the purchase of navy yards, the building of a navy, &c., I think I was more prudent than those who opposed me, though my popularity was sacrificed to it and my enemies rose to power by their imprudent opposition. Their prudence, I agree with Lee, was a rascally virtue.

I am anxious to see the progress of Burr's trial, not from any love or hatred I bear to the man, for I cannot say that I feel either. He is, as you say, a nondescript in natural history. But I think something must come out on the trial, which will strengthen or weaken our confidence in the general union. I hope something will appear to determine clearly whether any foreign power has or has not been tampering with our union. . . .

John Adams

To RUSH

September, 1807

DEAR FRIEND,

I want to write an essay. Whom shall I choose for a model? Plutarch, old Montaigne, Lord Bacon, Addison, Johnson, or Franklin? The last, if he had devoted his life to the study, might have equalled Montaigne in essays or La Fontaine in fables,[31] for he was more fitted for either or both than to conduct a nation like Rosny or Colbert.[32] I am, however, too round about to imitate the close, direct, and sententious manner of any of them. I am stumbled at the very threshold. My subject is disinterest or disinterestedness. I must leave you to decide, for I cannot say which is the most proper word.

Mirabeau[33] said of La Fayette, "Il a affiché désintéressement," and he added, "this never fails." You know the sense of the word "affiché"? It is as much as to say "he advertised" his disinterestedness. That is equivalent to saying that he employed a crier to proclaim through the streets "O Yes! O Yes! O Yes!" All manner of persons may have the benefit of my services, *gratis,* provided always and only that they will yield me their unlimited and unsuspecting confidence and make me commander in chief of five hundred thousand men, and after I shall have gained a few victories, make me a king or an emperor, when I shall take a fancy to be either. This has been the amount and the result of most of the disinterestedness that has been professed in the world. I say most, not all. There are exceptions, and our Washington ought to pass for one. La Fayette imitated his

31. Michel de Montaigne (1533–92), a great French essayist, was famous for his ability to find humor in the behavior of human beings. Jean de La Fontaine (1621–95), French poet and dramatist, was the author of the *Fables* (1678) and the *Contes* (1664–66).

32. Maximilien de Béthune, Duc de Sully, son of the Baron de Rosny, was known as Rosny before 1606. He was Henry IV's superintendent of finance for a time and diplomat at the court of James I in 1603. Better known is Jean Baptiste Colbert (1619–83), who was Louis XIV's famous financial expert and minister of marine.

33. Honoré Gabriel Riquetti, Comte de Mirabeau (1749–91), was an early leader of the French Revolution who worked for a reformed monarchy.

example. So have Jefferson, Hamilton, Governor Strong, Fisher Ames, and many others.[34]. . .

Washington had great advantages for obtaining credence. He possessed a great fortune, immense lands, many slaves, an excellent consort, no children. What could he desire more for felicity here below? His professions therefore of attachment to private life, fondness for agricultural employments, and rural amusements were easily believed; and we all agreed to believe him and make the world believe him. Yet we see he constantly betrayed apprehensions that he should not be seriously believed by the world. He was nevertheless believed, and there is not an example in history of a more universal acknowledgment of disinterestedness in any patriot or hero than there is and will be to the latest posterity in him.

La Fayette had not the same felicity. His fortune in France bore no proportion to Washington's in America; and Frenchmen had not the same faith with Americans in the existence or possibility of disinterestedness in any man. His professions, therefore, did not produce such an enthusiasm as Washington's. Jefferson resigned his office as Secretary of State and retired, and his friends said he had struck a great stroke to obtain the presidency. . . . The whole anti-Federal party at that time considered this retirement as a sure and certain step towards the summit of the pyramid and, accordingly, represented him as unambitious, unavaricious, and perfectly disinterested in all parts of all the states in the union. When a man has one of the two greatest parties in a nation interested in representing him to be disinterested, even those who believe it to be a lie will repeat it so often to one another that at last they will seem to believe it to be true. Jefferson has succeeded; and multitudes are made to believe that he is pure benevolence; that he desires no profit; that he wants no patronage; that if you will only let him govern, he will rule only to make the people happy. But you and I know him to be an intriguer.

Hamilton had great disadvantages. His origin was infamous; his place

34. Caleb Strong (1745–1819), a Massachusetts Federalist, was governor of the state from 1800 to 1808, and again from 1812 to 1816. He was United States senator during Adams' presidency.

of birth and education were foreign countries; his fortune was poverty it-self; the profligacy of his life—his fornications, adulteries, and his incests—were propagated far and wide. Nevertheless, he "affichéd" disinterestedness as boldly as Washington. His myrmidons asserted it with as little shame, tho' not a man of them believed it. All the rest of the world ridiculed and despised the pretext. He had not, therefore, the same success. Yet he found means to fascinate some and intimidate others. You and I know him also to have been an intriguer. . . .

Ames miscarried. He was obnoxious to one party and, by placing all his hopes on Hamilton, lost the confidence of the soundest portion of the other party and is now dying, as I fear, under the gloomy feelings of his disappointments.

I have sometimes amused myself with inquiring where Washington got his system. Was it the natural growth of his own genius? Had there been any examples of it in Virginia? Instances enough might have been found in his-tory of excellent hypocrites, whose concealments, dissimulations, and sim-ulations had deceived the world for a time; and some great examples of real disinterestedness, which produced the noblest efforts and have always been acknowledged. But you know that our beloved Washington was but very superficially read in history of any age, nation, or country. Where then did he obtain his instruction? I will tell you what I conjecture.

Rollin's *Ancient History,* you know, is very generally diffused through this country because it has been and is in England. The reading of most of our men of letters extends little further than this work and Prideaux's *Connections of the Old and New Testament.*[35] From Rollin I suspect Washington drew his wisdom, in a great measure. In the third chapter of the third book . . . there are in the character of Dejoces several strokes which are very curious as they resemble the politics of so many of our countrymen, though the whole character taken together is far inferior in purity and magnanimity to that of Washington. "He retired from public business, pretending to be over

35. Humphrey Prideaux (1648–1724), distinguished scholar and dean of Norwich Cathe-dral, was the author of *The Old and New Testament Connected in the History of the Jews and Neighbouring Nations* (1716–18) and *The Nature of Imposture Fully Displayed in the Life of Mahomet* (1697).

fatigued with the multitudes of people that resorted to him." "His own domestic affairs would not allow him to attend those of other people" &c. . . .

"There is nothing certainly nobler or greater than to see a private person eminent for his merit and virtue and fitted by his excellent talents for the highest employments, and yet through inclination and modesty preferring a life of obscurity and retirement; than to see such a man sincerely refuse the offer made to him of reigning over a whole nation, and at last consent to undergo the toil of government, upon no other motive than that of being serviceable to his fellow citizens. His first disposition, by which he declares that he is acquainted with the duties and consequently the dangers annexed to a sovereign power, shows him to have a soul more elevated and great than greatness itself; or, to speak more justly, a soul superior to all ambition. . . . But when he generously sacrifices his own quiet and satisfaction to the welfare and tranquility of the public, it is plain he understands what that sovereign power has in it, really good or truly valuable; which is that it puts a man in a condition of becoming the defender of his country, of procuring it many advantages, and of redressing various evils . . . and he comforts himself for the cares and troubles to which he is exposed by the prospect of the many benefits resulting from them to the public. Such a governor was Numa at Rome, and such have been some other emperors, whom the people have constrained to accept the supreme power. . . ."

"He commanded his subjects to build a city, marking out himself the place and circumference of the walls." "Within the last and smallest enclosure stood the king's palace. In the next there were several apartments for lodging the officers. The name of the city was Ecbatana," &c.[36] Tom Paine represents me as exulting at Washington [city]: "Is not this great Babylon that I have builded," &c. The scoundrel knew it was Washington and Jefferson that built this Ecbatana; and he might have known that I opposed it in every step of its progress and voted against it in Senate on all occasions. But truth has no esteem in his eyes. No more.

Tell me, has not our American system of politics and ambition been cop-

36. Charles Rollin, *Ancient History,* 11th edn. (London, 1808), II, 104–107, contains substantially the quoted material.

ied from this very passage? If not, from whence did it come? Read the chapter in Rollin. Washington was more sincere than Dejoces, but I am persuaded he had read this description of him.

John Adams

To ADAMS

October 31, 1807

DEAR SIR,

. . . I agree with you in your history of disinterestedness. It is indeed a rare virtue. . . . I do not think the gentleman you alluded to in your letter upon this subject formed himself or his conduct upon the model of the character described in Rollin. He was self-taught in all the arts which gave him his immense elevation above all his fellow citizens. An intimate friend of Colonel Hamilton's informed me that he once told him that he had never read a single military book except Simes's *Guide*.[37] Sir Hans Sloane[38] used to show among the curiosities of his museum a list of Dr. Radcliffe's library, which consisted only of half a dozen practical books upon medicine. A friend of Radcliffe's told him of this satire upon his medical character and spoke at the same time of the large size of Sir Hans' library. "That is all right," said Dr. Radcliffe. "D——n the fellow, he requires books." The same remark has been applied to many other men who possess learning and reading, and the same preeminence over them by men who never read has often been ascribed to the gentleman mentioned in your letter. While the resources of genius, reading, and reflection have each had their specific advocates for fame, perhaps Dr. Clark's[39] opinion of the means of becoming eminent in a profession deserves the most credit; it consists, he says, in

37. Thomas Simes, *The Military Guide for Young Officers* (London, 1772; Philadelphia, 1776), was widely read and consulted during the American Revolution. Adams owned a copy.

38. Sir Hans Sloane (1660–1753), court physician for Queen Anne and George II, collected a large body of books and manuscripts and bequeathed them to the nation for a consideration of £20,000 for his heirs.

39. John Clark (1744–1805) was a physician and philanthropist who wrote on fevers and the problems of medical care on voyages into humid climates. See *The Gentleman's Magazine*, LXXV (1805), Pt. II, 678.

"reading much, thinking much, and writing much." They mutually assist each other in giving the greatest expansion and correctness to the human mind. For this purpose they should bear a due proportion to each other.

Dr. Priestley read and wrote a great deal. Had he *thought* more, he would probably have corrected many of the errors which he defended upon several subjects. Dr. Franklin thought a great deal, wrote occasionally, but read during the middle and latter years of his life very little, and hence the errors of several of his opinions upon government. Our great man wrote a great deal, thought constantly, but read (it is said) very little, and hence the disrespect with which his talents and character have been treated by his aide-de-camp. But enough of great men! —especially to one who has ceased to believe in them from knowing so well how much littleness is mixed with human greatness, how much folly with human wisdom, and how much vice with the greatest attainments in human virtue. . . .

Benjn: Rush

P.S. My son Richard has just returned from Norfolk, where he went to take a part in the inquiry into the conduct of Captain Barron.[40] On his way home he stopped at Richmond, where he saw and heard many things which it is not lawful to tell. Federalism! Democracy! law! order! "Libertas et natale solum!" All fine, very fine words. I wonder, in the language of Dean Swift, "where we stole them."[41]

To RUSH

November 11, 1807

MY DEAR PHILOSOPHER AND FRIEND,

I have, long before the receipt of your favor of the 31 of October, supposed that either you were gazing at the comet or curing the influenza; and

---

40. James Barron (1769–1851) was commander of the *Chesapeake* at the time of its famous encounter with the *Leopard*. The court-martial found him guilty of gross neglect of duty.

41. See Swift's poem "Whitshed's Motto on His Coach," in which William Whitshed, who presided over the trial of Harding, printer of the *Drapier's Letters,* is criticized for his judicial behavior.

in either case that you was much better employed than in answering my idle letters. . . .

Self-taught or book-learned in the arts, our hero [Washington] was much indebted to his talents for "his immense elevation above his fellows." Talents! you will say, what talents? I answer. 1. An handsome face. That this is a talent, I can prove by the authority of a thousand instances in all ages: and among the rest Madame Du Barry, who said "Le véritable royauté est la beauté."[42] 2. A tall stature, like the Hebrew sovereign chosen because he was taller by the head than the other Jews. 3. An elegant form. 4. Graceful attitudes and movements. 5. A large, imposing fortune consisting of a great landed estate left him by his father and brother, besides a large jointure with his lady, and the guardianship of the heirs of the great Custis estate, and in addition to all this, immense tracts of land of his own acquisition. There is nothing, except bloody battles and splendid victories, to which mankind bow down with more reverence than to great fortune. . . .

Mankind in general are so far from the opinion of the lawyer that there are no disinterested actions, that they give their esteem to none but those which they believe to be such. They are oftener deceived and abused in their judgments of disinterested men and actions than in any other, it is true. But such is their love of the marvelous, and such their admiration of uncommon generosity, that they will believe extraordinary pretensions to it, and the Pope says, "Si bonus populus vult decipi, decipiatur."[43]

Washington, however, did not deceive them. I know not that they gave him more credit for disinterestedness than he deserved, though they have not given many others so much. 6. Washington was a Virginian. This is equivalent to five talents. Virginian geese are all Swans. Not a bairn in Scotland is more national, not a lad upon the Highlands is more clannish, than every Virginian I have ever known. . . . The Philadelphians and New Yorkers, who are local and partial enough to themselves, are meek and modest in comparison with Virginian Old Dominionism. Washington, of course, was extolled without bounds. 7. Washington was preceded by favorable

42. "The true royalty is beauty."
43. "If the good people wish to be deceived, let them be deceived," adapted from a saying of Cardinal Carlo Carafa (Pope Paul IV), ca. 1560, and apparently taken from De Thou.

anecdotes. The English had used him ill in the expedition of Braddock. They had not done justice to his bravery and good counsel. They had exaggerated and misrepresented his defeat and capitulation, which interested the pride as well as compassion of Americans in his favor. President Davies had drawn his horoscope by calling him "that heroic youth, Col. Washington."[44] Mr. Lynch of South Carolina[45] told me before we met in Congress in 1774 that "Colonel Washington had made the most eloquent speech that ever had been spoken upon the controversy with England, viz. that if the English should attack the people of Boston, he would raise a thousand men at his own expense and march at their head to New England to their aid.". . . 8. He possessed the gift of silence. This I esteem as one of the most precious talents. 9. He had great self-command. It cost him a great exertion sometimes, and a constant constraint, but to preserve so much equanimity as he did required a great capacity. 10. Whenever he lost his temper as he did sometimes, either love or fear in those about him induced them to conceal his weakness from the world. Here you see I have made out ten talents without saying a word about reading, thinking, or writing, upon all which subjects you have said all that need be said. You see I use the word talents in a larger sense than usual, comprehending every advantage. Genius, experience, learning, fortune, birth, health are all talents, though I know not how the word has been lately confined to the faculties of the mind. . . .

Now for that resolute word "No." I ought to have said No to the appointment of Washington and Hamilton and some others; and Yes to the appointment of Burr, Muhlenburg, and some others.[46] I ought to have appointed Lincoln and Gates and Knox and Clinton, &c. But if I had said Yes and No in this manner, the Senate would have contradicted me in every

44. Samuel Davies, *Religion and Patriotism the Constituents of a Good Soldier* (Philadelphia, 1755), p. 9n. Davies was president of the College of New Jersey.

45. The delegate from South Carolina to the Continental Congress, Thomas Lynch (1727–76), met Adams on his arrival in Philadelphia in 1774.

46. Adams refers to his embarrassment in 1798 when he was forced to follow the wishes of Washington in making Hamilton second in command of the army. Washington was so popular throughout the nation that alienation of the former President would have created a storm. But Washington refused to serve unless Hamilton, who had only the rank of a colonel at the end of the Revolution, was commissioned a general and jumped ahead of all other officers of the military establishment.

instance. You ask what would have been the consequence. I answer Washington would have [been] chosen President at the next election if he had lived, and Hamilton would have been appointed commander in chief of the army. This would have happened as it was if Washington had lived, and this was intended.[47] With all my ministers against me, a great majority of the Senate and of the House of Representatives, I was no more at liberty than a man in a prison, chained to the floor and bound hand and foot. . . . Washington ought either to have never gone out of public life, or he ought never to have come in again. . . .

John Adams

To ADAMS

December 15, 1807

MY VENERABLE AND DEAR FRIEND,

. . . I admire the correctness of your history of the *ten* talents committed to the subject of your letter. Upon the talent of his taciturnity, Mr. Liston[48] gave me the following anecdote: "That he was the only person he had ever known (and he had conversed with several crowned heads and many of the first nobility in Europe) who made *no reply* of any kind to a question that he did not choose to answer."

A clamor has lately broken out in our city against the perpetual residence of Congress at Washington. The dissolution of the Union in case of a war is predicted from it. To which of the generals, aides, secretaries, or major generals must that measure be ascribed?—for the author of it did no wrong.

Torrents of abuse are poured out in all the Virginia papers against J. Marshall and J. Randolph, but the authors of them all qualify their invectives with the most extravagant encomiums upon their "abilities." You have

47. At the time of Washington's death Hamilton and his followers were urging the former President to reenter politics as a candidate for the presidency, using the persuasive idea that Washington must run for office in order to retain his fame.

48. Robert Liston (1742–1836) was the British minister at Washington.

assigned the true reason for this conduct. They both possess the *talent* of being Virginians. . . .

To persons who read newspapers in the years 1774 and 1775 and remember the arguments with which the advocates for Great Britain defended her right to tax us, it is amusing to see how exactly those arguments are repeated in the attempts that are made to defend her right to tyrannize over our ships upon the ocean. Who after this can refrain from crying out with the parrot, "I have lost my labor"?[49] Let us in our retirement pity the bear-leaders who *now* occupy our places in those years.

Benjn: Rush

To RUSH

December 28, 1807

MY DEAR PHILOSOPHER AND FRIEND,

. . . The clamor in your city is too late. Pennsylvania may thank herself for the evil she feels. She has not only established the permanent residence of Congress at Washington, but she has established a perpetuity of absolute power at the southward of Potomac under which, however she may complain, she must suffer. The Union is not a palace of ice, nor a castle of glass. There must be an intense heat to melt it and very hard blows to break it. One war will not dissolve it. Deep and strong are its roots in the judgments and hearts of the people. A dozen Hamiltons and Burrs will be killed in duels or hanged, before the Union will be broken. Washington believed bona fide that the Federal City would . . . bind together not only the northern and southern states but the trans-Alleghenians with the Atlantic states. . . .

The resemblance you remark between the arguments in 1774 and 1775 and this time really exists. Who will argue and what will be the arguments in favor of the *Sovereign of the World,* to apply to Napoleon the epithet

---

49. This is one of Rush's frequent remarks. He may have taken the quotation from Shakespeare's *Macbeth,* V.viii.8, where Macbeth, on slaying MacDuff, says, "Thou losest labour," or from *All's Well That Ends Well,* III.v.8, where the widow sighs, "We have lost our labour."

which Dryden applies to Alexander in his *Feast?*[50] The Dutch once declared war against England, France, and Spain all at once and fought them all with great intrepidity. Shall we follow their example? Fight them all with 240 gunboats?

I wish you would cure our rulers of the hydrophobia![51] Yet if they should get well of it now, it seems to be almost too late. . . . If ever a nation was guilty of imprudence, ours has been so in making a naval force and maritime preparations unpopular. But anything, no matter what, to turn J. A. out and come under the dominion of Virginia. Huzza . . . for Virginia! Hail Massachusetts, New York, and Pennsylvania![52] Sacrifice loyally your commerce and clank your chains in harmonious concert with Virginia! She tells you commerce produces money, money luxury, and all three are incompatible with republicanism! Virtuous, simple, frugal Virginia hates money and wants it only for Napoleon, who desires it only to establish freedom through the world!

My friend, the times are too serious. Instead of the most enlightened people, I fear we Americans shall soon have the character of the silliest people under Heaven.

John Adams

50. Dryden, *Alexander's Feast,* line 33: "And stamp'd an image of himself, a sov'reign of the world."

51. Rush had recently sent Adams a copy of his lecture on veterinary medicine, in which he had strongly recommended study and prevention of animal diseases. The lecture is number thirteen in his *Sixteen Introductory Lectures* (Philadelphia, 1811).

52. An echo of *Macbeth,* I.iii.48–50, 62–69.

CHAPTER 5

A Game of Leapfrog

"OUR BELOVED COUNTRY, my dear Friend, is indeed in a very dangerous situation. It is between two great fires in Europe and between two ignited parties at home." The national crisis, Adams hastened to add, put an obligation upon honest men to declare their principles, to be true Americans. The "sordid stinginess" of the new rich in trade and agriculture must be rebuked; the people must be given the example of virtue by their leaders' lives and the party game of leapfrog ended. Rush was afraid there was little either man could do to check the greed and avarice of the new elite in party and nation. He felt pain, he admitted, and would have liked to erase his name from the Declaration of Independence and disassociate himself from the nation he helped to found. Adams, true to his nature, reminded Rush of their obligation as citizens: to work for the good of their country as long as they lived.

To ADAMS

February 18, 1808

MY VENERABLE AND DEAR FRIEND,

. . . Our citizens are making great preparations for celebrating the birthday of the first President of the United States. Is this not a unique [practice] in the history of nations *thus* to perpetuate the memories of their benefactors and deliverers? I exclude from this question the homage that has been paid by all nations to the birthday of the Saviour of the World. By such acts we shall gradually be prepared for much higher degrees of devotion to the name of our great man. What do you think of hearing the minister of our church seven years hence begin public worship by saying, "Let us sing to the praise and glory of G. W."?[1]

Great clamors are everywhere excited against the Embargo.[2] How different were the feelings and conduct of our citizens in 1774 upon the subject of the most oppressive nonimportation act of that memorable year! The clamors against the Embargo originated in our cities and chiefly among one class of citizens. "And he causeth all, both small and great, rich and poor, bond and free, to receive a mark in their right hand or in their foreheads, and that *no man might buy or sell* save he had the mark or the name of the beast or the number of his name."[3] It is easy to tell who are the persons alluded to that have received this mark, as also the nature of the impression made by it upon the hand or upon the forehead,[4] but who is the beast that has imposed this mark upon the buyers and sellers of our country? Is it Napoleon; or is *three* the number of his name—that is, George the Third; or is it the Lord and Master of them both, Lucifer the First?

What monuments of ignorance, folly, and pride will Congress leave behind them should they finally escape from the city of Washington! . . .

Benjn: Rush

To RUSH

February 25, 1808

MY DEAR PHILOSOPHER,

Your two last letters have puzzled me. In one you tell me that your citizens are clamorous against the residence of Congress at Washington. Now Washington was the father of the Columbian Territory, the city of Washington, and the residence of Congress in it; and Washington, Jefferson, and

1. Washington's birthday became a Federalist holiday much to the annoyance of Rush and Adams, who resented the excessive veneration as unrepublican. During his presidency Adams had caused public comment when he and Mrs. Adams declined an invitation to participate in a party to honor Washington's activities as a general.

2. The Embargo Act of 1807.

3. Revelation 13:16–17.

4. Note in letter by Rush: "An eagle and the figure of liberty."

L'Enfant[5] were the triumvirate who planned the city, the capitol, and the prince's palace. In your last, Feb. 18, you tell me that your citizens are making preparations for celebrating a kind of adoration to Divus Washington. How can these two clamors be reconciled? The celebration of the birthday I can account for by Blount's motion to repeal the funding system,[6] because Hamilton's adulation can be supported only by Washington's adoration. Another obvious motive is to cast disgrace upon Washington's two successors, Adams and Jefferson. Similar motives have produced a phenomenon in Boston. On the fourth of July, Washington's picture is placed behind the table of the principal magistrates, Hamilton's opposite to him in the most conspicuous spot in the whole hall, while the pictures of Samuel Adams and John Hancock are crowded away in two obscure corners. Thus is Faneuil Hall, which ought to be as sacred in Boston as the Temple of Jupiter was on the Capitol Hill in Rome, made the headquarters of fornication, adultery, incest, libeling, and electioneering intrigue. Yet Boston is the headquarters of good principles. One of the most superb blocks of brick buildings, too, erected lately by the richest man in the town, is called Hamilton Place, and twenty other proud palaces deserve the name as well.[7]

The clamors against the Embargo are no doubt intended to disgrace Jefferson's administration. France and England had embargoed our trade before we embargoed it. No prudent merchant would send a ship to sea unless she had the mark of one or other of the beasts, perhaps both, for some are capable of making their court to both.

My old acquaintance King George has broke his word. He promised me he would be the last to disturb our independence. But his tyrannical proclamation for impressing seamen from our merchant ships is a flagrant disturbance of our independence. . . .

You ask how different were our feelings and conduct in 1774? Different

5. Pierre Charles L'Enfant (1754–1825), soldier and artist, surveyed the future site of Washington, D.C., at President Washington's request.

6. Thomas Blount (1759–1812), soldier and merchant of North Carolina, was first elected to the House of Representatives in 1793. Blount's threat to lead a campaign against the funding system was given on Feb. 5, 1808.

7. Hamilton Place was built in 1806. It was a good example of how the new wealth was changing the appearance of American cities.

indeed. We then loved liberty better than money. Now we love money better than liberty. Then liberty meant security for life, liberty, property, and character. Now the word has changed its meaning and signifies money, electioneering, tricks, and libels, and perhaps the protection of French armies and British fleets.

When my parson says, "Let us sing to the praise and glory of G. W.," your church will adopt a new collect in its liturgy and say "Sancte Washington, ora pro nobis."[8]

But you know that all this adulation in the leaders of it is sheerly hypocritical. It would have added at Washington a mausoleum of an hundred feet square at the base and an hundred feet high to the other monuments of "ignorance, folly, and pride" to be left in that place when Congress shall remove from it.

I told my friend Powell of Virginia[9] at my own table that if that bill for a mausoleum passed, I should be obliged to do the most unpopular act of my whole unpopular life by sending it back with a negative and reasons. "Oh!" said Powell, "I hope not!"

I hope that when anarchy shall invade us, it will stumble on that rock and break its shins.

At the time of Hamilton's death, the Federal papers avowed that Hamilton was the soul and Washington the body, or in other words that Washington was the painted wooden head of the ship and Hamilton the pilot and steersman.

Thus the world goes, has ever gone, and ever will go. And so let it go.

John Adams

To ADAMS

April 5, 1808

MY VERY DEAR FRIEND,

. . . You have mistaken the church to which I belong in supposing that prayers will one day be offered up in it to the great man whose birthday has

8. "Saint Washington, pray for us"—a parody of the litany.
9. Levin Powell (1737–1810) was the only Virginia elector to vote for Adams in the 1796 election. Powell served in the House of Representatives from 1799 to 1801.

lately been celebrated in our country. During the life of Dr. Ewing,[10] whose influence was very extensive in the Presbyterian Church, I took refuge in the Episcopal Church from his malice and persecutions excited by my opposition to his holding by usurpation the provost's place in the College of Philadelphia. The Episcopal Church at that time had divested itself of many of its absurdities in doctrine and worship. By their restoration by Bishop Seabury,[11] I was thrown out of its pale and have never since visited with any other society, although I constantly worship with them all but chiefly with the society under the care of the Reverend Dr. Green.[12] I have often lamented the squeamishness of my . . . mind upon the subject of religious creeds and modes of worship. But accustomed to think for myself in my profession, and encouraged to believe that my opinions and modes of practice are just, from the success which has attended them even in the hands of their enemies, I have ventured to transfer the same spirit of inquiry to religion. . . .

I pass on to lament that not less than 47 vessels have lately arrived at the Havana with cargoes of flour, all of which cleared out of American ports and all of which pretend to have been driven from them by bad weather. Can a country stained with such crimes escape the judgments of heaven? And is such a country worthy of the patriotism of honest men? . . .

Benjn: Rush

P.S. . . . Do you not felicitate yourself in your retirement every time you view the present distracted and perilous state of our country? Were Mr. Jefferson now asked how he liked his present seat at the helm of our government, he would probably answer as Sancho did after having occupied a similar situation, "Give me (not my shoes and stockings, which were the words of Sancho) but give me my telescope and mathematical instruments.". . .

10. John Ewing (1732–1802), provost of the University of Pennsylvania, was a linguist, clergyman of repute, and author of scientific papers.

11. Samuel Seabury (1726–96) was the first bishop of the Protestant Episcopal Church in the United States.

12. Ashbel Green (1762–1848), eighth president of the College of New Jersey, was minister of the Second Presbyterian Church of Philadelphia from 1787 to 1812 and chaplain of Congress from 1792 to 1800.

To RUSH

April 18, 1808

DEAR RUSH,

. . . In my jocular prayer to the saint, I meant no reflection or insinuation against your church or any other.

I shall esteem you the more for having become a Christian on a large scale. Bigotry, superstition, and enthusiasm on religious subjects I have long since set at defiance. I have attended public worship in all countries and with all sects and believe them all much better than no religion, though I have not thought myself obliged to believe all I heard. Religion I hold to be essential to morals. I never read of an irreligious character in Greek or Roman history, nor in any other history, nor have I known one in life, who was not a rascal. Name one if you can, living or dead. I shall be very glad to receive your creed, as you give me encouragement to hope.

You have heard the mercantile maxim: "If it is necessary in the course of commerce to send a ship through the fire, you must run the risk of burning your sails." Not all the politicians of the world, the Pharisees, the Jesuits, the Brahmins, the Druids, the Romans, the Carthaginians, the Britons, or the French, have ever employed more subtilty in negotiation than merchants. We may depend upon it that every device that human wit can conceive will be employed to evade the Embargo. The 37 cargoes of flour at the Havana, therefore, are no surprise to me. I fear that a practice and habit of smuggling, too, will be introduced by this irksome stagnation. . . .

You and I have been deceived in conceiving too high an opinion of the sense and honesty of our nation. We are driven up in a corner, can retreat no farther. Bayonets and cannon mouths are at our bosoms. We are insulted and injured, ridiculed and scorned by the belligerent powers. We have no defense prepared by sea and land; and all this because Tench Coxe and a few other foolish knaves like him would have it so, and the people would say amen.[13]

13. Tench Coxe (1755–1824) was opposed to an American navy because he believed it would involve the United States in expensive and unnecessary wars. See his *Thoughts on the Subject of Naval Power in the United States of America* (Philadelphia, 1806), p. 9.

Mr. Jefferson has reason to reflect upon himself. How he will get rid of his remorse in his retirement, I know not. He must know that he leaves the government infinitely worse than he found it, and that from his own error or ignorance. I wish his telescopes and mathematical instruments, however, may secure his felicity. But if I have not mismeasured his ambition, he will be uneasy and the sword will cut away the scabbard. As he has, however, a good taste for letters and an ardent curiosity for science, he may, and I hope will, find amusement and consolation from them; for I have no resentment against him, though he has honored and salaried almost every villain he could find who had been an enemy to me.[14]

Our people will not suffer the Constitution to operate according to its true principles, spirit, and design. The President's office ought to mediate between the rich and the poor, but neither will have it so. Each party will have the executive and judiciary, too, wholly and exclusively to itself. . . .

John Adams

P.S. I have omitted to answer your close question, "Whether such a country is worthy of the patriotism of honest men?" I answer, such a country is as worthy as any other country. Our people are like other people. Our obligations to our country never cease but with our lives. We ought to do all we can. Instead of being Frenchmen or Englishmen, Federalists or Jacobins, we ought to be Americans and exert every nerve to convince and persuade our country to conquer its sordid stinginess, to defend our exposed cities and prepare a naval force. . . . The miserable struggle for place and power must be laid aside, and heart and hand united for defense.

The judgments of heaven cannot be averted, but Dr. Rush can mitigate the yellow fever, and he can do much to guard against that avarice which is our national sin, which is most likely to draw down judgments. An aristocracy of wealth, without any check but a democracy of licentiousness, is our curse. I wish that aristocracy was in a hole, guarded by Hercules with his club on one side and an honest people with their million hands on the

---

14. Nearly three years were to pass before Adams and Jefferson would resume their correspondence. Adams also reflects upon the difficulties of forgetting the rivalries of official life; his own memories still were fresh.

other.[15] The eternal intrigues of our monied and landed and *slaved* aristocracy are and will be our ruin. I will be neither aristocrat nor democrat without a mediator between the two. With such a mediator I will be both. Answer me candidly to this.

To ADAMS

June 13, 1808

MY VENERABLE AND DEAR FRIEND,

. . . I feel pain when I am reminded of my exertions in the cause of what we called liberty, and sometimes wish I could erase my name from the Declaration of Independence. In case of a rupture with Britain or France, which shall we fight for? For our Constitution? I cannot meet with a man who loves it. It is considered as too weak by one half of our citizens and too strong by the other half. Shall we rally round the standard of a popular chief? Since the death of Washington there has been no such center of Union. Shall we contend for our paternal acres and dwelling houses? Alas! how few of these are owned by the men who will in case of a war be called to the helm of our government. Their property consists chiefly in bank stock, and that to such an extent that among some of them it is considered as a mark of bad calculation for a man to live in a house of his own. I lately attended an old man who died under my care in the 81st year of his age. Of course he knew America in her youthful and innocent days. In speaking of the change in the principles and morals of our people which has taken place since the Revolution, he said: "They had all become idolaters; they worshipped but one god it is true, but that god was GOD DOLLARS." Were I permitted to coin a word suggested by my patient's remark, I would say we were a "bedollared nation." In walking our streets I have often been struck with the principal subjects of conversation of our citizens. Seldom have I heard a dozen words of which *"Dollar, dis-*

15. The first labor of Hercules was to kill the Nemean lion, which lived in a cave with two entrances. Hercules netted one opening, followed the beast into the other, and strangled the creature. See Robert Graves, *The Greek Myths* (London, 1955), II, 104.

count, and a *good Spec"* did not compose a part. "O Civitas mox peritura si emptorem invenias."[16] . . . But not only our streets but our parlors are constantly vocal with the language of a broker's office, and even at our convivial dinners "Dollars" are a standing dish upon which all feed with rapacity and gluttony. . . .

Benjn: Rush . . .

To RUSH

June 20, 1808

MY DEAR PHYSICAL AND MEDICAL PHILOSOPHER,

I give you this title for the present only. I shall scarcely allow you to be a political, moral, or Christian philosopher till you retract some of the complaints, lamentations, regrets, and penitences in your letter of the 13th. . . .

You and I, in the Revolution, acted from principle. We did our duty, as we then believed, according to our best information, judgment, and consciences. Shall we now repent of this? God forbid! No! If a banishment to Cayenne or to Botany Bay,[17] or even the guillotine, were to be the necessary consequences of it to us, we ought not to repent. Repent? This is impossible. How can a man repent of his virtues? Repent of your sins and crimes and willful follies, if you can recollect any; but never repent of your charities, of your benevolences, of your cures in the yellow fever. . . .

You ask, in case of a rupture with Britain or France, what shall we fight for? I know of no better answer to give than this—to get rid of the Embargo. This object, as I understand the politics of the times, is worth a war with all the world. But where are we to trade, when we are at war with all the world?

My friend! Our country is in masquerade! No party, no man, dares to avow his real sentiments. All is disguise, visard, cloak. The people are totally puzzled and confounded. They cannot penetrate the views, designs, or objects of any party or any individual. . . . Our Constitution operates as I al-

---

16. "O City soon to perish if you find a buyer." Cf. Sallust, *Jugurtha* XXXV.
17. These places were French and British penal colonies.

ways foresaw and predicted it would. It is a game at leapfrog.[18] The Federalists ruled for twelve years by very small majorities; then the Republicans leaped over their heads and shoulders and have reigned seven years; it is even uncertain whether their dominion will last another year, but every appearance indicates that it will not continue beyond twelve years, when the Federalists will leap over their heads and shoulders again. Thus from twelve years to twelve years we are to have a total revolution of parties; and the principle seems to be established on both sides that the nation is never to be governed by the nation, but the whole is to be exclusively governed by a party. Integrity is, as Tacitus says, *certissimum exitium,* most certain destruction, and impartiality is treason.

You ask, "Shall we rally round the standard of a popular chief?" I know not whom you mean. I am determined to rally round the standard of the President, as far as I can in honor, whether Mr. Pinkney, Mr. Clinton, or Mr. Madison be the man.[19] I will engage in no systematical and universal opposition to any man. We must rally round our government or be undone. Since the death of Washington, you say there has been no center of union. But what center was Washington? He had unanimous votes as President, but the two houses of Congress and the great body of the people were more equally divided under him than they ever have been since. . . .

Commerce and wealth have produced luxury, avarice, and cowardice. *Luxuria incubuit, victamque ulciscitur Britaniam.*[20] Our bedollared country has become a miser and a spendthrift, *alieni appetens, sui profusus.*[21] Former

18. Adams' use of the game of leapfrog to illustrate the rotation of parties in office may have been drawn from Swift: "For, some think, that the spirit is apt to feed on the flesh, like hungry wines upon raw Beef. Others rather believe there is a perpetual game at leapfrog between both; and sometimes the flesh is uppermost, and sometimes the spirit." *A Discourse concerning the Mechanical Operation of the Spirit,* Sec. 2.

19. Adams probably intended Charles C. Pinckney rather than William Pinkney. C. C. Pinckney (1746–1825) was the Federalist candidate for President in 1804 and 1808; he became famous as a participant in the XYZ Affair. George Clinton (1739–1812) was Vice-President of the United States from 1805 to his death.

20. "Luxury has laid her hand upon us and takes vengeance on a Britain [she has] conquered." Cf. Juvenal, *Satires* VI.293. Adams probably took the idea from Algernon Sidney's *Discourses concerning Government,* Ch. ii, Sec. 15.

21. "Covetous of others' possessions, lavish of his own." Cf. Sallust, *The War with Catiline* V.4.

ages have never discovered any remedy against the universal gangrene of avarice in commercial countries but setting up ambition as a rival to it. Military honors have excited ambition to struggle against avarice, till military honors have degenerated into hereditary dignities. You and I have no military ambition nor any great wealth, and both of us wish that ambition and avarice may be restrained by law and be subservient to liberty. But nature will have her course, and corruption is coming in like a flood, accelerated by English influence in the greatest degree and by French influence in a very considerable degree, and still more by the eternal internal struggle between debtor and creditor, which has overturned every republic from the beginning of time. . . .

John Adams

To ADAMS

July 13, 1808

MY DEAR OLD FRIEND,

The campaign of summer diseases being opened, and my duties calling me at all hours of the day into the field of sickness and distress, I have not had time till now to answer your last letter. . . . The Embargo becomes daily more and more unpopular among both farmers and mechanics. Its influence is in favor of a revolution of the power of our country.

I have lately heard that a life of General Hamilton is preparing for the press.[22] It will consist of many documents which will throw light upon the councils of the army and government of the United States during the time Mr. Hamilton acted as aide-de-camp and secretary of the treasury under General Washington. One of Hamilton's friends said in my presence a few days ago, "The intended publication would show General W. to be a *good* man but General Hamilton to be a GREAT man." Let this work end as it will, I shall continue to believe that "great men are a lie, and mean men vanity,"[23] and that there is very little difference in that superstition which leads

22. Apparently this biography was not completed.
23. Psalms 62:9.

us to believe in what the world call "great men" and in that which leads us to believe in witches and conjurors.

The papers will inform you of the death of my brother professor and old enemy, Dr. Shippen. He sent for me in his last illness and discovered after he was unable to speak that he carried no hostility out of the world against me. This was a great triumph of truth or of religion in his mind, for he was unfriendly to me ever since my settlement in Philadelphia in 1769. . . .

Benjn: Rush . . .

To RUSH

July 25, 1808

DEAR BENJAMIN,

Handsome Bradford of thy city alarmed me the other day at our Athenaeum in Boston, by telling me that Dr. Rush's business had amazingly increased and was increasing.[24] Knowing thine ardor in thy profession, I was apprehensive that thy zeal for the health of the sick would soon eat thee up and consequently that thine ether would escape from this colluvies of humanity to the regions of divinity before mine. . . .

But to change the style a little—not much. I look at the presidential election as I do at the squabbles of little girls about their dolls and at the more serious wrangles of little boys, which sometimes come to blows, about their rattles and whistles. It will be a mighty bustle about a mighty bauble.

In one of your letters you say that one half the people think the government too strong, and the other half too weak. The truth is it is too strong already without being just. In the hands of aristocrats it has been too strong without being sufficiently wise or just. In the hands of democrats it has been too strong without being either wise or just. Wisdom and justice can never be promoted till the President's office, instead of being a doll and a whistle, shall be made more independent and more respectable: capable of mediating between two infuriated parties. . . .

---

24. The Bradfords, William and Samuel, sons of Thomas Bradford, were in the publishing and bookselling business.

You justly observe that the Embargo operates in favor of a revolution of power. That is, the Embargo will enable the aristocrats to leap over the heads and shoulders of the democrats, as taxes &c. enabled the democrats eight years ago to leap over theirs. But if the aristocrats get the power, how will they use it? Will they submit to the proclamations, Orders in Council, &c. of the English and go to war with France, Spain, Portugal, Holland, Italy, Germany, Prussia, Denmark, and Russia? Such a war, I think, would be worse than the Embargo. Though my system has always been neutrality, and I have sacrificed everything to it, yet I have always been convinced that it was our true policy to preserve as long as possible a good understanding with France; and that if we were driven to extremities, we had better preserve peace with France. . . . If we get into a quarrel with France and the war passions are once excited between our people and the people of France and her allies, our Presidents will be mere statholders danced upon British wires.[25]. . .

Though the life of Hamilton will be a made-up picture, like Dean Swift's *Coelia,*[26] and rags will be contrived to prop the flabby dugs, lest down they drop, I shall be very glad to see it. I hope his famous letter which produced the army, the Sedition Law, &c., in which he recommended an army of fifty thousand men, ten thousand of them horse, will not be omitted.[27]. . .

The aristocratical tricks, the *coup de théâtre,* played off in the funerals of Washington, Hamilton, and Ames, are all in concert with the lives and his-

25. Adams often expressed the idea that the executive power should be separated from the legislative. "The people, then, ought to consider the President's office as the indispensable guardian of their rights. I have ever, therefore, been of the opinion, that the electors of President ought to be chosen by the people at large. The people cannot be too careful in the choice of their Presidents; but . . . they ought to expect that . . . [the Presidents] will act their own independent judgments, and not be wheedled nor intimidated by factious combinations of senators, representatives, heads of departments, or military officers." *Works,* IX, 302.

26. "The Lady's Dressing Room," lines 1–4:

> Five Hours, (and who can do it less in?)
> By haughty *Celia* spent in Dressing;
> The Goddess from her Chamber issues,
> Array'd in Lace, Brocades and Tissues.

27. See "Measures of Defence," *The Works of Alexander Hamilton,* ed. Henry Cabot Lodge, Federal edn. (New York, 1904), VII, 48–50.

tories written and to be written, all calculated like drums and trumpets and fifes in an army to drown the unpopularity of speculations, banks, paper money, and mushroom fortunes. You see through these masks and veils and cloaks, but the people are dazzled and blinded by them and so will posterity be. . . .

This our beloved country, my dear friend, is indeed in a very dangerous situation. It is between two great fires in Europe and between two ignited parties at home, smoking, sparkling, and flaming, ready to burst into a conflagration. In this state of embarrassment, confusion, and uncertainty, no genius appears, no comprehensive mind, no exalted courage. What shall we do? What will become of us? To you and me these things are of little consequence, but we have children and grandchildren and shall soon have great-grandchildren. . . .

The Embargo is a cowardly measure. We are taught to be cowards both by Federalists and Republicans. Our gazettes and pamphlets tell us that Bonaparte is omnipotent by land, that Britain is omnipotent at sea, that Bonaparte will conquer England and command all the British navy and send I know not how many hundred thousand soldiers here and conquer from New Orleans to Passamaquoddy. Though every one of these bugbears is an empty phantom, yet the people seem to believe every article of this bombastical creed and tremble and shudder in consequence. Who shall touch these blind eyes? The American people are not cowards nor traitors.

John Adams

To ADAMS

August 24, 1808

MY VENERABLE AND DEAR FRIEND,

In contemplating the events that have lately taken place in Spain and their probable consequences, I feel disposed to exclaim in the bold apostrophe of Jeremiah: "O! thou sword of the Lord, how long will it be ere thou be quiet?" [28] . . . I tremble at his name [Napoleon]. The levity of a

---

28. Jeremiah 47:6.

Frenchman, the phlegm of a German, the avarice of a Dutchman, the cold-heartedness of a Russian, the solidity of an Englishman, the gravity of a Spaniard, the subtlety of an Italian, and the cruelty of a Turk appear to be united in his character. In no one part of his conduct do we trace the least semblance of any one of the virtues that rescued the name of Alexander and Caesar from total infamy. He is devoid of the occasional magnanimity of the former and the habitual clemency of the latter. What do you think of all the Christian nations in the world uniting in a general fast day to take place six or nine months hence for the sole purpose of supplicating the Father of the human race to deliver them from the fangs of this beast of prey? . . .

Accident threw me a few days ago into the company of one of the leaders of the Democratic party in Philadelphia whose name I have more than once heard you mention with an abhorrence of his principles.[29] He addressed me privately in the following words. "Doctor, I have changed my opinion of your old friend Mr. Adams. I once thought him a weak man, but I now think him the wisest man in our country. He foresaw the present state of the parties that now distract our country and pointed out the only remedy to prevent them. I wish to heaven we could *now,* while the people possess all the power of the country, fix upon a *perpetual* and *hereditary* chief magistrate, and limit his powers. If this be not done *soon* and *by the people,* it will take place in *another* way." I submit the anecdote to your reflections. . . .

Benjn: Rush

To RUSH

─────────────────────────────

August 31, 1808

MY DEAR SIR,

. . . If I had ever heard that a pen of Tacitus had been preserved among the relics of antiquity, I should swear you had stolen it to draw the character of the most conspicuous moral, political, and military phenomenon of

---

29. The person is unidentified.

the age. I tremble not, however, at his name. All the ships in Europe he can procure could not transport an army to hurt us. I see in him a conqueror who resembles Alexander, Caesar, Mahomet, and Kublai Khan and the vices, follies, and madness as well as the genius, courage, and desperation which belonged to them all. In attention to the arts and sciences, he is equal to any of them. His religion and morality are very like that of all of them. I see nothing in him so very much superior to Dumouriez or Pichegru,[30] or several others of the generals now under him. The impetus of the revolution, setting all things at defiance, operated like a steam engine to bend the character of the French soldiers to the severest military discipline the world ever witnessed. All this was done and the French nation and armies formed by the national assemblies and their committees to the most absolute submission before he came to the command. With these instruments he has defended himself against a series of coalitions and combinations against him. In one point he has been more hardy and impudent than Caesar or Cromwell: he has thrown off a mask which they were obliged to wear and openly avowed his personal and family ambition.

But what is he now? I believe him to be the most miserable individual of the human species. He must be conscious that he is brandishing a beetle round his head upon the pinnacle of a steeple. His whole system must crumble under him. He is contending with England for a superiority of power, a glittering object for which the English and French nations have incessantly wrestled and fought for many ages. It is in vain to say the English are acting in self-defense, for so is Napoleon, and he is in more danger than the English. The truth is the English are contending to be the dominant power of the world, or, if you will, for universal empire as much as the French. . . . Unlimited despotism on the ocean, for which Britain avowedly and openly contends, would be a more dangerous domination over the civilized world than any that Napoleon ever can accomplish.

What is now the power of Napoleon? Compare it with that of the House

---

30. Charles François du Perier Dumouriez (1739–1823) served in various capacities in the French Revolution. He fled from France when his counter-revolutionary attempt failed in 1793. Charles Pichegru (1761–1804) was commander in chief of French armies in 1794 and 1795. At the height of fame he conspired to restore the monarchy and was forced to resign his commissions.

of Austria under Charles the 5th and his successors. . . . Compare the Napoleons with the Captain Rou[31] in the time of Charlemagne who had as vast views [and] as much skill in arms and policy and was as cruel as the present hairbrain.

There are so many in Philadelphia, tho' not more than in New York, Baltimore, or Boston, whose principles I thought not very generous, that I can not guess who was the blockhead who changed an orthodox opinion that I was a weak man for the heretical conceit that I am a wise one, at a time when he can have no temptation to it. My own opinion has always agreed with his old opinion, and I am not about to change it. . . .

Whoever he is, I pronounce him a weak man too. He never was capable of understanding, even me. I never was for fixing a "perpetual hereditary chief magistrate." This will never be done. Whenever, if ever, there is one such magistrate, there will be two or three. The U.S. will be divided into two or three sections, and all of them become vassals to European powers. Call them statholders if you will. Another thing! Whenever there is an hereditary chief, there must be an hereditary senate to check him, or he will soon be either guillotined like Charles 1 and Louis the 16 or become a despot like Napoleon.

If I had not been a weak man, I should have explained myself so as to be better understood; and if your man had not been a weak man, he would have understood me better. . . .

John Adams

To ADAMS

September 16, 1808

MY DEAR FRIEND,

    . . . I went to bed a few evenings ago at my usual hour, and during the night I dreamed that I had been elected President of the United States. At first I objected to accepting of the high and honorable station, but upon recollecting that it would give me an opportunity of exercising my long-cherished

---

31. Rou (or Rollo, Hrólfr) was a Norwegian chieftain who received Normandy from Charles the Simple of France in 911.

hostility to ardent spirits by putting an end to their general use in our country, I consented to accept of the appointment and repaired to the city of
Washington, where I entered upon the duties with spirit and zeal. . . . [Con-
gress] concurred in my determination, and a law was obtained for those purposes. It set forth the evils of ardent spirits in strong terms, and in the room
of them recommended simple water, molasses and water, and small beer.

Wise, humane, and patriotic as this law was, it instantly met with great
opposition, particularly in those states and counties in which spirits were
consumed in the greatest quantities. Petitions flowed in upon me from all
quarters to advise Congress to repeal the law, but I refused to comply with
them. One day sitting alone in my council chamber, a venerable but plain-
looking man was introduced to me by one of my servants. I offered him a
chair and delicately asked him what his business was with me. "I have taken
the liberty," said he, "Mr. President, to call upon you to remonstrate with
you against the law for prohibiting the importation, manufactory, and consumption of ardent spirits." He said the law was well enough for a month
or two, during which time all the drunken men in the country had become
sober, but, protracted as it was for nearly a year, it did such violence to the
physical and commercial habits of our citizens that it had not and could not
be carried into general effect; that many of the persons who had conformed
to it had been made sick from drinking nothing but cold water; . . . that all
the West India merchants, distillers, and tavern keepers in the country were
in an uproar; and that unless the water and small beer law were instantly repealed, we should soon have our country filled with hospitals and our jails
with bankrupts. "Hold, sir," said I. "You don't know the people of the
United States as well as I do; they will submit to the empire of Reason, and
Reason will soon reconcile them to the restrictions and privations of the law
for sobering and moralizing our citizens." "Reason! Reason! Mr. President.
Why, you forget that it was Reason in the form of a Goddess that produced all the crimes and calamities of the French Revolution, and that it
was by a book entitled *The Age of Reason* that Tom Paine demoralized half
the Christian world. You forget, too, that men are *rational only,* not reasonable creatures. . . ."

"Mr. President, in thus rejecting the empire of Reason in government,
permit me to mention an empire of another kind, to which men everywhere

yield a willing, and in some instances involuntary, submission, and that is the EMPIRE OF HABIT.[32] You might as well arrest the orbs of heaven in their course as *suddenly* change the habits of a whole people. . . . Indeed, Mr. President, I am sorry to tell you, you are no more of a philosopher than you are of a politician, or you never would have blundered upon your spirit law. Let me advise you to retire from your present station and go back to your professor's chair and amuse your boys with your idle and impracticable speculations, or go among your patients and dose them with calomel and jalap. . . ."

Do not suppose, my good friend, that I mean the least reflection by the contents of this letter upon any recent events in the administration of the government of the United States. I believe a republic to be the best possible government to promote the interest, dignity, and happiness of man. I believe the Embargo to be a wise, a just, and a necessary measure, and I believe simple water, molasses and water, and small beer to be the best ordinary drinks in the world; but if mankind will prefer a monarchy to a republic, commerce and war to an embargo, and drams, slings, grog, and toddy to the wholesome liquors above-mentioned, I can only testify my sorrow for the depravity of their political, moral, and physical inclinations by weeping over their folly and madness.

This letter must not be seen nor read out of your own house. . . .

Benjn: Rush

To RUSH

September 27, 1808

DEAR SIR,

That Rosicrucian sylph, that Fairy Queen Mab, or that other familiar spirit, whatever it is, that inspires your nightly dreams, I would not exchange, if I had it, for the Daemon of Socrates.[33] You have more wit and

32. See Publilius Syrus, *Sententiae,* line 236, "Gravissimum est imperium consuetudinis." See also David Hume, *A Treatise of Human Nature,* Bk. I, Pt. III, Sec. IX; Hume's ideas on habit had a great influence on that generation of Americans.

33. Socrates, in describing the demon or spirit that guided him, said: "My good friend, when I was about to cross the stream, the spirit and the sign that usually comes to me came—

humor and sense in your sleep than other people, I was about to say, than you have yourself when awake. . . .

I believe with you "a republican government," while the people have the virtues, talents, and love of country necessary to support it, "the best possible government to promote the interest, dignity, and happiness of man." But you know that commerce, luxury, and avarice have destroyed every republican government. England and France have tried the experiment, and neither of them could preserve it, for twelve years. It might be said with truth that they could not preserve it for a moment; for the Commonwealth of England from 1640 to 1660 was in reality a succession of monarchies under Pym, Hampden, Fairfax, and Cromwell.[34] And the Republic of France was a similar monarchy under Mirabeau, Brissot, Danton, Robespierre, and a succession of others like them down to Napoleon the Emperor. The mercenary spirit of commerce has recently destroyed the republics of Holland, Switzerland, and Venice. . . . When public virtue is gone, when the national spirit is fled, when a party is substituted for the nation, and faction for a party, when venality lurks and skulks in secret, and much more when it impudently braves the public censure, whether it be sent in the form of emissaries from foreign powers or is employed by ambitious and intriguing domestic citizens, the republic is lost in essence, though it may still exist in form. . . .

When commerce and luxury and dissipation had introduced avarice among the Greeks, the artful policy and military discipline of Philip and his son prevailed over all the toils, negotiations, and eloquence of Demosthenes. . . . The same causes produced the same effects in Rome, and the labors, eloquence, and patriotism of Cicero were to as little purpose as those of Demosthenes, and were equally rewarded. . . .

Americans, I fondly hope and candidly believe, are not yet arrived at the age of Demosthenes or Cicero. If we can preserve our Union entire, we may

---

it always holds me back from something I am about to do" (Plato, *Phaedrus* 242.B-C, trans. H. N. Fowler, Loeb Classical Lib. [London, 1926]).

34. These men were leaders in the English civil war against Charles I. John Pym (1584–1643) and John Hampden (1594–1643) were prominent in the Short and Long Parliaments. Thomas Fairfax (1612–71) was the leading Parliamentary general during the early stages of the war.

preserve our republic. But if the Union is broken, we become two petty principalities, little better than the feudatans [sic], one of France and the other of England.

If I could lay an embargo or pass a nonimportation law against corruption and foreign influences, I would not make it a temporal but a perpetual law, and I would not repeal it, though it should raise a clamor as loud as my gag law or your grog law or Mr. Jefferson's Embargo. . . .

I am weary of conjectures, but not in despair.

John Adams

To ADAMS

September 22, 1808

MY DEAR OLD AND TRIED FRIEND,

. . . Mr. Clymer[35] is almost the only citizen of Philadelphia with whom I converse upon political subjects. His mind retains the texture which the Revolution gave it. He is neither a Frenchman nor an Englishman and laments that Americans partake too much of the principles of both. He is no advocate for Mr. Jefferson, but he boldly defends the Embargo and acquits him of partiality to the French nation. . . .

Our papers teem with electioneering scandal. From all treason, sedition, conspiracies, and *party rage,* good Lord deliver us!—I have often heard, when a boy, of men's selling their souls to the Devil to relieve a pressing want of money. This practice is now in disuse, but we do the same thing in another way by selling our time, our talents, our tempers, our moral feelings and principles, and sometimes our *wills,* as well as our money, to a party. Under the constant pressure of the two powerful and opposite currents that divide our city, I am enabled to keep my feet. Sooner than float *after* either of them, I would quit my country and go where human folly and madness had exhausted themselves and where the extremity of despotism had left nothing to fear. I would in other words end my days in Constantinople or Paris.

35. George Clymer (1739–1813), Rush's close friend and patient, was then semiretired. He had been a member of the Continental Congress and the United States Congress.

Could the absurdities and contradictions in principle and conduct of our two great parties for the last 12 years be laid before the world in a candid and dispassionate manner, we should be ashamed to call ourselves MEN. The disputes of children about their nuts and gingerbread have less folly and wickedness in them.

From a dozen instances of what I allude to, I shall select but two. When the Spaniards shut the port of New Orleans against our vessels, the cry of the whole Federal party was for war and the acquisition of Louisiana by force. Its immense resources in West and East India produce were enumerated in long, sensible, and eloquent speeches and pamphlets. When that country was purchased by Mr. Jefferson, the same party condemned his conduct, depreciated the trade, soil, and people of that country, and represented it as a millstone about the neck of the United States. In the year 1798 the Democrats opposed the election of Mr. Ross[36] upon the ground of his being a deist. The Federalists either denied it or said his religious tenets had nothing to do with his qualifications for governor. In 1799 the Federalists opposed the election of Mr. Jefferson upon the ground of his being a deist. The Democrats denied it or said his infidel principles had nothing to do with his qualifications for President!!! "Non aula, non ecclesia, solum — sed totus mundus *histrionem* agunt."[37]

The Scriptures speak of nations being *drunk* and of all the individuals of the human race being *mad*. What *sober* man or what man in his *senses* would think of walking in company or reasoning with either of them? . . .

Benjn: Rush

To RUSH

October 10, 1808

MY DEAR SIR,

. . . I cannot . . . boldly defend the long continuance of the Embargo. I thought it at first a necessary measure, but was fully apprehensive it could

36. James Ross (1762–1847) was the United States senator for Pennsylvania from 1794 to 1803.

37. "Not the court, not the church, alone—but the whole world plays the actor." The quotation comes in part from Petronius Arbiter, *Fragments.*

not be long continued. I am neither an advocate nor an accuser of Mr. Jefferson without discrimination. I can acquit him of partiality to Napoleon, but not entirely to the French Nation. I have long known his bias to the French and his bitterness to the English. Of Napoleon I have reason to believe he thinks justly.

Mr. Jefferson in my opinion has long ago adopted two very erroneous opinions: 1. That England was tottering to her fall. That her strength and resources were exhausted.[38] That she must soon be a bankrupt and unable to maintain her naval superiority. This I never believed, and we shall yet have proofs enough and to spare of her tremendous power, though I dread it not. . . . 2. But the second opinion was still more erroneous and still more fatal. He did not study the French Nation nor consider the character of her court, her nobility, her clergy, her lawyers, her institutions, and much less the nature of her common people, not one in fifty of whom could write or read. He had studied so little the nature of man, and still less the nature of government, that he came from France and continued for years, fully persuaded that the nation would establish a free republican government and even a leveling democracy, and that monarchy and nobility would be forever abolished in France. I have reason to remember these things, for I have heard him assert them and enlarge upon them, with the utmost astonishment. I have reason to remember them, moreover, because these were the first topics upon which we ever differed in opinions upon political subjects. I have reason to remember them, too, because his opinions recommended him to the French Revolutionary Government and Nation, and especially to all the friends, ambassadors, consuls, and other agents as well as to all other Frenchmen in America, even to Talleyrand and the Duke de Liancourt,[39] who all exerted all their influence and all their praises to exalt Mr. Jefferson over my shoulders, and to run me down as an aristocrat and a monarchist. I have reason to remember it, too, because my opinion of the

38. Adams is very hard on Jefferson. Jefferson was critical of Great Britain, but he had a healthy respect for her vitality. See his letter to John Page, May 4, 1786, *The Writings of Thomas Jefferson,* ed. Paul Leicester Ford (New York, 1892–99), IV, 213–215. See also Dumas Malone, *Jefferson and His Time,* Vol. II: *Jefferson and the Rights of Man* (Boston, 1951), pp. 53–62.

39. François Alexandre Frederic, Duc de La Rochefoucauld-Liancourt (1747–1827), tried to save Louis XVI from execution and, when the Revolution advanced, fled to America.

French Revolution produced a coldness towards me in all my old Revolutionary friends, and an inclination towards Mr. Jefferson, which broke out in violent invectives and false imputations upon me and in flattering panegyrics upon Mr. Jefferson, till they ended in a consignment of me forever to private life and the elevation of him to the President's chair.[40]. . .

John Adams

[This letter was continued on Dec. 19, with an additional note on Dec. 20.]

To ADAMS

December 14, 1808

MY DEAR FRIEND,

Has your right hand forgotten its cunning from pain or sickness? Or have you ceased to contemplate the present interesting crisis of your beloved country? Or have you become fearful of committing your apprehensions of her future destiny to paper? If none of these events have come to pass, why am I not favored with answers to my . . . letters? . . .

Benjn: Rush

To RUSH

December 19, 1808

[MY DEAR BENJAMIN,]

. . . Your favor of December 14 has reminded me of the project I had begun. My right hand has not been palsied by pain or sickness to such a degree as to be wholly incapable of holding a pen, nor have I ceased to contemplate the crisis of our affairs. Nor am I fearful of committing my thoughts to paper. . . .

To what purpose, my friend, is it for me to give my opinion when every appearance indicates that it will not be followed now any more than it was in 1800? My opinion will not be regarded by any or either party.

40. Adams was also hitting at Rush's enthusiasm for the French Revolution.

Si velis pacem para bellum is by the Federalists said to be Washington's doctrine.[41] So it was and so it has been the maxim of every patriot and hero and indeed of every man of sense. . . .

My system has always been to prepare for war so far as to fortify our most important and most exposed places on the frontier and on the seaboard, and to prepare for war by sea so far as to build frigates and other smaller vessels, schooners and brigantines, by degrees as our revenues could afford, so that in case of an unforeseen rupture our immense commerce might not be all liable to be swept at once into the coffers of our enemies. . . . The Embargo, I presume, must be relaxed. If not, it will either produce a general violation of it, which will cost more than foreign war to suppress it, or it will turn out of office, at least in New England, every man who supports it. There will not be a selectman nor a representative left who will advocate the administration. The same spirit will increase in the middle and even in the southern and western states. Mr. Madison's administration will be a scene of distraction and confusion, if not of insurrections and civil war, and foreign war at the same time both with France and England, if the Embargo is not lightened. Why then are not orders given to equip and man all the frigates we have and to build more in all our great seaports? . . .

My opinion of embargoes . . . has never varied. In 1774 Congress was unanimously sanguine . . . that the nonimportation agreement would procure the ample redress of all our complaints. I went with the rest because the people everywhere were of the same opinion. . . . When Mr. Madison sent up to Senate his resolutions of nonimportation, I decided the question in a divided Senate against them. When the present embargo was laid, I was of the same opinion that we could give laws neither to England nor France by such means. Yet I have raised no clamor against these measures, being determined to support the government in whatever hands as far as I can in conscience and in honor. . . .

41. The saying "If you wish for peace, prepare for war" ("Si vis pacem, para bellum") was popular in Boston during the disturbance immediately prior to the outbreak of hostilities against Britain in 1774. See Abigail to John Adams, Sept. 22, 1774, and John to Abigail Adams, Oct. 7, 1774, *Adams Family Correspondence,* ed. Lyman H. Butterfield et al. (Cambridge, Mass., 1963), I, 161, 165.

December 22, 1808

. . . I may now explain my long silence. For three or four months I have been in company with such great personages as Moses, Zoroaster, Sanchoniathan, Confucius, Numa, Mahomet, and others of that rank. In that period I have read four volumes of Voltaire's *Essai sur les moeurs et l'esprit des nations* and three of his *Louis 14* and *Fifteen,* and these led me to read his Bible *expliquée,* his philosophy of history, his sermons, homilies, dialogues, and a multitude of other pieces in which his whole stock of learning, wit, humor, satire, scurrility, buffoonery were exhausted. . . .

The vast extent and variety of talents which this mortal possessed had given him a reputation through the world, and his wit and style attracted readers of all nations. Everybody read his works. . . . This reputation gave him power to propagate through the world the miserable spoils which he borrowed or stole from the English infidels with an effrontery more unjustifiable and inexcusable than that of the Hebrews which he censures so bitterly, when they borrowed gold and silver and jewels of the Egyptians. . . .

Although I have been so highly entertained as to neglect my most precious correspondent, I would not advise him ever to spend his time so idly, at least unless he should ever have as much leisure as I have, and that I am very sure can never happen. . . .

John Adams

CHAPTER 6

Parties, French and English

"I SEE OUR AMERICAN PARTIES precisely in the same light with you. I am determined to swallow American garlic enough to defend me against French and English onions, let their odor be as strong as it will." This response Adams made to Rush, who had complained that to be on easy terms with either of the two American parties one had to swallow either pro-French or pro-English propaganda, just as a man had to eat onions to endure the smell of a room full of onion eaters. Rush and Adams deplored the spirit of factionalism that infected American politics. The Washington's birthday celebrations, the feasts, the state funerals given Hamilton and other patriots were instances of hypocritical pageantry designed by a party to keep systems of privilege in existence, and public acceptance of these political rituals was a mark of moral depravity in America. Such ceremonials, drugging men's reason with emotionalism, blinded the people to the selfish aims of party programs. Adams desired Dr. Rush to use his "salutiferous" pen like a lancet to attempt to cure the nation's delusions and advance the cause of political truth.

To ADAMS

January 13, 1809

MY DEAR FRIEND,

. . . In the clamors which have been excited lately against commerce, I have been led to consider the absurdity of deriving human depravity from any other source than that recorded in the Bible. It has been ascribed not only to commoners but to kings, to different forms of government, to the clergy, and by Rousseau and some members of the legislature of Pennsylvania to science and to colleges. Legislation founded upon any one of these opinions must necessarily be erroneous and productive of misery. In the Bible alone man is described as *he is*. He can be governed of course only by accommodating law to his nature as developed in that sacred book. . . .

Our Constitution will I believe be safe. Our new governor, too, I believe aims well. But if, as you once told me, George the 3rd is not king of Great Britain but ruled by a varying aristocracy, how can we expect Simon Snyder to be an independent governor of Pennsylvania?[1]

It would seem as if there was but *two* vices in the United States—and that is the *vice* of Federalism and the *vice* of Democracy. My worthy brother has given great offense to the ruling powers by voting for Mr. Ross.[2] The judiciary system of the state, it is said, is to undergo a change. If so, he may probably expiate his vote by a change in his situation. . . .

Benjn: Rush

To RUSH

January 23, 1809

DEAR SIR,

What signify clamors against commerce, property, kings, nobles, demagogues, democracy, the clergy, religion? For to each and all of these has the depravity of man been imputed by some philosophers. Rousseau says the first man who fenced a cabbage yard ought to have been put to death.[3] Diderot says the first man who suggested the idea of a god ought to have been treated as an enemy of the human race.[4] Tom Quelqu'un of Clapham in England said he believed [in] no God, no Providence, no future state, but he loved life so well that if he could but be assured of immortal existence,

---

1. Simon Snyder was Republican governor of Pennsylvania from 1808 to 1817.

2. James Ross campaigned for governor regularly from 1799 to 1808.

3. For Rousseau's argument that private property brought crime, war, misfortune, and horror, see *A Discourse upon the Origin and Foundation of the Inequality among Mankind* (London, 1761), p. 97.

4. Denis Diderot (1713–84) was a French *philosophe* and editor of the *Encyclopédie*.

he would consent to be pitched about in fire and brimstone by the devils with their forks to all eternity. Some of our religionists say that before a man can be fit to be saved he must be willing to be damned to all eternity. It is a pity that men of sense will give any attention to any of these ravings which are fit only for Bedlam. Philosophy, morality, religion, reason, all concur in your conclusion that "Man can be governed only by accommodating laws to his nature." . . .

As I know your political pen to be as salutiferous as your medical or chirurgical instruments, I will run the risk to ask you why in this momentous crisis you and other philosophers in Philadelphia will not write sometimes to help us out of our difficulty. The Embargo must be removed.[5] It is Pennsylvania and New York who still keep it on. If it is kept on till doomsday, it will not bend France or England. We are in a shocking delusion not only in our opinion of the efficacy of the Embargo but in our unaccountable aversion to naval preparations. The one thing needful is a navy. The expense is held up as a bugbear. Mr. Searle told me in Holland that the accounts of our whole naval armaments and preparations during the Revolutionary War had been made up.[6] And the United States' shares in the prizes they had made amounted to thirteen millions of dollars more than their whole cost. These were paper dollars no doubt, but if they paid their way, besides the necessary military munitions and protection to our shores and commerce they procured and afforded, this was a great thing.

Whatever vices there are, Federalism and Republicanism will cover them all. An infamous birth, a more infamous life, and a contemptible death will at any time be canonized as a saint by the former, and folly, ignorance, stupidity, and debauchery will be adored in their lifetime by the latter. No vir-

---

5. The Embargo was intended as a substitute for war. Since neither Britain nor France would recognize the United States' "right" to trade as a neutral with both belligerents, the Jefferson administration hoped that withholding American commerce from the warring nations would force them to accept the American position. However, Jefferson badly misjudged the effect of the Embargo both on the belligerents and on American commercial interests. Historians are generally agreed that, though a noble experiment in intention, it was a blunder as practiced.

6. James Searle (1733–97), Pennsylvania merchant and member of the Continental Congress, served a short time in Europe as the state's envoy in negotiating military supplies.

tues, no talents will make atonement with either for honor and justice, when maintained against the party will.

We may flatter ourselves that a numerous legislature will be favorable to the people and bulwarks to liberty, but it will be found that in all countries and under all forms of government a very few men rule the whole. In company with Mr. Eden[7] at a diplomatic dinner he took me aside and said, "I am anxious about affairs between my country and yours." So am I. "Two honest men sitting down together might in two or three hours arrange everything to mutual satisfaction." I am fully of that opinion, but this nation, by what I can observe, does not think so. "This nation! This nation thinks exactly as two or three of us would have it think, at most four or five of us!"

The same, I fear, may be said of our complicated government of seventeen sovereignties within one sovereignty.

Our parties would not be dangerous, if it were not for foreign influences. To deny that there has been a French influence and an English influence in this country ever since the peace is to deny that the sun and moon have shone upon the earth. They have played with our parties and run the game of leapfrog with them. Look back upon the history of Europe for the last thirty years. You will see French influence and English influence constantly at work in Russia, Sweden, Denmark, Prussia, Germany, Holland, Spain, Portugal, Sardinia, Naples, and Turkey. When two nations so powerful and rich as England and France have been for ages in the habit of negotiating and intriguing with all nations, how can we expect to be out of the reach of their arts? . . . The great body of our nation is divided in affection—by fear between the two. Very few men are really impartial, and they have no influence because nothing but party has influence. . . .

A navy is the only object that can form an independent American party. France and England are both sensible of this tho' we are not, and accordingly both powers set their faces against a navy in this country and do all they can to discourage it.

7. William Eden, 1st Lord Auckland (1744–1814), was a member of the Carlisle Commission in 1778 and a distinguished diplomat in the Pitt administrations.

Our legislature meets the day after tomorrow, and we shall have stormy weather. Federalism grows every day more and more triumphant and Mr. Jefferson and his successor more and more unpopular. Nothing will check this career but a repeal of the embargo laws, nonimportation laws, nonintercourse laws, and beginning in earnest a naval force. . . .

John Adams

To ADAMS

February 20, 1809

MY DEAR AND EXCELLENT FRIEND,

Soon after the receipt of your last letter, in which you advise me to shake off my retired habits and prejudices and to come forward in support of the petitions of my fellow citizens for a repeal of the Embargo laws, I went to bed at my usual hour and dreamed that I had yielded to your advice, and in consequence of it determined to appear at a Federal town meeting which was to be held the next day in company with my worthy friend and only surviving colleague in subscribing the Declaration of Independence, Mr. George Clymer.[8] I thought I had agreed to speak in favor of the measures that were to be proposed by the meeting, and for that purpose prepared a speech which was amply larded with the Federal phrases of "the immortal Washington, the disciples of Washington, the ghost of Washington, &c., &c."

At the proposed hour of the meeting (which was 11 o'clock in the forenoon) I imagined I set off for the Statehouse yard, and that on my way my attention was drawn to a small frame house between 4th and 5th Streets in Chestnut Street in which I saw a number of men busily employed in a manner which excited my curiosity to a very high degree. I begged permission to sit down in the room in which they were assembled. This was read-

8. Though retired from politics, Clymer continued to be interested in community projects, serving as first president of the Philadelphia Bank, president of the Academy of Fine Arts, and vice-president of the Philadelphia Agricultural Society.

ily granted. Never did I witness such a scene. The man nearest to the door was engaged in placing a number of wheels within wheels. I was told he was attempting to find out perpetual motion. On one side of the fireplace I saw a man surrounded with crucibles with a small furnace before him. I was told that he was endeavoring to change a piece of copper into gold. On the opposite side of the fireplace I saw a man shaking a bottle in which were infused a number of rare gums and roots. He said he was preparing an elixir, a teaspoonful of which taken every morning in a tumbler of cold water would prevent the pains and all the deformities of old age and restore man to his original antediluvian longevity. In a corner of the room sat a meager-looking young man covered with goose down, with a basket of feathers on each side of him. I asked what he was about to do with those feathers. He said he was making a pair of wings with which he intended to amuse the citizens of Philadelphia shortly by flying from the top of the newly erected shot manufactory upon Schuylkill to the one lately erected in Southwark upon the Delaware. In another corner of the room sat a little squat fellow with a table before him upon which he was trying to make an egg stand upon one of its ends. In the middle of the floor I saw a stout man with a flushed face standing with both his feet upon a stick, with his two hands grasped round each end of it, straining with all his might to lift himself from the floor.

"What! What means all this?" said I. "I am certainly in a madhouse." After this declaration I rose suddenly from my seat and walked towards the door. "Stop!" said a little old man who appeared to be the master of the house, "and tell me where are you going." "To the town meeting," said I. "You are at it already," said he. "What! in this receptacle of madmen?" said I. "Yes," said he, "they are an epitome of all public bodies, whether assembled in town meetings, state legislatures, congresses, conventions, or parliaments, and of all the statesmen and philosophers, whether at courts or in a closet, who expect to produce by their labors *wisdom, justice, order* and *stability* in human governments."

Struck with the good sense of this speech, I instantly returned to my house, strongly impressed with a sense of my obligation to the little old man who *thus,* as I thought, saved me from adding to the list of the follies of my political life. While congratulating myself upon this escape, a midnight rap at my door awoke me and confirmed my pleasure by satisfying me that my *relapse* into the vices of party and the vexations of public life was nothing but a DREAM. . . .

Benjn: Rush

To RUSH

───────────────────────────

March 4, 1809

RUSH,

If I could dream as much wit as you, I think I should wish to go to sleep for the rest of my life, retaining, however, one of Swift's flappers to awake me once in 24 hours to dinner, for you know without a dinner one can neither dream nor sleep.[9] Your dreams descend from Jove, according to Homer.[10]

Though I enjoy your sleeping wit and acknowledge your unequalled ingenuity in your dreams, I cannot agree to your moral. I will not yet allow that the cause of "Wisdom, justice, order, and stability in human government" is quite desperate. The old maxim *Nil desperandum de Republica*[11] is founded in eternal truth and indispensable obligation.

Jefferson expired and Madison came to life, last night at twelve o'clock. . . . I pity poor Madison. He comes to the helm in such a storm as I have seen in the Gulf Stream, or rather such as I had to encounter in the government in 1797. Mine was the worst, however, because he has a great majority of the officers and men attached to him, and I had all the officers and half the crew always ready to throw me overboard. Our candidate for governor, Mr. Gore, has brought forward in our legislature a proposition

---

9. See *Gulliver's Travels,* Pt. III, Ch. iv.

10. Dreams are inspired by Zeus, but may have ends that would lead the dreamer to his doom. See Homer, *Iliad* II.1–75.

11. "Let us not despair of the Republic."

for war against France.[12] I hope their constituents are not for that measure. But if a majority of them is, I am not. . . .

Mr. Lincoln, our Republican candidate, is one of our old whigs and a man of sense and learning.[13] He has given offense to our clergy and grieved multitudes of our good Christians. Both candidates are unpopular. Party only will decide, and neither party will be fully satisfied, whatever the decision may be. The English party is very confident of success in the choice of Mr. Gore. The French party is very diffident of their man. If the Federalists prevail, Mr. Madison will have New England states very powerfully against him, through his whole four years. Mr. Jefferson's appointments in New England have been so entirely on party motives and have fallen upon such characters as have brought the national government into contempt. I hope Mr. Madison will be more prudent. If he is not, he will have a terrible navigation of it.[14]

We have been serenaded this morning with the roar of cannon from the Castle and from Republican collections in the neighboring towns, on the accession of the new monarch to his throne, but there is a great gloom and a great rage among the people. I am very anxious to know the final result of the Tenth Congress. Our peace will depend very much upon that result. Whatever is to be the destiny of our country, you will always find a friend in

John Adams

12. Christopher Gore (1758–1827), an influential Massachusetts lawyer, diplomat, and politician, was elected Federalist governor in 1809 and served two years.

13. Levi Lincoln (1749–1820), acting governor of Massachusetts from December 1808 until May 1809, was succeeded by Gore.

14. An Adams pun. Adams and his son supported Jefferson's Embargo as a temporary expedient, and John Quincy Adams actually voted for it in the United States Senate. In doing so he irritated other Federalist leaders and was subjected to much abuse in the party's newspapers. The tension was heightened when he joined the Republican caucus which nominated Madison and Clinton for President and Vice-President of the United States. The Federalist legislature of Massachusetts retaliated by bringing up prematurely the question of John Quincy Adams' renomination as United States senator. Their choice of James Lloyd, Jr., for his seat brought his decision to resign six months before the expiration of his term. See Worthington C. Ford, "The Recall of John Quincy Adams in 1808," *Proceedings of the Massachusetts Historical Society*, XLV (1912), 354–375.

"The Temple of Liberty," displaying medallions of great legislators. Frontispiece from *The Oceana and Other Works of James Harrington* (London, 1771), one of the editions owned by John Adams.

"Benjamin Rush" (1745–1813), by Charles Willson Peale, in Independence Hall, Philadelphia. Reproduced by courtesy of the Independence National Historical Park.

"John Adams" (1735–1826), by Charles Willson Peale, in Independence Hall, Philadelphia. Reproduced by courtesy of the Independence National Historical Park.

Marguerite Gerard's etching "Au Genie de Franklin" ("To the Genius of Franklin"),
1778, after Honoré Fragonard, illustrating Turgot's epigram "He snatched the
lightning from heaven and the scepter from tyrants." Reproduced with permission
of the Philadelphia Museum of Art: given by Mrs. John D. Rockefeller.

"L'Amérique Indépendante," engraved by J. C. le Vasseur, after a design by A. Borel, 1778. America, a comely Indian, kneels at the foot of the statue of liberty under Franklin's protection, while Gallia defeats the tyrannical aims of Britain. From the Huntington Library.

"The Apotheosis of Washington," lithographed by H. Weishaupt, after a painting by Samuel Moore, ca. 1800. Borne on the arms of faith and love, surrounded by the virtues, Washington is carried to heaven as he is mourned by Columbia and the orphaned states of the Union. From the Huntington Library.

"Commemoration of Washington," lithographed by J. J. Barralet, artist unknown. The general has burst from his tomb, which is surrounded by mourning America and Liberty, to be immortalized and enthroned on high. From the Huntington Library.

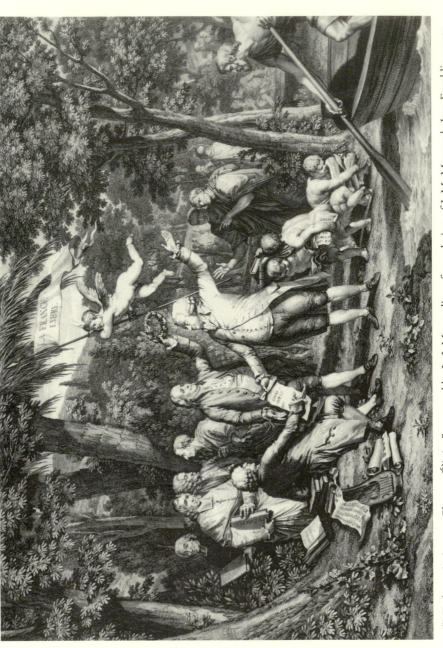

"Mirabeau Arrive aux Champs Élisées," engraved by L. J. Masquelier, after a design of J. M. Moreau le Jne. Franklin greets Mirabeau and crowns him with laurels as he debarks from Charon's boat in the Elysian Fields. Cicero and Demosthenes admire the French orator, who is welcomed to the company of Rousseau, Montesquieu, Voltaire, Mably, and Fénelon,

To ADAMS

MY DEAR AND VENERABLE FRIEND,

. . . The papers will inform you that our government is about to yield to the clamors of your part of the United States against the Embargo laws. Had our legislators been better historians, they would have promptly saved their honor and preserved the peace of our country. Augustus repealed a law to compel bachelors to marry, as soon as he discovered that it could not be carried into effect.[15] One of the kings of Spain issued an edict to oblige the citizens of Madrid to build and make use of privies in order to defend the streets of that city from the ordure which covered them every morning.[16] This edict was resisted and repealed, and the inhabitants of Madrid continue to this day to enjoy in their old and filthy habit the triumph of their ancestors over the despotism of their government. . . .

The 22nd of last month, the birthday of General Washington, was celebrated with great festivity in our city.

We are advised to eat onions in order to prevent our being offended with the breath of persons who have eaten them. Is there no method of infecting persons with madness in order to prevent their being offended and distressed with the madness of their friends and the public? Nathaniel Lee, the poet, was asked in a cell in Bethlehem hospital what brought him there. He answered, "He had said the world was mad, but that the world had said the same thing of him, and that he had been *outvoted*."[17] Do and say what we will, we shall I fear always be *outvoted* by the fools and knaves and madmen of our country.

Tomorrow I expect to close my lectures. The subject of my last lecture

---

15. Baron de Montesquieu, *The Spirit of Laws,* trans. Thomas Nugent (London, 1900), II, 13–14.

16. A reform of Charles III and his great minister, Florida Blanca. See William Coxe, *Memoirs of the Kings of Spain of the House of Bourbon* (London, 1815), V, 200–201, 271.

17. Lee (ca. 1653–92), writer of verse tragedies, was an inmate of Bedlam from 1684 to 1688.

will be "the diseases of the *eyes* and *ears.*" Difficult as they are to cure in the human body, they are far less so than when they affect those two senses in public bodies. . . .

Benjn: Rush

To RUSH

March 14, 1809

MY DEAR FRIEND,

Your anecdotes are always extremely apropos and none of them more so than those in your letter of March 2d. . . .

I remember our Massachusetts legislature once made a law for the extirpation of barberry bushes, upon severe penalties. Not a single bush was ever injured in obedience to it, and at the next election seven eighths of the members were turned out and friends to barberries elected, who instantly repealed the law.[18]

Another time in my memory our legislature made a law to compel bachelors to marry, upon pain of paying double taxes. The people were so attached to the liberty of propagating their species or not, as they chose according to their consciences, that at the next election they left out all the advocates for the bill and chose men who respected the right of celibacy enough to repeal the law.[19]

Legislators! Beware how you make laws to shock the prejudices or break the habits of the people. Innovations even of the most certain and obvious utility must be introduced with great caution, prudence, and skill.

I am very anxious about your state because I think the fate of American union and independence depends more upon its policy than its wisdom or virtue qualifies it to adopt.

18. The Massachusetts General Court passed a bill to extirpate the colony's barberry bushes in December 1754. The law remained on the books until 1764, when it expired. See Andrew McFarland Davis, "Barberry Bushes and Wheat . . . ," Publications of the Colonial Society of Massachusetts, XI, *Transactions 1906–1907* (Boston, 1910), pp. 82–85.

19. This law has not been identified. Adams may have confused reforms in France during the French Revolution with those in Massachusetts.

You and I remember the times when Virginia and Massachusetts agreed very well and acted cordially together. And other times when Pennsylvania and Massachusetts associated very well; but I fear these were the times when the old Constitutional Party was predominant. At other times Massachusetts and New York have drawn together sincerely and amicably.

But Burr by his intrigues with Clintons and Livingstons and Gateses threw New York into the scale of Virginia, and McKean by his intrigues with Gallatin, Dallas, Swanwick, and other foreigners,[20] the French, the Spaniards, the Irish, and the Germans, has alienated Pennsylvania entirely from Massachusetts and thrown her blindfold into the arms of Virginia. There is now, therefore, and has been for eight years a combination of Virginia, Pennsylvania, and New York against Massachusetts, and their domination has been so hardhearted that if it should be much longer continued and be much more cruel, I really do not know but the people of New England would petition the King of England to take them under his protection again and appoint their governors, senators, and judges. The royal appointments in New England before the Revolution were as respectable as Mr. Jefferson's appointments have been. . . .

The birth of Washington was celebrated in Boston, too. The feasts and funerals in honor of Washington, Hamilton, and Ames are mere hypocritical pageantry to keep in credit, banks, funding systems, and other aristocratical speculation.[21] It is as corrupt a system as that by which saints were

20. This is Adams' view of the interstate coalition that Jefferson led to victory in the election of 1800, with Burr sewing up New York and McKean, Pennsylvania. There was truth in Adams' charge that Jefferson was the beneficiary of "the immigrant vote," but it was petty of Adams to call the immigrants "foreigners" when they had come to this country of their own free will and had pledged their allegiance in order to become citizens. Moreover, it was the xenophobic attitude of the Federalists toward first-generation citizens that impelled immigrants to vote Republican. Ironically, John's great-grandson Henry in his classic history of the era would judge Albert Gallatin (1761–1849)—the "foreign" Jeffersonian most vilified by the Federalists—the ablest statesman of his generation.

21. The most ironic manifestation of these partisan fetes relates to the Fourth of July, the birthday of the nation. From 1788 until 1800 the Federalists monopolized the day and turned it into a strictly party occasion, Jefferson's name rarely being mentioned. After 1800, the campaign which stressed Jefferson's authorship of the Declaration, the Republicans made the Fourth theirs, and Adams' name—he who was most responsible for leading Congress to take

canonized and cardinals, popes, and whole hierarchical systems created. I allow Washington, Hamilton, and Ames all their real merit, but many others much more important and deserving than either of them, instead of being honored, are studiously and systematically driven into oblivion.

Our New England Federal papers have been celebrating the dear love of Old England towards us and the horrible dangers that Napoleon will conquer England and then conquer America, till they have frightened the people into their party.[22] As I believe none of these tales, I cannot approve much of the conduct that has been produced by them. I have children and grandchildren and little to leave them besides their liberty. I am sometimes more anxious for this than my philosophy approves. I wish you could allay my fears. . . .

John Adams

To ADAMS

March 13, 1809

MY EXCELLENT FRIEND,

When a young man I read Sidney upon government.[23] In one of his chapters he agitates the following question, "Whether a civil war or slavery be the greatest evil?" and decides in favor of the latter. In revolving that sub-

---

the step—then ceased to figure in the toasts. The Republican monopoly of the Fourth after 1800 was one reason for the Federalist alternative focus on Washington's birthday. See Charles Warren, "Fourth of July Myths," *William and Mary Quarterly,* 3rd Ser., II (1945), 254–272.

22. Fisher Ames (1758–1808) was the author of a series of articles attacking France. Many of these were republished as a memorial tribute in 1809. His fear of Napoleon led to exaggerated statements: "He [Napoleon] wants nothing but the British navy to realize the most extravagant schemes of his ambition. A war that should give him possession of it, or a peace, like the last, that should humble England, and withdraw her navy from any further opposition to his arms, would give the civilized world a master" ("The Successes of Bonaparte," *Works of Fisher Ames,* ed. Seth Ames [New York, 1869], II, 285). John Quincy Adams reviewed the memorial volumes in 1809. His hostile comments reveal what the Adams family thought of their fellow Federalists: "While we drop a tear of compassion upon the political weakness of Mr. Ames's declining days let us rejoice that the maintenance of our national rights against Great Britain has been committed to men of firmer minds" (*American Principles: A Review of Works of Fisher Ames* [Boston, 1809], p. 24).

23. Rush may have been reminded of Algernon Sidney's ideas by Adams' earlier reference (June 20, 1808). See *Discourses concerning Government,* Ch. ii, Sec. 15.

ject in my mind, I have been led to suppose there are evils more afflicting and injurious to a country than a foreign war. The principal evil of war is death. Now vice I believe to be a greater evil than death, and this is generated more by funding systems, banks, embargoes, and nonintercourse laws than by war. Dr. Price calculates the perjuries in Great Britain from the excise and customs at three millions annually. What do you suppose was the number of the false oaths produced by our late Embargo? And what will be the number of the same crimes from the operation of our present nonintercourse law? Greater probably than the amount in number and in enormity of all the crimes that are perpetrated by the *fighting* part of an army in twenty years, and even by its quartermasters, commissaries, and directors of hospitals in half that time.[24] . . .

You have properly distinguished the two great parties which divide your state into French and English. The history of Massachusetts is the history of all the states in the Union as far as it respects political zeal and party principles. We are not "all Federalists and all Republicans," but we are (with the exception of a few retired and growling neutrals) all Frenchmen or all Englishmen.[25] The men of both those nations have immense advantages over you and me. By not eating of the onions of either of them, we are constantly exposed to the offensive breath of them *both*. . . .

Benjn: Rush

To RUSH

March 23, 1809

MY SENSIBLE AND HUMOROUS FRIEND,

I agree with Sidney as quoted in your favor of the 13th, that civil war is preferable to slavery, and I add that foreign war and civil war together at the same time are preferable to slavery.

We hear very often declamations on the demoralizing tendency of war,

24. Rush is referring to his famous exposé of Dr. William Shippen, Jr. (1736–1808), whom he charged with lax administration of military hospitals during the Revolution.
25. Rush is recalling Jefferson's inaugural address, in which Jefferson sought the support of Americans regardless of party affiliation.

but as much as I hate war, I cannot be of the opinion that frequent wars are so corrupting to human nature as long peaces. In a peace of an hundred years and sometimes of fifty, and I have some suspicions of twenty-five, a nation loses its honor, integrity, and most of its other virtues. It sinks into universal avarice, luxury, volupty, hypocrisy, and cowardice. War necessarily brings with it some virtues, and great and heroic virtues, too. Holland, Denmark, and Italy ought to be warnings to us. Those nations by long peace were sunk below the character of man. What horrid creatures we men are, that we cannot be virtuous without murdering one another? . . .

I was not displeased to see by Mr. Madison's nomination of my son that he was not totally renounced, abjured, and abhorred by all parties like his father; but I have no inclination to see him banished into Siberia.[26] I rejoice that he is not to go, though I thank not the Senate for preventing it. That vote was an aristocratical usurpation. There has been a constant inclination in the Senate for twenty years to interfere with the President in appointments to foreign embassies. In Washington's reign there were motions made several times to pass similar resolutions. They were always evaded by the previous question. The secret pride of aristocracy lurked in the heart with so much influence as to prevent the majority from passing a resolution, as in my opinion they ought, that the Senate had no constitutional authority to judge of the necessity or expediency of any proposed embassy. In my distracted times I believe the Senate never went so far upon record, though they sent private committees to overawe me upon several occasions and negatived some of my nominations because I would not give way to their secret cabals. The power of the Senate in executive affairs is in my opinion the rotten part of the Constitution and requires an amendment in the constitutional way more than any other thing. That power overturned the federal administration and will embarrass if not destroy every future one.

Mr. Jefferson's nomination of a minister to Russia at the end of his term was a wise measure; and Mr. Madison's repetition of it, at the beginning of his, shows that his views are too extensive to be bounded by the expense of

26. After John Quincy Adams' break with the Federalist party, many Republicans urged his appointment to some post in the Jefferson administration, but the President did not act. Two days after Madison became President, however, he offered Adams the post of minister to Russia. The appointment was finally cleared by the Senate in June 1809.

a mission. It is of great importance that our President should be informed of the views and politics of the northern courts and cabinets at this dangerous conjuncture.

As to my son, I would not advise him to refuse to serve his country when fairly called to it; but as to myself I would not exchange the pleasure I have in his society once a week for any office in or under the United States.

I see our American parties precisely in the same light with you. I am determined to swallow American garlic enough to defend me against French and English, Federal and Republican onions, let their odor be as strong as it will.

The most modern reproach against me that has come to my knowledge is that "misinterpretations and misrepresentations of my opinions have done great injuries to my country." . . . I am weary, my friend, of that unceasing insolence of which I have been the object for twenty years. I have opposed nothing to it but stoical patience, unlimited submission, passive obedience, and nonresistance. Mausoleums, statues, monuments will never be erected to me. I wish them not. Panegyrical romances will never be written, nor flattering orations spoken, to transmit me to posterity in brilliant colors. No, nor in true colors. All but the last I loathe. Yet I will not die wholly unlamented. Cicero was libeled, slandered, insulted by all parties — by Caesar's party, Catiline's crew, Clodius' myrmidons, aye, and by Pompey and the Senate too. He was persecuted and tormented by turns by all parties and all factions, and that for his most virtuous and glorious actions. In his anguish at times and in the consciousness of his own merit and integrity, he was driven to those assertions of his own actions which have been denominated vanity. Instead of reproaching them with vanity, I think them the most infallible demonstration of his innocence and purity. He declares that all honors are indifferent to him because he knows that it is not in the power of his country to reward him in any proportion to his services.[27]

Pushed and injured and provoked as I am, I blush not to imitate the

27. Adams may have taken his generalization from Conyers Middleton, *The History of the Life of Marcus Tullius Cicero* (London, 1741), II, 518: "It is not . . . the empty blast of popular favor, or the applause of a giddy multitude . . . but the consenting praise of all honest men, and the incorrupt testimony of those, who can judge of excellent merit; which resounds always to virtue, as the eccho to the voice."

Roman and to say to these snarlers against me that if, to avoid misrepresentations of my words, I had omitted to speak and write, they would never have been wealthy and powerful as they are. This country would never have been independent.[28] Three hundred millions of acres of excellent land which she now holds would have been cut off from her limits. The cod and whale fisheries, those inexhaustible sources of wealth and power, would have been ravished from her; the Massachusetts Constitution, the United States Constitution, the Constitution of New York, that of Philadelphia, and every other constitution in the United States which is fit for any but brutes to live under would never have been made. Our armies could not have been fed or clothed for a long time nor our ambassadors, Franklin and Jefferson, supported but with my money; an American navy would never have existed, the Barbary Powers would have captivated and plundered; and without my treaty in 1800 which I made by force against all the arts and opposition of those who pretended to be my friends, we should have been now involved in a foolish war with France and a slavish alliance with Great Britain. All this in my conscience I believe to be true.[29]

28. Adams refers to his advocacy of negotiations with Great Britain independent of France. Vergennes, the French minister, admitted that the Americans received concessions as to boundaries, fishing rights, and Loyalist claims that were better than anticipated by the French government. See Vergennes to Rayneval, Dec. 4, 1782, *The Revolutionary Diplomatic Correspondence of The United States,* ed. Francis Wharton (Washington, D.C., 1899), VI, 107.

29. This sweeping statement of Adams' history-making role during the Revolution and its aftermath, together with his nine points in the letter of April 12, is his personal appraisal of his right to fame. Historians will make one qualification. While Adams more than any other man was the architect of the Massachusetts constitution of 1780, and while this did provide a most important model for later constitution makers, he does overstate his claim when he says that neither the United States Constitution nor other state constitutions would have been correctly designed without the Massachusetts example and without the theoretical teachings of his *Defence.* As any reader of that book will recognize, Adams' massing of authorities to show that history proved that there was only one good form of government—a mixed type with bicameral legislature—was in itself evidence against originality and novelty. Madison's judgment in a letter to Jefferson, June 6, 1787, on Adams' *Defence* is thus more balanced: "Men of learning find nothing new in it. . . . It will, nevertheless, be read and praised, and become a powerful engine in forming the public opinion." Madison's full comments and a representative sample of other contemporary judgments on the *Defence* in 1787 can most easily be consulted in Charles Warren, *The Making of the Constitution* (Boston, 1928), Appendix C, pp. 815–818; cf. pp. 156–157. However, Robert R. Palmer in his *The Age of the Democratic Revolution* (Princeton, 1959—), I, Ch. ix, argues that the example of the Massachusetts con-

Let the Federalists then talk about misinterpretations and misrepresentations of my words or actions. None have done more of them than themselves. I appeal to foreign nations. I appeal to my own countrymen within a year after my death. And there let the appeal rest for the present. . . .

John Adams

To ADAMS

April 1, 1809

MY DEAR AND VENERABLE FRIEND,

. . . In your letter of the 23rd of March you mention Cicero as a precedent for a man's doing justice to his services to his country. You might have added the conduct of St. Paul for the same purpose. The calumnies of the Jews and the ingratitude of his pagan converts compelled him to enter into a long detail of his sacrifices, sufferings, and exploits in advancing the glory of his Master and the interests of his gospel;[30] There is, it is true, great difficulty in a man's speaking or writing of himself so as to avoid giving offense. The King of Prussia in his *Posthumous Works* says this difficulty is so great that even a public justification for supposed offenses should be avoided, inasmuch as it cannot be made without some self-praise,[31] but this opinion is by no means a correct one. A reverence for religion and a regard for truth, liberty, family honor, and the interests of society may make it indispensably necessary for a man who has been wronged by the country or the age in which he has lived to appeal to the world at large and to posterity for an acquittal of the follies or crimes with which he has been charged. Knowing that you feel your obligations to all these objects, and your desire to maintain a fair and just character, I have formerly suggested to you to employ the evening of your life in writing "the history of your own times"

stitution had a far greater impact on French and European liberal thought than even Adams realized.

30. II Corinthians 11:22–23.

31. *Posthumous Works of Frederic II, King of Prussia,* trans. Thomas Holcroft (London, 1789), I, xx–xxi. The preface (p. xi) opens: "Most of our historians are compilers of falsehood interspersed occasionally with truth."

as far as you were an actor in them. Let it be published by your sons after your death. It will be more than a patent of nobility to your descendants to the end of time. I shall follow the advice I am now giving you as far as it relates to volumes of scandal that have been printed against me for my medical opinions and practice since the year 1793, to no one of which I have ever replied even by a single paragraph in a newspaper. My sons expect this act of justice to them with more solicitude than they would an independence in property, were it possible for me to bequeath it to them.[32] . . .

Our legislature has exhibited prodigies of folly and madness. They have passed an arbitration law which is to supersede, if possible, trials by jury. They have made several attempts to sweep the benches of the state of federal judges. . . .

O Liberty! liberty! I have worshipped thee as a substance.—But—but—but—"Where are my shoes and stockings?"—Where is my lancet?—Where are my gallipots?[33] . . .

In the year 1800 I stood nearly alone in refusing to be led by either of the two parties that were then contending for the power of our country. This is not the case now. Hundreds of our citizens now think and act with me, more especially the whigs of the Revolution. The most active men of both parties were brought into life by the sunshine and safety of the peace of 1780 or by the prosperity or poverty which have been produced by it. . . .

Are the labors and virtues of the patriots and heroes of 1774, 1775, and 1776 to perish without bringing forth any other fruit than what we have gathered from the transient duration of our general government? Or are their sleepless nights, their midnight addresses to the power and justice of Heaven for their oppressed and injured country, their sacrifices of time and property, and their "cruel mockings" (often worse than bodily sufferings) to be rewarded only in "another and a better world"? Let us believe

32. This undoubtedly refers to the *Autobiography,* pp. 78–109, in which Rush records for his family his political career and his professional experiences.

33. Rush is again thinking of Don Quixote. "Liberty, Sancho, is one of the most precious gifts given of the skies to men; with it no treasures the sea covers or the earth confines can be compared." Miguel de Cervantes Saavedra, *The Visionary Gentleman Don Quijote de la Mancha,* trans. Robinson Smith (New York, 1932), II, 480 (Ch. lvii).

The firm patriot *there*,
Who made the welfare of mankind his care,
Though here with envy and with faction tost,
Shall find the generous labor was not lost.[34]

Adieu. Always yours most sincerely, . . .

Benjn: Rush . . .

To RUSH

April 12, 1809

[DEAR RUSH,]

Thank you for your favor of the 1st. I might have quoted Job as well as St. Paul as a precedent; but as I mix religion with politics as little as possible, I chose to confine myself to Cicero. You advise me to write my own life. I have made several attempts, but it is so dull an employment that I cannot endure it. I look so much like a small boy in my own eyes that with all my vanity I cannot endure the sight of the picture. I am glad you have resolved to do yourself justice. I am determined to vindicate myself in some points while I live. Inclosed is a whimsical specimen. In future I shall not be so *goguenard.*

The dialogue between Diodati and me is literal truth,[35] that is, it is a literal translation from the French, in which language the conversation was held and which I reduced to writing. You may ask what reasons I had for foreseeing such consequences. I will give you a few hints among a thousand.

1. When I went home to my family in May 1770, from the town meeting in Boston, which was the first I had ever attended,[36] and where I had

34. Joseph Addison, *Cato,* IV.iv.157–160.

35. The dialogue enclosure is missing. Fortunately, Adams in a letter to Daniel Wright and Erastus Lyman, Mar. 13, 1809 (*Works,* IX, 613–615), gives an account of the conversation. Diodati says, "You will experience all the ingratitude, all the injustice of the ancient republicans. . . . You will be ill-treated, hated, despised and persecuted." Diodati was then Saxony's ambassador to France.

36. Adams' description of his state of mind in 1770 seems overdramatized. Nevertheless, 1770 was a year of unresolved tensions that produced something like a nervous breakdown in

been chosen in my absence, without any solicitation, one of their representatives, I said to my wife, "I have accepted a seat in the House of Representatives, and thereby have consented to my own ruin, to your ruin, and the ruin of our children. I give you this warning that you may prepare your mind for your fate." She burst into tears, but instantly cried out in a transport of magnanimity, "Well, I am willing in this cause to run all risks with you and to be ruined with you if you are ruined." These were times, my friend, in Boston which tried women's souls as well as men's.

2. I saw the awful prospect before me and my country in all its horrors and, notwithstanding all my vanity, was conscious of a thousand defects in my own character as well as health, which made me despair of going through and weathering the storms in which I must be tossed.

3. In the same year, 1770, my sense of equity and humanity impelled me, against a torrent of unpopularity and the inclination of all my friends, to engage in defense of Captain Preston and the soldiers.[37] My successful ex-

---

1771. The problem for Adams, as Massachusetts politics became increasingly polarized between two intransigent parties, was that by nature he was a nonparty man. So while he had worked with the Patriots against the Bernard administration since 1765, he had never joined the Sons of Liberty and continued to hold mental reservations about their methods though approving most of their aims. At the same time he was a declared enemy of the Hutchinson group, whose program he deemed subversive of the Charter and divisive for the Empire. What Adams reports to Rush is his memory of his mental anguish in 1770; what he forgets or conceals is that the anguish grew out of his "trimming" role of 1770 — serving as a Patriot representative in the House and defending the soldiers that the Patriots were trying to punish legally for the Boston Massacre. Adams did not resolve his internal conflict and align himself completely with the Patriots until December 1772. See Page Smith, *John Adams* (Garden City, N.Y., 1962), I, 135–140; David Hawke, *A Transaction of Free Men: The Birth and Course of the Declaration of Independence* (New York, 1964), pp. 89–96.

37. The defense of Captain Preston and the "Massacre soldiers" by Adams and Josiah Quincy did indeed bring down on his head an avalanche of popular criticism. Officially the Patriots' publicly announced program never shifted from demanding the death penalty. It is probable, however, that secretly they were not sorry to see the defense in the hands of lawyers who would not turn the trial into an investigation of the upper class and Patriot management of the Boston mob. And with the public sincerely convinced that the soldiers were guilty, the political aims of the "Massacre" were served; it did not matter whether the wretched creatures swung or not. That Adams was elected Boston representative in 1770, at the very time he was the subject of widespread popular disapproval, is suggestive evidence also of how powerful the Patriot caucus was. The populace might condemn Adams for associating himself with the defense, but Patriot leadership had decided that he should represent Boston in the House, and that decision was carried out.

ertions in that cause, though the result was perfectly conformable to law and justice, brought upon me a load of indignation and unpopularity which I knew would never be forgotten nor entirely forgiven. The Boston newspapers to this day show that my apprehensions were well founded.

4. You can testify for me that in 1774 my conduct in Congress drew upon me the jealousy and aversion not only of the tories in Congress, who were neither few nor feeble, but of the whole body of Quakers and proprietary gentlemen in Pennsylvania. I have seen and felt the consequences of these prejudices to this day.

5. I call you to witness that I was the first member of Congress who ventured to come out in public, as I did in January 1776, in my "Thoughts on Government, in a Letter from a Gentleman to his Friend," that is, Mr. Wythe, in favor of a government in three branches with an independent judiciary.[38] This pamphlet, you know, was very unpopular. No man appeared in public to support it but yourself. You attempted in the public papers to give it some countenance, but without much success. . . .

Mr. Thomas Paine was so highly offended with it that he came to visit me at my chamber at Mrs. Yard's to remonstrate and even scold at me for it, which he did in very ungenteel terms. In return, I only laughed heartily at him and rallied him upon his grave arguments from the Old Testament to prove that monarchy was unlawful in the sight of God. "Do you seriously believe, Paine," said I, "in that pious doctrine of yours?" This put him in good humor and he laughed out. "The Old Testament!" said he, "I do not believe in the Old Testament. I have had thoughts of publishing my sentiments of it, but upon deliberation I have concluded to put that off till the latter part of my life." Paine's wrath was excited because my plan of government was essentially different from the silly projects that he had published in his *Common Sense*. By this means I became suspected and unpopular with the leading demagogues and the whole Constitutional Party in Pennsylvania.

6. Upon my return from France in 1779, I found myself elected by my native town of Braintree a member of the convention for forming a consti-

38. North Carolina delegates William Hooper and John Penn asked Adams to put his thoughts on government into writing. George Wythe saw Hooper's manuscript copy and asked to read it. He and others encouraged its publication, but it did not receive the circulation that Paine's *Common Sense* achieved.

tution for the state of Massachusetts. I attended that convention of nearly four hundred members. Here I found such a chaos of absurd sentiments concerning government that I was obliged daily before that great assembly, and afterwards in the grand committee, to propose plans and advocate doctrines which were extremely unpopular with the greater number.[39] Lieutenant-Governor Cushing was avowedly for a single assembly like Pennsylvania.[40] Samuel Adams was of the same mind. Mr. Hancock kept aloof in order to be governor. In short, I had at first no support but from the Essex Junto, who had adopted my ideas in the "Letter to Mr. Wythe." They supported me timorously and at last would not go with me to so high a mark as I aimed at, which was a complete negative in the governor upon all laws. They made me, however, draw up the constitution, and it was finally adopted with some amendments very much for the worse. The bold, decided, and determined part I took in this assembly in favor of a good government acquired me the reputation of a man of high principles and strong notions in government, scarcely compatible with republicanism. A foundation was here laid of much jealousy and unpopularity among the democratical people in this state.[41]

7. In Holland I had driven the English party and the Statholder's party before me like clouds before the wind and had brought that power to unite cordially with America, France, and Spain against England. If I had not before alienated the whole English nation from me, this would have been enough to produce an eternal jealousy of me; and I fully believe that whenever a free intercourse should take place between Britain and America, I might depend upon their perpetual ill will to me and that their influence would be used to destroy mine.

39. The Massachusetts constitutional convention assembled on Sept. 1, 1779, and chose almost immediately a committee of thirty-one to write the proposed constitution. As a member of the committee, Adams is credited with drawing up the original draft, except for the article on religion.

40. Thomas Cushing (1725–88) served as lieutenant governor of Massachusetts from 1780 to 1788. He was a member of the Continental Congress and a founding member of the American Academy of Arts and Sciences.

41. Professor Samuel E. Morison has described Adams' role as draftsman and analyzed the debate on this 1780 constitution. See his "The Struggle over the Adoption of the Constitution of Massachusetts, 1780," *Proceedings of the Massachusetts Historical Society,* L (1917), 353–412.

8. In all my negotiations in France and Holland … I had so uniformly resisted all the arts and intrigues of the Count de Vergennes and M. de Sartine and all their satellites,[42] and that with such perfect success that I well knew, although they treated me with great external respect, yet in their hearts they had conceived an ineradicable jealousy and aversion to me. I well knew, therefore, that French influence in America would do all in its power to trip me up.

9. Dr. Franklin's behavior had been so excessively complaisant to the French ministry and, in my opinion, had so endangered the essential interests of our country that I had been frequently obliged to differ from him and sometimes to withstand him to his face; so that I knew he had conceived an irreconcilable hatred of me and that he had propagated and would continue to propagate prejudices, if nothing worse, against me in America from one end of it to the other.[43] …

With all these reflections fresh in my mind, you may judge whether my anticipations in the good-humored conversation with Diodati were rash, peevish, or ill-grounded. …

John Adams

To ADAMS

May 5, 1809

DEAR SIR,

I am much pleased with the specimen you have given of the use of *your wings* upon a certain subject in your last letter. Your publications in the

42. Charles Gravier, Count de Vergennes (1717–87), became minister of foreign affairs for Louis XVI in 1774 and negotiated the famous alliance of 1778 with the United States. Antoine Sartine, Count d'Alby (1729–1801), was minister of marine during Adams' negotiations for military aid.

43. There is much evidence that Franklin found Adams a provoking colleague, but there is no evidence to show that he hated him. Franklin characterized the New Englander as "always an honest man, often a wise one, but sometimes, and in some things, absolutely out of his senses." Franklin was older than Adams, wiser in recognizing what aid could and could not be gotten from the French ministry, and infinitely wiser in recognizing that a begging diplomat catches more flies with honey than with vinegar. However, the Pennsylvanian's unabashed enjoyment of French manners and his acceptant attitude toward French morals out-

newspapers show still further how important to the public, to posterity, and to your family honor are the words you have preserved of your political life. Your defense of the rights of our seamen is much admired. It discovers, with the experience and wisdom of 70, the fire and eloquence of five-and-twenty. The *place* from which it was dated induced me to read it. It is many years since I have read a political essay of half its length. It inspired me with the feelings of 1774 and 1776. . . .

Some of your tory enemies in Boston have endeavored to prove that your country has canceled the immense debt it owes you by drafts upon the Treasury of the United States. They forget that the obligations due to patriots, heroes, and other benefactors of mankind can never be canceled by millions of dollars, especially when that acknowledgement of their services is opposed by calumny, falsehood, and persecution. The proper and the dearest compensation for the labors, sacrifices, and achievements of public spirit is *justice to character.* Everything short of this is nothing but Shakespeare's purse—"all trash."[44]

Benjn: Rush

To RUSH

June 7, 1809

DEAR SIR,

Your letters are not apt to lie a month unacknowledged. That of May 5th is before me, since which I have received an *Aurora* under your envelope. . . .

It would divert you if I were to amuse myself with writing an answer to the tory enemy you mention. That wretch's father stepped into my practice in Boston when I was sent to Congress and by my business made a fortune of two or three hundred thousand dollars. [He had] left him a splendid fortune, a palace in Boston, a superb country seat, and very large sums in banks

---

raged Adams' Puritanism, while the adulation of Franklin by the French people filled the awkward and unpopular New Englander with envy. See Verner W. Crane, *Benjamin Franklin and a Rising People* (Boston, 1954), p. 194.

44. See *Othello,* III.iii.157.

and stocks. A fortune accumulating now every day, whereas I have not added a shilling to my property these eight years. He is worth, I suppose, four times as much as I am. His uncle by my appointment made as navy agent in three or four years more than I am worth.[45] If I was allowed two and an half per cent on a million sterling that I borrowed and passed thro' my hands in Holland as he was for 4 or 500 thousand dollars he spent as navy agent, it would amount to twice the sum I am worth. For this I was never allowed a farthing. Two others of his connections I promoted. This is Essex Junto gratitude. . . .

John Adams

45. Adams easily could have been confused about the relationship of George Cabot (1752–1823) and Stephen Higginson (1743–1828), because they were first cousins and brothers-in-law. Adams appointed Higginson to the post of naval agent at Boston in 1797 and offered Cabot the secretaryship of the navy in 1798. Higginson was already rich before he took the agency, and Cabot, who was influential in the United States Bank and the Suffolk Insurance Company, had also made a substantial fortune. See Thomas Wentworth Higginson, *Life and Times of Stephen Higginson* (Boston, 1907), pp. 14–15, 187–216.

CHAPTER 7

The Corruption of Tradition

"THE YOUNG PEOPLE of our country born since the year 1774, and who compose a majority of our citizens, would receive everything that came from your pen upon the subject of American independence." Rush was again urging Adams to write an autobiography and publish some of his correspondence and was reminding him of his obligation to leave a record of the Revolution for posterity. Adams replied immediately, assuring Rush that he had "solemn notions of the sanctity of history" and would compel historians, if he had the power, to take an oath to tell only the truth. Nevertheless, he wondered whether history could be written objectively and whether anyone could capture the spirit of the Revolution. Surely, the history they would write to tell the true story would be far different from the accounts already in existence, but they, too, would be prejudiced. At their age for the sake of tranquility they should become politically passive and abjure the intensity of patriotic emotions, but such an idea, Adams declared, "strikes us both with horror."

To RUSH

August 7, 1809

MY DEAR FRIEND,

. . . You have frequently . . . advised me to write my own life. I shall never have resolution or time to accomplish such a work; but having been called before the public most undesignedly and unexpectedly and excessively reproached with one of the wisest, most virtuous, most successful and most important actions of my life, the Peace with France in 1800, I undertook an apology for it. You may see by the manner in which that is executed, how large a work it would require to vindicate all the actions of my life.[1]

I am now upon the Peace of 1783. That I shall exhibit chiefly in copies of documents and a few extracts from my own letters. How it will be received I know not. The printers in Boston talk of an edition of them in a book. That is their affair. I have nothing to do with it.[2] . . .

Parents must have their trials. I am now experiencing another. My oldest son sailed on Saturday, the 5th of this month, for St. Petersburg with his family. The separation was like tearing me to pieces. A more dutiful and affectionate son there cannot be. His society was always a cordial and a consolation under all circumstances. I maintain my serenity, however. I can only pray for his safety and success. The objects of his mission I know only by conjecture. I have thought these thirty years that we ought to have a minister at that court. . . .

John Adams

To ADAMS

August 14, 1809

MY DEAR OLD FRIEND,

. . . It was from a conviction that you saw things with other eyes than most of the persons that cooperated with you in establishing the independence of the United States, and that your opinions and conduct would bear the scrutiny of posterity at that eventful time, that I have so often urged you to bequeath to your country memoirs of your life. . . . Suppose you take up the state of the public mind with respect to that great measure in 1774, 1775, and 1776, and the private and public part you took in it.

I once heard you say the *active* business of the American Revolution began in Philadelphia in the act of her citizens in sending back the tea ship, and that Massachusetts would have received her portion of the tea had not

---

1. These letters and documents were printed in the Boston *Patriot* and reprinted in Adams' *Works,* IX, 241–311.

2. Apparently these letters were never published.

our example encouraged her to expect union and support in destroying it. Perhaps you have never heard that Colonel Bradford first suggested to General Mifflin the necessity of opposing landing of the tea in an accidental interview they had at the old man's door. The General received the proposition coolly and said it would be impossible to awaken our citizens to a sense of the importance of such a measure. The old man said, "Leave that business to me. I will collect a few active spirits at my house tomorrow evening. Do you be one of them, and we will soon set the city in motion." The next evening six or eight citizens (of whom I was one) met at his house. A number of resolutions were drafted. A town meeting was called a few days afterwards. Dr. Cadwalader[3] (an aged and highly respected whig) was applied to, to preside at it, which he cheerfully agreed to do. A large meeting was held. The business was conducted with prudence, spirit, and unanimity. The flame kindled on that day soon extended to Boston and gradually spread throughout the whole continent. It was the first throe of that convulsion which delivered Great Britain of the United States.

J. Cheetham is now employed in writing the life of Thomas Paine. He applied to me for the history of the origin of his *Common Sense.* In reply to his letter I informed him that Mr. Paine wrote that pamphlet at my suggestion and that I gave it its name. I did not suggest a single idea contained in it, and I believe Dr. Franklin's head and hand were equally distant from the author while he wrote it. Mr. Cheetham intends to do Paine justice. He will expose his errors and crimes as well as extol his talents and services to our country.[4]

The young people of our country born since the year 1774, and who compose a majority of our citizens, would receive everything that came from your pen upon the subject of American independence with great avidity. The history of the prejudices and fears that were gradually written and spoken down before that measure took place would form an interesting view of the human mind in its relation to liberty and government. One

3. Thomas Cadwalader (ca. 1707–99), a Philadelphia physician, was a member of the city and provincial councils from 1751 to the Revolution.
4. James Cheetham (1772–1810), a New York journalist, published a biography of Paine in 1809.

thing would be very striking in the history of the time alluded to, and that is the sameness of the prejudices and fears of a certain class of our citizens with respect to the ministry, the government, the commerce, and the power of Great Britain. . . .

A safe passage to both our sons across the ocean! With love to all who still surround your table, I am . . .

Benjn: Rush . . .

To RUSH

August 31, 1809

MY DEAR OLD FRIEND,

. . . I have very solemn notions of the sanctity of history. Every historian ought to be able to take the oath of Thuanus, *pro veritate historiarum mearum Deum ipsum obtestor.*[5] This was an oath taken to I know not how many volumes, forty or fifty perhaps. I should not dare to take such an oath to any history I could write. I pretend to nothing more than to furnish memorials to serve historians. It is their business and duty to detect my errors and appreciate everything according to its true value. Amid all my avocations I have found time to read Mr. Fox's morsel of history;[6] and I can scarcely refrain from wishing that his whole parliamentary life had been employed in writing history. It is but a morsel of one single year of James the Second; but it displays an industry, a discernment, a reflection beyond Robertson, Hume, Gibbon, and all the rest.[7] . . .

I doubt whether faithful history ever was or ever can be written. 300 years after the event it cannot be written without offending some powerful and popular individual family party, some statesman, some general, some prince,

5. Another reference to De Thou's vow to write impartial history.
6. Charles James Fox, *A History of the Early Part of the Reign of James the Second* (London, 1808). Adams was impressed with this history because it was written by an active politician.
7. William Robertson (1721–93) was as famous in the eighteenth century for his histories of Scotland and America and his great *History of the Reign of the Emperor Charles V* as was Edward Gibbon (1737–94) for the *History of the Decline and Fall of the Roman Empire.* Fox's work would not today be mentioned in the same breath with Gibbon and Hume.

some priest or some philosopher. The world will go on always ignorant of itself, its past history, and future destiny. If you were to write the history of our Revolution, how different it would appear from the histories we have!

The anecdotes you mention I have no doubt are true. In Holland I wrote some observations on my friend, the Abbé Raynal, in which an account is given of the sending back the ships and destroying the tea very conformable to what you remember I said to you. If I had time, I would sent it [to] you.[8]

Mr. Cheetham's project is of uncertain utility. The sooner Paine is forgotten, perhaps, the better. I fear he has done more harm than good. This is, however, speaking after the manner of men, with submission to higher Powers. . . .

September 1, 1809

. . . You pretend that you have outlived your patriotism; but you deceive yourself. Your feelings contradict your assertions. You can never get rid of your *amor patriae* and attachment to your *natale solum*. At your age and mine it would perhaps be better for our tranquility if we could outlive all our public feelings. Yet the very thought of this strikes us both with horror. . . .

Pray how comes Parson Caldwell to be so very rich? I suppose he was another Witherspoon or another MacWhorter who thought a part of Christ's kingdom was of this world.[9] My friend, the clergy have been in all ages and countries as dangerous to liberty as the army. Yet I love the clergy and the army. What can we do without them in this wicked world? But to dismiss

8. The French editor and historian Guillaume Thomas Raynal (1713–96), most famous for his best-selling history of the European settlements in the East and West Indies (1770), also wrote an account of the American Revolution which appeared in English translation and was published in Dublin in 1781. Both books were republished under the general title *A Philosophical and Political History of the Settlements and Trade of the Europeans in the East and West Indies*, 6 vols. (Edinburgh, 1804). Raynal gave Boston credit for creating the disturbance over tea (VI, 54–55).

9. James Caldwell (1734–81), a graduate of the College of New Jersey, was a Presbyterian clergyman who served in the American Revolution as a commissary. John Witherspoon (1723–94) was president of the College of New Jersey, a signer of the Declaration of Independence, and a member of the Continental Congress, 1776–82. Alexander MacWhorter (1734–1807), Presbyterian clergyman, was a Revolutionary War chaplain, president of Charlotte Academy, and trustee and fund-raiser for the College of New Jersey.

all this, what shall we say of public affairs? The hounds have all been in fault, wholly lost and bewildered. They could not yet scent the track of the fox. They know not which way to pursue the game. I expect the master huntsmen will soon point out the path; one will cry war with France and the other war with England. But they cannot get a vote in Congress for either.

I have no hope of any settlement with France or England at present. It is impossible. England asserts a sovereignty at sea and France almost claims an absolute dominion at land. We ought not to agree to either. We never can agree to the claims of England. What shall we do? . . . The *unum necessarium* is a navy. . . . One year would produce at less expense than the gunboats a little power that would secure us more consideration than an hundred thousand disciplined veteran land forces.[10]

John Adams

To ADAMS

September 6, 1809

MY DEAR FRIEND,

Although for many years past I have read nothing but books upon medicine on weekdays and upon religion on Sundays and have expected to continue to do so as long as I live, yet you have almost persuaded me to read Fox's *History of James the Second.* . . .

You wonder how Parson Caldwell became possessed of certificates! He acted as a deputy quartermaster in the army at a time when purchases were made *only* with that species of paper money, and when the pay of quartermasters was a commission upon all purchases made with them. . . .

You charge me with the feelings of *patriotism.* I grant that man is naturally a domestic, a social, and a political or rational animal, and that Horace's line is in general true, "naturam expellas furca, tamen usque re-

---

10. Jefferson considered the navy primarily a defensive force and had therefore recommended to Congress the construction of 200 gunboats, but the ravages of pirates in Tripoli and engagements with invading foreign warships prior to the War of 1812 revealed the need for offensive vessels.

currit."[11] But those tribal passions have been and may be subdued. There are political as well as social and domestic monks. Happy the man that in the present state of our country has put on the hood and that can look upon a newspaper and the history of town meetings as an old friar looks upon a blooming young woman. If I have not attained to this felicity, I have in a great measure deserved it, for I generally hear and read with the same indifference of the proceedings of the leaders of both the great parties that now agitate and divide our country. . . .

I am now busily engaged in revising the proof sheets of an edition of the celebrated Dr. Sydenham's *Works,* with notes, and the 3rd edition of my *Medical Inquiries.*[12] To the latter I have made considerable additions. They will both be published I hope sometime in November. Such is the physical and moral influence of a man's constant employment upon his body and mind, that it is said in England "a button maker becomes a button and a buckle maker a buckle in the course of his life." Do not wonder then if you should hear of my habits of bookmaking having converted me into proof sheets and calfskin, or of my habits of feeling pulses into a pulse glass or a stop watch. I exist almost wholly in those two employments. . . .

Benjn: Rush

To RUSH

September 27, 1809

DEAR FRIEND,

. . . Fox was a remarkable character. I admire the morsel of history. Pitt was another. He has left nothing but speeches taken down by stenographers. I cannot pronounce either of them wise statesmen; yet perhaps they were as wise as they could be in their circumstances. Great men they both were, most certainly. Pitt, I think, was more correct in his knowledge of the English constitution and of the subject of government in general than ei-

11. "Though you drive out nature with a fork, it will incessantly return." Horace, *Epistles* I.x.24.
12. A four-volume edition was published in Philadelphia in 1809.

ther Fox or Burke. Both of these have uttered and published very absurd notions of the principles of government. . . .

Have a care! Deceive not thyself. There is not an old friar in France, not in Europe, who looks on a blooming young virgin with *sang-froid.* Your *naturam expellas furca* is mere infallible nature. I do and will insist upon it, you are still a patriot, and you never can cease to be so. . . .

If a button maker becomes a button at last, the Lord knows what I am to be: a newspaper, I fear. I had rather be anything else. You are infinitely better off, if you are to become Sydenham's and Rush's *Works.* Oh! What would I not give to be a Sydenham or a Rush in preference to being a newspaper writer!

Your present employment is patriotism and, what is more and better, philanthropy; far superior to mine, as I not only fear but believe. In my line, I fear, it is impossible to do any good. I hope I shall do no harm. . . .

October 8, 1809

Bacon, the great Bacon, was fond of paradoxes. What could [he have meant when he said that great men have] neither ancestors nor posterity? Was not Isaac the son and Jacob the grandson and Joseph the great-grandson of Abraham? Was not Julius Caesar the posterity of Anchises and Aeneas? . . . Was not William Pitt, a great soul surely, the son of Chatham? And Richard, the son of Benjamin, I hope will be as great a man as his father. . . .

John Adams

To ADAMS

October 16, 1809

MY DEAR FRIEND,

Who were the ancestors and posterity of Homer, Demosthenes, Plato, and Aristotle? Who were the ancestors and posterity of Cicero, Horace, and Virgil? Were any of them philosophers, orators, or poets? Who were the ancestors and posterity of Walsingham, Sully, Marlborough, and Wolfe? Were any of them statesmen, generals, or heroes? I do not ask whether they were descended from gentlemen or whether they left gentle sons behind them. I ask, were their ancestors GREAT in the same elevated walks in life as themselves? I believe history and common observation will furnish many more instances of the truth of Lord Bacon's remark than of the reverse of it. . . .

"What book is that in your hands?" said I to my son Richard a few nights ago in a DREAM.[13] "It is the history of the United States," said he. "Shall I read a page of it to you?" "No, no," said I. "I believe in the truth of no history but in that which is contained in the Old and New Testaments." "But, sir," said my son, "this page relates to your friend Mr. Adams." "Let me see it then," said I. I read it with great pleasure and herewith send you a copy of it.

"1809

"Among the most extraordinary events of this year was the renewal of the friendship and intercourse between Mr. John Adams and Mr. Jefferson, the two ex-Presidents of the United States. They met for the first time in the Congress of 1775. Their principles of liberty, their ardent attachment to their country, and their views of the importance and probable issue of the struggle with Great Britain in which they were engaged being exactly the same, they were strongly attracted to each other and became personal as well as political friends. They met in England during the war while each of them held commissions of honor and trust at two of the first courts of Europe, and spent many happy hours together in reviewing the difficulties and success of their respective negotiations. A difference of opinion upon the objects and issue of the French Revolution separated them during the years in which that great event interested and divided the American people. The predominance of the party which favored the French cause threw Mr. Adams out of the Chair of the United States in the year 1800 and placed Mr. Jefferson there in his stead. The former retired with resignation and dignity to his seat at Quincy, where he spent the evening of his life in literary and philosophical pursuits surrounded by an amiable family and a few

13. See Lyman H. Butterfield, "The Dream of Benjamin Rush: The Reconciliation of John Adams and Thomas Jefferson," *Yale Review*, XL (1950–51), 297–319.

old and affectionate friends. The latter resigned the Chair of the United States in the year 1808, sick of the cares and disgusted with the intrigues of public life, and retired to his seat at Monticello in Virginia, where he spent the remainder of his days in the cultivation of a large farm agreeably to the new system of husbandry. In the month of November 1809, Mr. Adams addressed a short letter to his friend Mr. Jefferson in which he congratulated him upon his escape to the shades of retirement and domestic happiness, and concluded it with assurances of his regard and good wishes for his welfare. This letter did great honor to Mr. Adams. It discovered a magnanimity known only to great minds. Mr. Jefferson replied to this letter and reciprocated expressions of regard and esteem. These letters were followed by a correspondence of several years, in which they mutually reviewed the scenes of business in which they had been engaged, and candidly acknowledged to each other all the errors of opinion and conduct into which they had fallen during the time they filled the same station in the service of their country. Many precious aphorisms, the result of observation, experience, and profound reflection, it is said, are contained in these letters. It is to be hoped the world will be favored with a sight of them when they can neither injure nor displease any persons or families whose ancestors' follies or crimes were mentioned in them. These gentlemen sunk into the grave nearly at the same time, full of years and rich in the gratitude and praises of their country (for they outlived the heterogeneous parties that were opposed to them), and to their numerous merits and honors posterity has added that they were rival friends." [14]

Benjn: Rush

14. With no immediate success, Rush later wrote Jefferson (Jan. 2, 1811) urging him to renew friendship with Adams: "Your and my old friend Mr. Adams now and then drops me a line from his seat at Quincy. His letters glow with the just opinions he held and defended in the patriotic years 1774, 1775, and 1776. . . . When I consider your early attachment to Mr. Adams, and his to you; when I consider how much the liberties and independence of the United States owe to the concert of your principles and labors; and when I reflect upon the sameness of your opinions at present upon most of the subjects of government and all the subjects of legislation, I have ardently wished a friendly and epistolary intercourse might be revived between you before you take a final leave of the common object of your affections. Such an intercourse will be honorable to your talents and patriotism and highly useful to the course of republicanism not only in the United States but all over the world. Posterity will

To RUSH

October 25, 1809

MY DEAR SIR,

. . . Whether there are more instances in favor of Bacon's observation or against it, I believe that almost all great men have mothers at least. I read in a *Journal de Paris* many years ago a list of almost all the great men who had lived and been famous in France, with an account of their births, and they were almost all the sons of tradesmen, bakers, brewers, masons, carpenters, clothiers, shoemakers, cabinetmakers, and some of them from laborers, livery servants, and the lowest and meanest occupations in society. I regret that I did not preserve and copy this catalogue. It was a proof irrefragable that there is some truth in Bacon's apophthegm. . . .

I believe there is as much in the breed of men as there is in that of horses. I know you will upon reading this cry out. Oh the Aristocrat! The advocate for hereditary nobility! For monarchy! and every political evil! But it is no such thing. I am no advocate for any of these things. As long as sense and virtue remain in a nation in sufficient quantities to enable them to choose their legislatures and magistrates, elective governments are the best in the world. But when nonsense and vice get the ascendency, command the majority, and possess the whole power of a nation, the history of mankind shows that sense and virtue have been compelled to unite with nonsense and vice in establishing hereditary powers as the only security for life, property, and the miserable liberty that remains. Let my countrymen, therefore, have a care how they confide in Callender, Paine, Burr, or Hamilton for their political guides. If they do not, calamities, devastations, bloodshed, and carnage will convince them that there is no special providence for them. They will go the way of all the earth.

---

revere the friendship of two ex-Presidents that were once opposed to each other. Human nature will be a gainer by it. I am sure an advance on your side will be a cordial to the heart of Mr. Adams. Tottering over the grave, he now leans wholly upon the shoulders of his old Revolutionary friends. The patriots generated by the funding system, &c., are all his enemies. . . ." *Letters,* II, 1075–76.

A DREAM AGAIN! I wish you would dream all day and all night, for one of your dreams puts me in spirits for a month. I have no other objection to your dream but that it is not history. It may be prophecy. There has never been the smallest interruption of the personal friendship between me and Mr. Jefferson that I know of. You should remember that Jefferson was but a boy to me. I was at least ten years older than him in age and more than twenty years older than him in politics. I am bold to say I was his preceptor in politics and taught him everything that has been good and solid in his whole political conduct. I served with him on many committees in Congress, in which we established some of the most important regulations of the army &c., &c., &c.

Jefferson and Franklin were united with me in a commission to the King of France and fifteen other commissions to treat with all the powers of Europe and Africa. I resided with him in France above a year in 1784 and 1785 and met him every day at my house in Auteuil, at Franklin's house at Passy, or at his house in Paris. In short, we lived together in the most perfect friendship and harmony.

I was sent to England in 1785. He came to me in England, and I travelled over the kingdom with him. He met me afterwards in Holland. I there instructed him in the situation of all my money matters before I left Europe. I have a bushel of letters from him. If I were disposed to be captious, I might complain of his open patronage of Callender, Paine, Brown, and twenty others, my most abandoned and unprincipled enemies.

But I have seen ambition and party in so many men of the best character of all parties that I must renounce almost all mankind if I renounce any for such causes. Fare them all well. Heaven is their judge and mine. I am not conscious that I ever injured any of them in thought, word, or deed to promote my own interest or reputation or to lessen theirs. Let them one and all say the same if they can. . . .

January 21, 1810

. . . I never asked my son any questions about . . . his mission to St. Petersburg. If I had been weak enough to ask, he would have been wise enough to be silent; for although a more dutiful and affectionate son is not in existence, he knows his obligations to his country and his trust are superior to all parental requests or injunctions. I know, therefore, no more of his errand than any other man. If he is appointed to be a Samson to tie the foxes' tails together with a torch or firebrand between them, I know nothing of it.[15] One thing I know, we ought to have had an ambassador there these thirty years; and we should have had it if Congress had not been too complaisant to Vergennes. Mr. Dana was upon the point of being received and had a solemn promise of a reception, when he was recalled.[16] Under all the circumstances of those times, however, I cannot very severely blame Congress for this conduct, tho' I think it was an error. It is of great importance to us at present to know more than we do of the views, interests, and sentiments of all the northern powers. If we do not acquire more knowledge than we have of the present and probable future state of Europe, we shall be hoodwinked and bubbled by the French and English. . . .

I have not seen, but am impatient to see, Mr. Cheetham's *Life* of Mr. Paine. His political writings, I am singular enough to believe, have done more harm than his irreligious ones. He understood neither government nor religion. From a malignant heart he wrote virulent declamations, which the enthusiastic fury of the times intimidated all men, even Mr. Burke, from answering as he ought. His deism, as it appears to me, has promoted rather than retarded the cause of revelation, at least in America and indeed in Europe. His billingsgate, stolen from Blount's *Oracles of Reason,*[17] from Bolingbroke, Voltaire, Bérenger, &c., will never discredit Christianity, which will hold its ground in some degree as long as human nature shall have anything moral or intellectual left in it.

The Christian religion, as I understand it, is the brightness of the glory and the express portrait of the character of the eternal, self-existent, independent, benevolent, all-powerful and all-merciful Creator, Preserver, and Father of the universe; the first good, first perfect, and first fair. It will last

15. Judges 15:4.

16. Francis Dana (1743–1811) was in St. Petersburg from 1781 to 1783, presenting arguments in favor of recognition of the rebellious colonies.

17. Charles Blount (1654–93) was the author of many books; the most famous, his deistic *The Oracles of Reason* (London, 1693), was condemned and burned by the public hangman.

as long as the world. Neither savage nor civilized man, without a revelation, could ever have discovered or invented it. Ask me not, then, whether I am a Catholic or Protestant, Calvinist or Arminian. As far as they are Christians, I wish to be a fellow-disciple with them all. . . .

John Adams

To ADAMS

February 1, 1810

MY DEAR AND EXCELLENT FRIEND,

With this letter you will receive a bundle of *Auroras* and another of the same size by the post of the next day. They are filled very much of late with our state politics, but you will find many columns still filled with complaints against Great Britain. So my son Richard tells me, for I assure you I have not read a column in any one of them this six months. My wife asked me a few days ago what was the object of Macon's bill.[18] I could not tell her. . . . But let our rulers do what they will, I shall patiently submit to them.

Do we not, my friend, mistake the nature of government and the business and rank of the men who rule us? Was not government one of the causes of the fall of man? And were not laws intended to be our chains? Of course. Are not our rulers who make and execute those laws nothing but jailers, turnkeys, and Jack Ketches[19] of a higher order? We give them titles, put them into palaces, and decorate them with fine clothes only to conceal the infamy of their offices. As labor, parturition, and even death itself (the other curses of the Fall) have been converted by the goodness of God into blessings, so government and rulers have in some instances become blessings to mankind. But this does not exempt them from the charge which I have brought against them. Let us do what we will to meliorate our government and to choose wise rulers, we cannot frustrate the designs of

18. Nathaniel Macon of North Carolina introduced the Macon Bill No. 1 in January 1810, but the Senate rejected it. The bill provided for a repeal of the Nonintercourse Act of 1809 and allowed American-built and -registered ships to transport merchandise to Britain and France.

19. "Jack Ketch" was the nickname for the public executioner.

heaven. The former will always carry in their construction marks of their being other forms only of jails, stocks, whipping posts, cells, and dungeons, and the latter will always exhibit, notwithstanding the disguise of their titles, palaces, and dresses, the insignia of the offices I have already ascribed to them. . . .

Your short but sublime description of the objects and nature of Christianity delighted me. I care not whether you are Calvinist or Arminian or both, for both believe the truth, and a true system of religion I believe can only be formed from a union of the tenets of each of them. But after all that has been said of doctrines, they only "who *have done good* shall come forth to the resurrection unto life, and they only who *have done evil* to the resurrection of damnation."[20] . . .

Benjn: Rush

To RUSH

February 11, 1810

DEAR SIR,

Thanks for yours of the first and the two packets. Who are they who furnish the *Aurora* with such an infinite quantity and variety of compositions? There must be many hands of no small capacity or information. In one you sent me before, there was an anecdote of a plan of Washington to attack Philadelphia, which was communicated to General Howe by a person in his confidence. The narrator affirms he was intimate with Washington and daily at his quarters.[21] I have a curiosity to know who this old man may be. I can think of no human being who can support the pretension.

Your letter is so grave a mixture of religion and politics that I wish I had eyes, fingers, and time to write you an answer to it of a mile long.

You will "patiently submit to our rulers, let them do what they will." Not so Tittle Top I. No factious opposition for me. No lying down of govern-

20. John 5:29.
21. The article in the Philadelphia *Aurora,* Jan. 3, 1810, was signed "Pennypacck" and implied that Hamilton was guilty of giving campaign plans to the British.

ment for me. But if our government will substitute Virginia fence for the wooden walls of Columbia as our Friend Jefferson did, I will not applaud. I will disapprove and modestly complain; and I cannot answer for myself that I shall not say in some unguarded moment to a confidential friend who may betray me, "Midas! Le Roy Midas a les oreilles d'ane."[22]

You seem to have borrowed, my friend, from Tom Paine a kind of hatred to government and to take pleasure in representing it in an odious and disgusting light. "Was not government one of the curses of Adam's fall?" If I were disposed to be merry, I would ask you was not the fall of man owing to the want of government in paradise? Had Adam possessed and exerted the proper authority and power of government, he would have tamed the shrew who betrayed him and us. Pardon this appearance of levity on a subject which ought always to be treated with reverence. . . .

February 23, 1810

Our electioneering racers have started for the prize. Such a whipping and spurring and huzzaing! Oh, what rare sport it will be! Through thick and thin, through mire and dirt, through bogs and fens and sloughs, dashing and splashing and crying out, the Devil take the hindmost. . . .

John Adams

To ADAMS

April 26, 1810

DEAR SIR,

. . . I send you herewith a few of Duane's papers. The character of J. Randolph is well drawn and I believe just.[23] I have long considered him as a mischievous boy with a squirt in his hands, throwing its dirty contents into the

22. "King Midas has the ears of an ass."

23. The criticism of Randolph appeared in the Philadelphia *Aurora*, Apr. 26, 1810: "He is turbulent, impetuous, and ambitious. He has a spirit so dogmatic and overbearing that the records of all parliamentary history afford no parallel to his career. Some men are content to advise. Mr. Randolph always dictates. Upon all occasions he usurps and exercises the authority of an arbiter."

eyes of everybody that looked at him. A kicking or a horsewhipping would be the best reply that could be made to his vulgar parliamentary insolence. It is only because the body which he insults *is what it is* that he has been so long tolerated. In the Congress of 1776 and 1777 he would soon have fallen and perished with his brother insects upon the floor of the house. . . .

Benjn: Rush

To RUSH

May 14, 1810

Dear Sir,

   . . . How can I turn my thoughts . . . to that glossamour [gossamer] that idles in the wanton summer air, John Randolph! The character of him in the *Aurora* is well drawn and in some respects just; but makes too much of him. You have expressed in two or three lines the truth, the whole truth, and nothing but the truth. A boy with a mischievous syringe in his hand, full of dirty water. . . .

   This letter will be full of sentiment, sympathy, and feeling. The day before yesterday I went to Hingham to convoy to the tomb my ancient, my invariable and inestimable friend Lincoln.[24] . . . A cold, unanimated, and ignorant sketch of his life and character was pronounced by his own parson in a funeral sermon. A long train, to be sure, of relations and neighbors walked in procession. No arms, no militia, no regulars! A few, a very few gentlemen from Boston. Governor Gore, to do him justice, attended.

   Recollect the mock funerals of Washington, Hamilton, and Ames. Lincoln's education, his reading, his general knowledge, his talent at composition was superior to Washington's; his services more arduous, dangerous, and difficult than Washington's.

   How long will fraud prevail over honesty? Hypocrisy over sincerity in this sublunary chaos? . . .

John Adams . . .

---

24. General Benjamin Lincoln (1733–1810), revolutionary soldier and statesman, was collector of the port of Boston from 1789 to 1809.

To ADAMS

July 4, 1810

DEAR AND VENERABLE FRIEND,

. . . And is this the 4th of July? What a group of ideas are associated with those words! Patriots and heroes rise before me, some of them just emerging from their graves. They ask the news of the day. They hear of British and French insults and aggressions and of our dismantled navy and unprotected commerce. They inquire into the conduct and characters of the members of the present Congress. They visit the extensive arbor under which several hundred of the Federal citizens of Philadelphia are now assembled to celebrate the anniversary of the day which announced our independence. They listen to the orator appointed by them to commemorate the great events connected with it.[25] They hear with astonishment that he has quietly acquiesced in the charges made in a public newspaper of having committed fraud and forgery, and having exposed one of his illegitimate children at the door of a respectable citizen of Philadelphia. They recover the paleness of death in hearing the details of the degeneracy and depravity of the country for which they toiled or bled. Their looks indicate a mixture of grief and indignation. Behold, they tread back their steps and descend with haste and pleasure to their graves, now become agreeable and welcome to them inasmuch as they conceal from their view the base and inglorious conduct of some of their contemporaries and of all their posterity. . . .

Benjn: Rush

---

25. Charles Caldwell was the orator. A former pupil and then foe of Rush, he was anti-French and anti-Madison in his remarks.

CHAPTER 8

The Dead Languages

"Were every Greek and Latin book (the New Testament excepted) consumed in a bonfire, the world would be the wiser and better for it." A rash statement, indeed, but Rush was reopening his case against the overemphasis of the classics in grammar schools. Too many young men, he felt, wasted their school years learning Latin and Greek, only to forget the languages upon graduation, when a knowledge of religion and history would be more appropriate. Adams met these arguments in good humor by erecting straw men for his friend to knock down: Were they not the model for heroes and conquerors? Were they not the source of liberty? The American Revolution itself, Adams observed, was responsible for turning men's thoughts again to the classics and dispelling the ignorance of centuries. Would we dare minimize this heritage of our Revolution?

To ADAMS

September 8, 1810

My dear Friend,

. . . I have sometimes amused myself by enumerating the different kinds of hatred that operate in the world. They are the "odium theologicum," the "odium politicum," the "odium philologium," and the "odium medicum." It has been my lot—I will not call it my misfortune—to be exposed to them all. The divines hate me for holding tenets that they say lead to materialism and that are opposed to the rigid doctrines of Calvin. The politicians hate me for being neither a democrat nor a monarchist, neither a Frenchman nor an Englishman. The philologists hate me for writing against the dead languages;[1] and the physicians for teaching a system of medicine that has robbed them by its simplicity of cargoes of technical lumber by which they imposed upon the credulity of the world. The last I believe is the most deadly hatred of them all. Cobbett acknowledged when he left Philadelphia that he was not my enemy; he even spoke well of me and said that all he had written against me was dictated to him by three physicians. The publications thus dictated against me in the year 1797 were compared by a clergyman in the Delaware State to the "mouth of hell being opened against me."[2] . . .

In the catalogue of hatreds to which I have been exposed, I neglected to mention the "odium mercatorium" and the "odium sanguiphobium." The former has rendered me so obnoxious to our merchants that some of them have proposed to drown me or drive me out of the city. My offense against them was deriving the yellow fever from domestic sources. The "odium sanguiphobium" has rendered me an object of more than hatred—of horror—to many of our citizens. Some have said they felt fainty at the sight of my carriage, and others have left sickrooms as soon as I entered them to avoid my company. This species of hatred against me has abated very much in Philadelphia in consequence of the practice which provoked it having become general. I am now the physician of a family the mistress of which has since confessed that she had often left company as soon as I came into it, only because my presence gave her pain. I was her "raw head and bloody bones."[3]

But where am I? and with what have I stained my paper? Alas! with a worthless subject—that is, myself—but away with me. With love and re-

---

1. Rush had long been a critic of the classics as they were then taught. His "Observations upon the Study of the Latin and Greek Languages" was reprinted in his *Essays, Literary, Moral & Philosophical* (Philadelphia, 1798), pp. 21–56.

2. Lyman H. Butterfield gives an account of the Rush-Cobbett feud in the *Letters of Benjamin Rush,* II, 1213–18. The Rush-Light articles are reprinted in William Cobbett, *Porcupine's Works* (London, 1801), XI, 211– 434. These vicious articles probably had no equal in the city's journalism and represent a climax to the attacks Cobbett had made upon Rush since 1797. "The novel system, adopted by Rush, is most aptly denominated, the system of *Depletion;* for the merit of it entirely consists in *emptying* the veins and the intestines with an expedition heretofore unknown and unheard of" (p. 251).

3. "Why does the Nurse tell the Child of Raw-head and Bloudy-bones, to keep it in awe?" John Selden, *Table-Talk* (London, 1689), p. 49, "Priests of Rome."

spects as usual, in which the faithful companion of my persecutions and triumphs joins me, I am, dear sir, ever yours,

Benjn: Rush

To RUSH

September 16, 1810

DEAR SIR,

. . . I have felt as well as you the Odium Theologicum, the Odium Politicum, and the Odium Mercatorium. Happily I have escaped as far as I know the Odium Philologium, the Odium Medicum and the Odium Sanguiphobium. I have escaped these hatreds because I never knew enough about any of them to excite any other man's jealousy or envy.

But now I must tell you a great and grave truth. I am one among your most serious haters of the philological species. I do most cordially hate you for writing against Latin, Greek, and Hebrew.[4] I never will forgive you until you repent, retract, and reform. No never! It is impossible. . . .

Rush! Every persecuted man, persecuted because he is envied, must be an egotist or an hypocrite. You and I must therefore cordially embrace the character of egotists and acknowledge the imputation of vanity or be totally overborne or become lying hypocrites, which you will swear you will not. So will I.

Pardon me for concluding this rhodomontade by a very serious paragraph. Yesterday were committed to the tomb the remains of William Cushing, a judge of the National Supreme Court.[5] Fifty-nine years has he been known to me and esteemed and beloved as an invariable friend. A judge for forty years of unblemished character. My contemporaries are almost all gone and left me almost alone. I wait in silence and resignation for

4. Adams had irritated Rush two decades earlier by challenging these ideas. Though Rush would de-emphasize the classics in school, he had great respect for them as the basis of thought for educated men.

5. William Cushing (1732–1810) served as an associate justice of the United States Supreme Court from 1789 to his death.

my turn. Until it arrives I shall cherish Rush at least, as another invariable friend to

John Adams...

To ADAMS

October 2, 1810

MY DEAR FRIEND,

Hate on, and call upon all the pedagogues in Massachusetts to assist you with their hatred of me, and I will after all continue to say that it is folly and madness to spend four or five years in teaching boys the Latin and Greek languages. I admit a knowledge of the Hebrew to be useful to divines, also as much of the Greek as will enable them to read the Greek Testament, but the Latin is useless and even hurtful to young men in the manner in which it is now taught. We do not stand in need now of Greek and Roman poets, historians, and orators. Shakespeare, Milton, Thomson, Pope, Hume, Robertson, Burke, Curran, Fénelon, Bourdaloue, and a dozen others that might be named *more* than fill their places.[6] Were every Greek and Latin book (the New Testament excepted) consumed in a bonfire, the world would be the wiser and better for it. . . . "Delenda, delenda est lingua Romana"[7] should be the voice of reason and liberty and humanity in every part of the world.

Our election comes on next week. Both parties are active. Federal and Democratic principles and measures are the *ostensible* objects of contention. But the true objects of strife are a "mercantile bank" by the former and a "mechanics' bank" by the latter party. I have seen this spirit pervade and govern our elections ever since the establishment of the funding system, and

6. In this assortment of modern poets, historians, and orators, two are almost completely forgotten today: John Philpot Curran (1750–1817) was an Irish patriot and orator; Louis Bourdaloue (1632–1704) a French orator.

7. "The Latin language must be destroyed—yea, destroyed!" Rush here parodies the phrase which Cato the Elder is said to have reiterated at the end of all of his speeches in the Senate, whatever their subject, *Delenda est Carthago* (Carthage must be destroyed), which became a cliché of Rush's time.

hence I have been unable to give a vote for either party since that event so inauspicious! to the morals and liberties of our country. Were I to compose an epitaph for the latter, it should be as follows.

> Here lie interred the liberties of the United States. They were purchased with much treasure and blood, and by uncommon exertions of talent and virtues. Their dissolution was brought on by the cheapness of suffrage in some of the states, by a funding system which begat banks and lotteries and land speculations, and by the removal of Congress to the city of Washington, a place so unfriendly to health, society, and instructing intercourse, and so calculated to foster party and malignant passions, that wise and good men considered a seat in it as a kind of banishment, in consequence of which the government fell into the hands of the young and ignorant and needy part of the community, and hence the loss of the respect and obedience due to laws, and hence one of the causes of the downfall of the last and only free country in the world.

While writing the above, the venerable Charles Thomson called to take a family dinner with me. He is now in his 81st year. . . . He mentioned the name of your excellent lady with uncommon respect. On the characters and conduct of public men he was silent. . . .

Benjn: Rush

To RUSH

October 13, 1810

DEAR SIR,

Mrs. Adams says she is willing you should discredit Greek and Latin because it will destroy the foundation of all the pretensions of the gentlemen to superiority over the ladies and restore liberty, equality, and fraternity between the sexes. What does Mrs. Rush think of this?

Hobbes calumniated the classics because they filled young men's heads with ideas of liberty and excited them to rebellion against Leviathan.[8]

---

8. Hobbes condemned the influence of the classical republican authors who attacked monarchy and sanctioned violence against authority. See *Leviathan,* Ch. xxi, "Of the Liberty of Subjects."

Suppose we should agree to study the oriental languages, especially the Arabic, instead of Greek and Latin. This would not please the ladies so well, but it would gratify Hobbes much better. According to many present appearances in the world, many useful lessons and deep maxims might be learned from the Asiatic writers. There are great models of heroes and conquerors fit for the imitation of the emperors of Britain and France. For example, in the Life of Timur Bec, or Tamerlane the Great, we read, Vol. I, p. 202: "It was Timur's ambition of universal empire which caused him to undertake such glorious actions. He has been often heard to say that it was neither agreeable nor decent that the habitable world should be governed by two kings; according to the words of the poet, as there is but one God, there ought to be but one King, all the earth being very small in comparison of the ambition of a great prince." [9]

Where can you find in any Greek or Roman writer a sentiment so sublime and edifying for George and Napoleon? There are some faint traces of it in the conduct of Alexander and Caesar but far less frank and noble, and these have been imprudently branded with infamy by Greek and Roman orators and historians. There is an abundance more of such profound instruction in the life of this Tamerlane as well as in that of Genghis Khan, both of which I believe Napoleon has closely studied. With Homer in one pocket, Caesar's *Commentaries* in the other, Quintus Curtius under his pillow, and the lives of Mahomet, Genghis Khan, and Tamerlane in his portfolio, and Polybius, Folard, Montecuccoli, Charlemagne, Charles Twelfth, Charles 5th *cum multis aliis* among his baggage, this man has formed himself; [10] but the classics among them have damped his ardor and prevented his rising as yet to the lofty heights of the Asiatic emperors. Would it not be better that George and Napoleon should forget all their classics and mount

9. The quotation has not been located. The same material is used by Joseph White, *Institutes Political and Military . . . by the Great Timour* (Oxford, 1783), p. 89: " 'Timour, God Almighty hath declared, that if there were two Gods in the heavens and in the earth, the order of the universe would end in horror and confusion.' And I took warning by his words."

10. These men are writers on the art of war and the creation of empire. Jean Charles de Folard (1669–1752) was a French soldier and author of a commentary on Polybius. Raimondo, Count de Montecuccoli (ca. 1609–80), was an Austrian general; his memoirs were published in 1770. Quintus Curtius Rufus, a Roman historian of Claudius' time, wrote a history of Alexander the Great.

at once to all sublimities of Mahomet, Genghis Khan, and Tamerlane? In that case one or the other must soon succumb; and would it not be better that one such should govern the globe than two?

October 15, 1810

Thus far I had written, when your favor of the 8th with your invention, a tranquilizer, was given to me from the post office. The tranquilizer is a very ingenious mechanical invention, and I hope will be beneficial to that most deplorable portion of our species for whom it is intended. But to be serious, if I were possessed of sovereign power over your hospital (provided I could do it secretly so that no mortal should know it but you and I), I would put you into your own tranquilizer till I cured you of your fanaticism against Greek and Latin. . . .

My friend, you will labor in vain. As the love of science and taste for the fine arts increases in the world, the admiration of Greek and Roman science and literature will increase. Both are increasing very fast. Your labors will be as useless as those of Tom Paine against the Bible, which are already fallen dead and almost forgotten. . . .

John Adams

To ADAMS

December 21, 1810

MY DEAR FRIEND,

. . . You have made no impression upon me by your arguments in favor of the dead languages. Napoleon would have been just what he is had he never read a page of ancient history. Rulers become tyrants and butchers from instinct much oftener than from imitation. As well might we suppose the human race would have been extinct had not Ovid bequeathed to modern nations his "arte amandi," [11] as suppose that modern villains are made by ancient examples. Royal crimes, like yellow fevers, spring up spon-

---

11. After Adams lists authors whom Napoleon might have consulted, Rush playfully refutes his argument by citing Ovid's manual on seduction, *Ars amatoria.* Lust, he implies, needs no textbooks.

taneously in similar circumstances in every country and in every age. The adoption of the former from antiquity is as contrary to truth and reason as the importation of the latter from foreign countries.

A bank mania pervades our city. I know not what is proper with respect to the Bank of the United States, but I am sure our country banks are preparing our citizens for a new form of government. They are everywhere drawing into their vortex farms and houses, and thus converting independent freeholders into obsequious and venal electors. The funding system was the "pomum Adami" of all the evils which now threaten the liberties and happiness of the United States. It created our canine appetite for wealth. It reduced regular industry and virtuous economy to the rank of sniveling virtues, and rendered "enterprise and successful speculation" the only mark of civic worth in our country. I would have filled my paper, but my better half begins to nod in her chair and tells me 'tis time to subscribe myself yours truly and affectionately,

Benjn: Rush

To RUSH

December 27, 1810

DEAR SIR,

. . . You and I are so much better employed that I presume political pamphlets are beneath your notice as well as mine. You are employed in healing the sick and extending the empire of science and humanity; I, in reading romances in which I take incredible delight. I have read within a few weeks, let me see: in the first place *Oberon*, in two translations, one by John Quincy Adams and the other by Sotheby, two refined translators, though neither has as yet acquired a reputation as an original poet.[12] This romantic, heroic poem of Wieland is all enchantment in every sense of the word. In the next

12. While John Quincy Adams was United States minister to Prussia, he studied German literature and developed a fondness for Christoph Martin Wieland (1733–1813), whose *Oberon* he translated. Before his translation was ready for the press, William Sotheby's appeared, which seemed more poetical than his, and he put his aside. It was not published in its entirety until Albert B. Faust edited it as *Oberon: A Poetical Romance in Twelve Books* (New York, 1940).

place, *The Scottish Chiefs*, which is superior to *Oberon* and beyond all comparison the noblest romance in the world.[13] It is better tho' not so classical as *Don Quixote* or *Telemachus*[14] or *Sir Charles Grandison*. In the third place, *The Lady of the Lake*. In the fourth place, *The Lay of the Last Minstrel*. In the fifth place, I intend to read *Marmion* as soon as I can get it.[15] In the sixth place, *The Edinburgh Reviews*, as entertaining romances to me as any of the former.[16] These fellows pretend to all knowledge, and they have a great deal. But they resemble their Creolian countryman Alec Hamilton. They can hammer out a guinea into an acre of leaf gold. . . .

Have the Scots monopolized all the genius of the three kingdoms? All the literature comes from them at present. I neither read nor hear of any Englishman of any fame.

These Scottish and German romances show in a clear light the horrors of the feudal aristocracy, as the histories of Genghis Khan and Tamerlane show the same anarchy in the Asiatic aristocracy. In Europe and in Asia they all ended in despotism or in simple monarchy.[17]

And how will our aristocracy proceed and end? Will our state governors become Abthanes? Virginia, Pennsylvania, and Massachusetts have given broad hints.

Every government is an aristocracy in fact. The despotism of Genghis Khan was an aristocracy. The government of the most popular French convention or national assembly was an aristocracy. The most democratical canton in Switzerland was an aristocracy. The most leveling town meeting

13. Jane Porter's *The Scottish Chiefs* (London, 1810) recounts the heroic deeds of William Wallace, the famous Scottish patriot.

14. Fénelon's didactic novel *Télémaque*, published in 1699, was reprinted in innumerable editions and translations in the eighteenth century. Book V, describing the utopian laws of Crete, so impressed Jeremy Bentham as a child that it fixed his determination to be a legal and social reformer in the classical tradition of the "semi-divine legislator."

15. Sir Walter Scott was the author of the poems Adams mentions. Samuel Richardson wrote *Sir Charles Grandison* (1753–54).

16. *The Edinburgh Review* (1802–1929), the famous Whig journal of literature and opinion. The August issue of 1810 carried a review of Scott's work.

17. The theme of feudal tyranny was an old one for Adams, as his earliest major writing, "A Dissertation on the Canon and Feudal Law" (1765), argued that it was the greatest glory of the first settlers of America to reject any feudalistic features in their new-world establishments.

in New England is an aristocracy. The empire of Napoleon is an aristocracy. The government of Great Britain is an aristocracy. But as they, The Aristocrats, are always ambitious and avaricious, the rivalries among them split them into factions and tear the people to pieces. The great secret of liberty is to find means to limit their power and control their passions. Rome and Britain have done it best. Perhaps we shall do better than either. God knows.

The pretty little warbling canary bird, Fisher Ames, sang of the *Dangers of American Liberty*. I had preached in "The Defence" and the "Discourses of Davila" and held up in a thousand mirrors all those dangers and more, twenty years before him. Ames had got my ideas and examples by heart. There was not a man in the world who read my books with more ardor or expressed so often an admiration of them.[18] But Ames's misfortune was that the sordid avarice which he imputes to the whole body of the American people belongs chiefly if not exclusively to his own friends, The Aristocrats, or rather, The Oligarchs, who now rule the Federal Party. . . .

December 27, 1810

[Your letter of December 21st is now before me.] . . . I agree that rulers become tyrants from passion, not instinct; but Aristocrats and Democrats have the same passions with kings and become tyrants from those passions whenever they have opportunity, as certainly and often more cruelly than kings. Aristocratical tyrants are the worst species of all; and sacerdotal tyrants have been the worst of aristocratical tyrants in all ages and nations. I can never too often repeat that aristocracy is the monster to be chained; yet so chained as not to be hurt, for he is a most useful and necessary animal in his place.[19] Nothing can be done without him.

It is to no purpose to declaim against the crimes of kings. The crimes of Aristocrats are more numerous and more atrocious. And are almost univer-

18. Ames wrote his "The Dangers of American Liberty" in 1805; see *Works of Fisher Ames,* ed. Seth Ames (New York, 1869), I, 344–399. Ames denounced party rivalry as an inherent weakness of democratic government and predicted that no security would be possible until the United States established a monarchy.

19. Adams is reversing the symbol of monster (which traditionally was associated with the people) in applying it to the aristocrats. He had just read Scott's *Lady of the Lake.* See Canto v, st. 30, where the traditional image is used: "Thou many-headed monster-thing / O who would wish to be thy king!"

sally, at least generally, the cause of the crimes of kings. Bind Aristocracy then with a double cord. Shut him up in a cage, from which, however, he may be let out to do good but never to do mischief.

The banking infatuation pervades all America. Our whole system of banks is a violation of every honest principle of banks. There is no honest bank but a bank of deposit. A bank that issues paper at interest is a pickpocket or a robber. But the delusion will have its course. You may as well reason with a hurricane. An Aristocracy is growing out of them that will be as fatal as the feudal barons, if unchecked in time.

The banks were anterior to [the] Funding System, and therefore I cannot attribute all our evils to that. Paper money was better than this bank money because the public reaped the benefit of the depreciation; but the depreciation of bank money accrues wholly to the profit of individuals. There is no honest money but silver and gold.

Think of the number, the offices, stations, wealth, piety, and reputations of the persons in all the states who have made fortunes by these banks, and then you will see how deeply rooted the evil is. The number of debtors who hope to pay their debts by this paper united with the creditors who build palaces in our cities and castles for country seats by issuing this paper form too impregnable a phalanx to be attacked by anything less disciplined than Roman legions. . . . You suggest danger to our elections. I could tell you very curious anecdotes of elections carried by these banks and elections lost. . . .

To leave off a letter to Dr. Rush is a much harder task than to begin one, to your old friend

John Adams . . .

To ADAMS

January 10, 1811

MY VENERABLE AND DEAR FRIEND,

I thank you for your son's pamphlet.[20] Much as I loathe political discussions of all kinds, I was induced by your request and my great respect for

20. John Quincy Adams had published four short essays in the Boston *Patriot* and then republished them with an introduction as *American Principles: A Review of Works of Fisher*

the genius of its author to read it. I thank you for the pleasure I derived from it. It is a masterly performance, overflowing with argument and eloquence. He places Mr. Ames where he ought to have stood in the meridian of his political glory. He seems to have died, if not *of,* certainly *with* the same kind of monarchical mania which raged with so much violence in the year 1776 as to carry off many of our citizens to Nova Scotia, Canada, and other parts of the British empire. . . .

I was much struck with your strictures upon banks. They have long governed all our state legislatures. A few weeks will determine whether the general government has strength enough to resist the power of one of them. Is there any difference in point of criminality between bribing public bodies and individuals? The funding system was carried by bribing both. The assumption of the state debts seduced the former, and many of the latter were seduced by certificates previously purchased at 2/6 in the pound. Among these Mr. Boudinot and Mr. Ames were so conspicuous that your friend characterized their speeches in defense of the funding system in one of our newspapers in the following lines:

> "Pay the poor soldier! He's a sot,"
> Cries our grave ruler, Boudinot.
> "No pity from us now he claims,"
> In artful accents echoes Ames.
> "A soldier's pay are rags and fame.
> A wooden leg, a deathless name.
> To specs, both in and out on Cong,
> The three and six percents belong."

. . . You say an attention to the dead languages has revived in Europe. This is true, and Napoleon is at the head of the junto confederated to restore and establish them. It is one among many other of his acts that are calculated and perhaps intended to bring back the darkness and ignorance of the 14th and 15th centuries. Cardinal Richelieu created and diffused a love for music, dancing, and other amusements among the people of France on purpose to divert them from prying into the machinations and oppressions

---

Ames (Boston, 1809). Adams was hostile to Ames's supposedly perverted ideas of American development, noting that Ames was sick and his judgment poor.

of the government of Louis the XIV. The study of the Latin and Greek languages will serve the same purpose to Napoleon and George the Third. . . .

Benjn: Rush

To RUSH

January 18, 1811

DEAR SIR,

. . . You allow that "an attention to the dead languages has revived in Europe," but allege that "Napoleon is at the head of the junto confederated to restore them."

I will not deny him the glory that is due to him. It is true that no man, prince or subject, has distinguished himself more by the patronage of science, literature, and the fine arts than Napoleon. This and toleration are the brightest jewels in his crown. I cannot, however, do so much honor to him as to ascribe this second resurrection of learning to him; it is rather due to the American Revolution. That great event turned the thoughts and studies of men of learning to the ancient Greeks, their language, their antiquities, their forms of government. Anacharsis, Gillies, Mitford, La Harpe, and a thousand other works in France, England, Holland, Germany, and Italy were produced by the American Revolution before Bonaparte made any figure.[21] . . .

We need not fear that Latin and Greek will ever be too much studied. Not one in ten thousand of those who study them in schools and colleges ever make any great proficiency in them. In general, scholars are enabled to understand their own languages the better for the smattering they acquire in the classics, and to examine a passage occasionally in Latin. . . .

21. Jean Jacques Barthélemy (1716–95), a French writer and antiquarian, was known for his *Voyage du jeune Anacharsis en Grèce, dans le milieu du quatrième siècle avant l'ère vulgaire* (1788). John Gillies (1747–1836), a Scottish historian, was author of *The History of Ancient Greece, Its Colonies and Conquests* (1786) and *The History of the World* (1807). William Mitford (1744–1827), an English historian influenced by Edward Gibbon, was famous for his great *History of Greece*, published in five volumes from 1784 to 1818. Frederic de La Harpe (1754–1838) was an inspired republican who wrote pamphlets urging the Swiss to revolt.

But you must be weary by this time of commonplace thoughts of your friend,

John Adams

To ADAMS

February 4, 1811

DEAR SIR,

. . . I have no objection to the *reading* the dead languages being still taught in our schools. Dr. Franklin used to say the acquisition of a language might be divided into ten parts, *five* of which only were necessary to read it, *seven* to speak it, and the whole *ten* to write it. By thus saving the time spent in teaching the *speaking* and *writing* of Latin and Greek, much time would be saved at school which might be employed in communicating the knowledge of *things* instead of the sounds and relations of *words.* Never will men walk erect until this is more generally the case. The human intellects are brutalized by being stuffed in early life with such offal learning. It is the more necessary to banish it from our schools since the late wonderful increase of knowledge in all useful arts and sciences. . . .

Benjn: Rush

To RUSH

February 13, 1811

DEAR SIR,

In your favor of the 4th, according to my judgment, you have given up the whole controversy. You have no objection, you say, to teaching the youth in our schools to *read* the dead languages. By reading them, no doubt you meant that they should so read them as to understand them, and they can be read to be understood in no way so well as by writing and speaking them. I therefore regret very much the discontinuance in the universities of Europe and America of the practice and fashion of talking in Latin. I regret, too, the exchange of French for Latin as the language of courts, camps, travellers, merchants, science, and letters. If Franklin's division of the labor of acquiring a language into ten parts be correct, I think the five for reading, the two for speaking, and the three for writing should all be employed, and the whole ten will be little enough to acquire a language as it should be mastered. The late wonderful increase of knowledge in all useful arts and sciences will facilitate the acquisition of languages as much as other things. The profound investigations of the principles of all languages and universal grammar and the great variety of excellent translations into English, French, Italian, German, &c., will make the progress more easy and delightful than ever it has been. . . .

John Adams

CHAPTER 9

A Farewell Address

WHILE ENJOYING GOOD HEALTH AND SPIRIT, advised Rush, Adams should prepare a posthumous address to the citizens of the United States in which he would inculcate the religious, domestic, and national virtues that would make them free, great, and happy. "No one," he added, "can suspect you . . . of aiming at any honor or profit by it." The advice brought tears to Adams' eyes, a fifteen-point refusal, and a suggestion that Rush himself might have a better right to address the United States than Adams had. On second thought, Adams wondered about the value of farewell addresses. Washington's was quoted as an oracle for the politicians, but "neither party cares one farthing about it." His message for the nation, Adams observed, was contained in all he had written. Everything depended on the proper form of government; without it, he said, "you may declaim on religion, morality, union, constitution to all eternity to no purpose."[1]

To RUSH

June 21, 1811

[MY DEAR FRIEND,]

. . . I am well, my appetite is as good as ever. I sleep well o'nights; no burdens, whether grasshoppers or mammoths of body or mind, affect me. I still enjoy a chair in this study, but avoid close thinking from principle. My nat-

1. Adams to Rush, Sept. 12, 1811, *Old Family Letters,* p. 361.

ural vision is not bad, but I use glasses for ease to my eyes, which you have known to be weak and subject to inflammations for almost forty years. My hearing, for anything that I perceive or my friends have remarked to me, is as good as ever. So much for the bright side.

On the other I have a "quiveration." What in the name of the medical dictionary, you will say, is a "quiveration"? A wild Irish boy, who lives with my son T. B. A., let a horse run away with a chaise. One of the family ran out and cried out, "Nat! Why did you not scream and call for help?" "Sir! Sir!" said Nat, "I was seized with such a *quiveration* that I could not speak." Nat's quiveration is the best word I know to express my palsy. It does not as yet much incommode me in writing, although my hands are chiefly affected. Another circumstance on the dark side is, my organs of speech are gone. It would divert you to witness a conversation between my ancient friend and colleague, Robert T. Paine,[2] and me. He is above eighty. I cannot speak, and he cannot hear. Yet we converse. . . .

And now how shall I turn my thoughts from this good-humored small talk to the angry, turbulent, stormy science of politics. . . .

I am sorry to find from your letter that the Boston tories who gave the tone to those of all the continent from 1761 to 1783 continue to give it to those of Philadelphia in 1811. At the same time forget not that the whigs of Boston gave the tone to the whigs of the continent. Let not the importance of Boston to this union be forgotten. . . .

"Louis 14, if not the greatest king, was the best actor of majesty that ever wore a crown," said Bolingbroke.[3] Our citizens in our great commercial cities, if they are not the greatest politicians that ever lived, are great masters of the theatrical exhibitions of politics. Were there ever more striking *Coups de Théâtre* than mock funerals? Or our celebrations of the rock on which my great, great, great, great (and I know not how many more greats) grandfather John Alden at twenty years of age first leaped at Plymouth in

2. Robert Treat Paine (1731–1814), a Massachusetts politician, jurist, and amateur scholar, lived most of his life in Boston, retiring from the bench because of age and deafness in 1804.

3. "If he was not the greatest king, he was the best actor of majesty at least that ever filled a throne." Henry St. John, Viscount Bolingbroke, *Letters on the Study and Use of History* (London, 1752), I, 262 (Letter VII).

1620. . . . Washington understood this art very well, and we may say of him, if he was not the greatest President, he was the best actor of presidency we have ever had. His address to the states when he left the army, his solemn leave taken of Congress when he resigned his commission, his Farewell Address to the people when he resigned his presidency: these were all in a strain of Shakespearean and Garrickal excellence in dramatical exhibitions.[4]

We whigs attempted somewhat of the kind. The Declaration of Independence I always considered as a theatrical show. Jefferson ran away with all the stage effect of that. . . and all the glory of it.

The exception from pardon of Hancock and Adams [by George III] had a like effect. This, however, was not their contrivance nor any device of our party. It was an incident in the play that was not prepared by the author or actors. It was considered by the people, and justly, as decisive proof of sin, in the sense of their enemy, and of saintship in their own sense.

We never instituted mock funerals for Warren, Montgomery, Mercer, Wooster, Hancock, Franklin, or Sam Adams, or Patrick Henry, or R. H. Lee, or James Otis, or John Dickinson.[5] This is a more modern discovery and improvement of the great art of aristocratical trick, intrigue, manoeuvre or what you please to call it. . . .

But all these arts are not equal to that of making immense fortunes, however scandalous, *per saltum,* in a twinkling of an eye, by a financiering operation which substitutes a paper money whose immense depreciations go into the pockets of a few individuals in lieu of a paper money whose depreciations are in favor of the whole people. A curse on paper money of all kinds.

But enough! Enough! of this ill nature. It restores all my good nature to bid you adieu as your old friend. . . .

John Adams

4. David Garrick (1717–79), famous actor and manager of Drury Lane Theatre.

5. In this list of Revolutionary heroes, Mercer and Wooster are the least known. Hugh Mercer (ca. 1725–77), a Scottish physician living near the present Mercersburg, Pa., was fatally wounded at the Battle of Princeton. David Wooster (1711–77) succeeded Montgomery in the Canadian expedition but resigned soon afterward to take command of the militia in Connecticut, where he was killed in action.

To ADAMS

July 20, 1811

DEAR OLD FRIEND,

The 4th of July has been celebrated in Philadelphia in the manner I expected. The military men, and particularly one of them, ran away with all the glory of the day. Scarcely a word was said of the solicitude and labors and fears and sorrows and sleepless nights of the men who projected, proposed, defended, and subscribed the Declaration of Independence. Do you recollect your memorable speech upon the day on which the vote was taken?[6] Do you recollect the pensive and awful silence which pervaded the house when we were called up, one after another, to the table of the President of Congress to subscribe what was believed by many at that time to be our own death warrants? The silence and the gloom of the morning were interrupted, I well recollect, only for a moment by Colonel Harrison of Virginia, who said to Mr. Gerry at the table: "I shall have a great advantage over you, Mr. Gerry, when we are all hung for what we are now doing. From the size and weight of my body I shall die in a few minutes, but from the lightness of your body you will dance in the air an hour or two before you are dead." This speech procured a transient smile, but it was soon succeeded by the solemnity with which the whole business was conducted.[7]

Of the farewell addresses you mention in your letter it is hardly safe to speak, they are so popular in our country; but I cannot help mentioning a remark I heard made by one of our Democrats a day or two after the last of them was published. "He has treated us as a master would do his slaves, were he about to transfer them to a new master. As a *servant* of the public, he should have been more modest." . . .

6. Adams gives his account of the episode in his autobiography (*Works,* III, 54–59). He describes the crucial moment thus: "All was silence; no one would speak; all eyes were turned upon me. Mr. Edward Rutledge came to me and said, laughing, 'Nobody will speak but you upon this subject. You have all the topics so ready, that you must satisfy the gentlemen from New Jersey.'"

7. Benjamin Harrison's inappropriate remarks were later verified by Elbridge Gerry. See Rush to Adams, Sept. 4, 1811, *Letters,* II, 1102.

Let us, my dear friend, console ourselves for the unsuccessful efforts of our lives to serve our fellow creatures by recollecting that we have aimed well, that we have faithfully strove to tear from their hands the instruments of death with which they were about to destroy themselves, that we have attempted to take off their fancied crowns and royal robes and to clothe them with their own proper dresses, and that we have endeavored to snatch the poisoned bowl from their lips and to replace it with pleasant and wholesome food. We shall not, I hope, lose our reward for these well-intended labors of love. . . .

Benjn: Rush

To RUSH

July 31, 1811

DEAR SIR,

. . . I was too wise to go to the great celebration. The heat would have killed me. It was here as with you. The fashion rules all. . . .

At the moment when independence was declared you know there were full one third of the people who detested it in their hearts, though they dared not confess it. In Pennsylvania and New York I have always thought there was at least one half. At the time I believed that these two states would have abandoned us if they had not been afraid of the union and their neighbors on both sides.

Among our secret enemies were many of old families and very wealthy people who, with their descendants and connections, were and will be the haters of all who early acted a part in the Revolution. These have sometimes had the government of the nation in their hands as well as many of the particular states. They always have and always will endeavor to blast the characters of all who they think had any active and efficient agency in the Revolution. These labor to obliterate all gratitude, esteem, and affection in the people towards the really operative whigs by lavishing an hypocritical adoration on Washington, whom they have always considered as the mere painted [figure]head of the ship. . . .

John Adams

To ADAMS

August 6, 1811

MY DEAR OLD FRIEND,

. . . Your account of the state of parties in New York and Pennsylvania at that memorable period I believe is chiefly just, and your remark referred to in one of your early letters to me has been verified in a thousand instances in our country. You have forgotten part of it. It was—"the whigs have done too much, suffered too much, and succeeded too well ever to be forgiven."

It is scarcely safe to mention Dr. Franklin's name with respect in some companies in our city. An old Quaker tory in walking by his statue which stands over our Library door a few years ago gave the true reason for the hostility to his name which I have mentioned, in the following words: "But for *that* fellow, we never should have had independence."[8] . . .

I *continue* to feel the malice of the people you have alluded to. Not more than a dozen families among them have ever been my patients at one time since the peace. During the war many of them permitted me to feel their pulses, but it was only to secure my influence with the whigs to save them from banishment and the worse evils that impended them. The services I rendered them by that influence is, I believe, another cause of their hostility to me. . . .

Dr. Franklin's son-in-law, Richard Bache,[9] died a few days ago and has left an estate of 530,000 dollars to his children, 400,000 of which were left to him by the Doctor. The rest were added from the interest of the principal. This immense estate has accumulated chiefly from lots and houses owned by the Doctor *before* the American war. At the time of his death

8. The statue of Franklin was presented to the Library Company of Philadelphia by William Bingham. Franklin may have been criticized, but his writings were in constant demand. His essays appeared in two volumes in 1793 and were frequently republished—in three volumes in 1806, then in a large edition that grew to six volumes of essays and letters by 1818. Single volumes of his *Autobiography* and *Almanac* were published almost yearly beginning in 1791.

9. Richard Bache (1737–1811) married Franklin's daughter Sara in 1767. He and his brother operated a substantial trading firm before the Revolution. Differences in politics separated them for a time, but in the 1780's and 1790's their business again reaped huge profits.

Mr. Hill, one of his executors, said his whole estate amounted only to £50,000, Pennsylvania currency. Adieu! Ever yours,

Benjn: Rush

To RUSH

August 14, 1811

[MY DEAR FRIEND,]

. . . You know there were but two whigs in the Revolution, Franklin and Washington. Franklin's sacrifices we learn in your account of Richard Bache's fortune of 530,000 dollars; and Washington's sacrifices we learn from his will, in which it appears he left four or five hundred thousand dollars to his nephews; and from the Federal City, by which he raised the value of his property and that of his family a thousand per cent, at an expense to the public of more than his whole fortune.

Poor Hancock, who was once worth four times more than both of them, was not a whig. He spent a fortune instead of making one.[10]

Dr. Rush! I request you, or your son Richard, to write a treatise or at least an essay on the causes of the corruption of tradition and consequently of the corruption of history. For myself I do believe that both tradition and history are already corrupted in America as much as they ever were in the four or five first centuries of Christianity, and as much as they ever were in any age or country in the whole history of mankind. This is bold and strong, but is it exaggeration? I know your prudence, your reserve, your caution, your wisdom; and therefore, as I cannot blame you, I have for a long time given up all hope and expectation of frank answers to such home questions.

I have been severely attacked for too much candor in acquitting Franklin in the affair of the "Secrete de Cabinet" and in the "Affair of Beaumarchais."[11] . . . But I had no idea of 530,000 dollars.

However, your account of lots and houses in Philadelphia and my knowl-

---

10. When John Hancock inherited the estate of his uncle Thomas in 1764, it was estimated at £75,000. John at his death in 1794 left an estate estimated at £72,000 (Suffolk County Probate Court Record, Boston, Files 13,484 and 20,215).

11. Pierre Augustin Caron de Beaumarchais (1732–99) arranged for and handled the secret aid that France and Spain gave to the American Colonies.

edge and conjectures of other things may still account for the whole, without the supposition of peculation. . . .

John Adams

To ADAMS

August 19, 1811

MY DEAR OLD FRIEND,

It is possible Dr. Franklin's estate when sold in order to be divided may not produce the sum mentioned in my last letter. It consists chiefly of real property, purchased in the early part of his life. . . . The Doctor was a rigid economist, but he was in every stage of his life charitable, hospitable, and generous. In his private intercourse with his fellow citizens he was honest even above suspicion, and from all I have ever seen and known of him I believe he was strictly upright and correct as a servant of the public. I recollect he once told me that a large sum of money passed through his hands for the purchase of stores for the British army during the last French war in America. When he settled his accounts with the quartermaster of the army, he said to him, "I wait now for my commissions." "Commissions," said the quartermaster. "Why, have you not paid yourself?" "No, sir, you see from the statement of my accounts I have not," said the Doctor. "I am sorry for it," said the quartermaster; "I have no power to allow you anything. You ought to have taken care of *yourself.*" [12]

I have no hesitation in expressing a general want of belief not only in tradition but in recorded history and biography. The events of the American Revolution opened my eyes upon these subjects. A few nights before the capture of the Hessians at Trenton, Colonel Samuel Griffin with a company of volunteer militia from Philadelphia alarmed a regiment of Hessians at Mount Holly. A reinforcement was sent from Trenton to support them. After the capture of the Hessians, this mode of weakening the enemy was ascribed to the consummate military skill of General Washington. Colonel

12. The story is told in *The Autobiography of Benjamin Franklin,* ed. Max Farrand (Berkeley and Los Angeles, 1949), pp. 201–202.

Griffin to my knowledge acted without any concert with the General. It was altogether a volunteer piece of business.

What do you think of Colonel Joseph Reed's name not being mentioned in the histories of our Revolution as the person who suggested the retreat and escape of our army by the Quaker road after the second battle at Trenton?[13] That wise measure gained the victory at Princeton, saved our army from annihilation, and perhaps, considering the desponding state of the public mind at the time, it saved our country.

Time and chance happen to all things as they appear to short-sighted mortals. Fame like money *seems* to be given with an undistinguishing hand. But all is just as it should be. Infinite wisdom and justice direct all the affairs of the children of men. In rejecting history and biography, I wish always to except the events and characters recorded in the Old and New Testaments. They are true because they are natural, for they ascribe the former to a divine hand, and they never fail to mention the weaknesses and vices of the latter. There is not a single Washington among all the heroes of the Bible. . . .

Benjn: Rush

P.S. There was scarcely a single deceased person that was active in our Revolution that has not died poor in Pennsylvania. Witness Reed, Mifflin, Morris, Wilson and many others of less note.

To RUSH

August 25, 1811

DEAR RUSH,

. . . In Massachusetts, as in Pennsylvania, those who were active in the Revolution have died poor. Hancock once owned houses, lands, lots, and wharves in the town of Boston and landed estates in almost all parts of New England which, if he had held them to this day, would be worth more than

13. During the war Rush did military duty as a medical officer in this area. See his *Autobiography*, ed. George W. Corner (Princeton, 1948), p. 128.

Washington and Franklin were both worth, as I believe. Yet he died not absolutely but comparatively poor. [T.] Cushing [and] S. Adams died poor. [R.T.] Paine, J. Adams, and Gerry will die poor enough, though I hope not insolvent. Lincoln, Knox, Brooks, Sullivan were not rich.[14] The great James Otis, Junior, added nothing to his property, but sacrificed immensely to the public.

I hope you will excuse me if I say a few words of myself, because you have read in some of our candid Federal papers that I have been "overpaid."

My father, now fifty years a saint in heaven, was at the expense of my education at a grammar school and at Harvard College. By keeping a public grammar school in Worcester, I defrayed the expense of my education to the bar. In 1758, I . . . took the oath and was admitted as an attorney. In 1761, I was called to the bar as a barrister by the Supreme Court. In May 1761, my ever honored and beloved father died and by his will left me a house and barn and forty acres of land, besides one third of his personal estate. If I had converted that real estate into money, it would in the fifty years that have passed since, at legal interest, have amounted to more, I believe, than I am now worth.

In 1764, I married the daughter of the richest clergyman[15] in the province, as his brother clergymen used to say. . . .

From 1758 to 1775, seventeen years, I was in practice at the bar; seven years of it, at the head of the bar. In this period, I am bold to say, no lawyer was ever more laborious. I was concerned in all the greatest causes and rode most of the circuit of the province. Though I was never so greedy of great fees as some others, and though our fees in those times were not so high as they are now and as they were in the Revolutionary times when rum, sugar and molasses, Madeira wine, and English goods were given in profusion to the lawyers, yet I got money, as I thought, very fast, as fast as I desired. This I laid out in a house in Boston, now of great value, in lands in my own

14. The least well known of these Massachusetts patriots is John Brooks (1752–1825), who served at the siege of Boston and at the Battle of Saratoga.

15. Adams' father-in-law, William Smith (1707–83), minister of the First Church of Weymouth from 1743, had married into the influential Quincy family.

neighborhood in the country, and in the purchase of my brother's share of my father's estate, and lent at legal simple interest on bonds and mortgages to private persons. . . .

When I was called to Congress in 1774, I left as full practice as any lawyer ever held in this state. I left debts due to me on books to a large amount and many other debts on notes and bonds. My friend and agent collected what he could and lent to the public. I have been ten years ambassador abroad, eight years Vice-President of the United States, and four years President.

John Lowell,[16] in 1776 or 1777, removed from Newbury Port to Boston, stepped into my shoes, undertook my business, engaged in the employment of my clients, and died lately worth several hundred thousand dollars; [he] left a very handsome fortune to all his sons and daughters, and that very Spartacus [John Lowell, Jr.], that leader of rebel slaves, that very "Rebel" who lately reproached me with being overpaid, has a magnificent seat in Boston, a splendid villa in the country, and large sums in funds, banks, and insurances all derived from his father, for he never earned much, if anything, himself. . . . Is not this insolence too great for philosophical or Christian patience to bear? No. It is not, and I bear it with much indifference, whether philosopher or Christian or not. . . .

John Adams

Near a million sterling passed through my hands in Amsterdam on which I never received a farthing as commissions or in any other way. . . .

To ADAMS

August 20, 1811

MY DEAR OLD FRIEND,

The time cannot be very distant when you and I must both sleep with our fathers. The distinguished figure you have made in life and the high

---

16. John Lowell, Sr. (1743–1802), served many years in the Massachusetts House of Representatives and in the Continental Congress.

offices you have filled will render your removal from the world an object of universal attention. Suppose you avail yourself while in health of the sensibility which awaits the public mind to your character soon after your death by leaving behind you a posthumous address to the citizens of the United States, in which shall be inculcated all those great national, social, domestic, and religious virtues which alone can make a people free, great, and happy. You will not be suspected of insincerity nor of selfishness in this address, for no one can suspect you of sinning in the grave nor of aiming at any honor or profit by it.

In such a performance you may lay the foundation of national happiness *only* in religion, not by leaving it doubtful "whether morals can exist without it" but by asserting that without religion morals are the effects of causes as purely physical as pleasant breezes and fruitful seasons. Under this head may be included public worship and the observance of the Sabbath, with which national prosperity has always been intimately connected. Recollect here your definition of a New Englander given to one of your friends in Amsterdam. It was: "He is a meeting-going animal." This is strictly true of the whole human race. . . .

Next to the duties nations owe to the Supreme Being may be inculcated the influence of early marriage and fidelity to the marriage bed upon public happiness. Much may be said to discourage the use of ardent spirits and to lessen the number of taverns and grocery stores, both of which are sapping the virtue of our country. The influence of female education upon morals, taste, and patriotism should not be passed over in silence.[17] In exposing the evils of funding systems and banks, summon all the fire of your genius as it blazed forth on the 2nd of July in the year 1776 upon the floor of Congress. The benefits of free schools should not be overlooked. Indeed, suffrage in my opinion should never be permitted to a man that could not write or read. I have only hinted at a few of the subjects that an address such as I have mentioned should embrace. Be assured it will be well received. You stand

17. Rush often refers to the education of women as both necessary and beneficial for society: ". . . let the ladies of a country be educated properly, and they will not only make and administer its laws, but form its manners and character." "Thoughts upon Female Education," reprinted in Rush's *Essays, Literary, Moral & Philosophical* (Philadelphia, 1798), p. 87.

nearly alone in the history of our public men in never having had your *integrity* called in question or even suspected. Friends and enemies agree in believing you to be an honest man. I fancy I hear a cry for a sight of your voice from the tomb such as was excited by Mark Antony for the reading of Caesar's will. . . .

Excuse the liberty I have taken in the subject I have chosen for this letter. Your name and fame have always been dear to me. I wish you to survive yourself for ages in the veneration, esteem, and affection of your fellow citizens and to be useful to them even in the grave. None but those persons who knew you in the years 1774, 1775, and 1776 will ever know how great a debt the United States owe to your talents, knowledge, unbending firmness, and intrepid patriotism. Adieu! Ever yours,

Benjn: Rush

To RUSH

August 28, 1811

MY DEAR FRIEND,

Your letter of the 20th . . . has filled my eyes with tears and, indurate stoic as I am, my heart with sensations unutterable by my tongue or pen. Not the feelings of vanity, but the overwhelming sense of my own unworthiness of such a panegyric from such a friend. Like Louis the 16, I said to myself, "Qu'est ce que J'ai fait pour le meriter?"[18] Have I not been employed in mischief all my days? Did not the American Revolution produce the French Revolution? And did not the French Revolution produce all the calamities and desolations to the human race and the whole globe ever since? I meant well, however. My conscience was clear as a crystal glass without a scruple or a doubt. I was borne along by an irresistible sense of duty. God prospered our labors; and awful, dreadful, and deplorable as the consequences have been, I cannot but hope that the ultimate good of the world, of the human race, and of our beloved country is intended and will be accomplished by it. . . .

18. "What have I done to merit this?"

If, by dedicating all the rest of my days to the composition of such an address as you propose, I could have any rational assurance of doing any real good to my fellow citizens of United America, I would cheerfully lay aside all other occupations and amusements and devote myself to it. But there are difficulties and embarrassments in the way which to me, at present, appear insuperable.

1. "The sensibility of the public mind," which you anticipate at my decease, will not be so favorable to my memory as you seem to foresee. By the treatment I have received and continue to receive I should expect that a large majority of all parties would cordially rejoice to hear that my head was laid low.

2. I am surprised to read your opinion that "my integrity has never been called in question" and that "friends and enemies agree in believing me to be an honest man." If I am to judge by the newspapers and pamphlets that have been printed in America for twenty years past, I should think that both parties believed me the meanest villain in the world.

3. If they should not "suspect me of sinning in the grave," they will charge me with selfishness and hypocrisy before my death, in preparing an address to move the passions of the people and excite them to promote my children and perhaps to make my son a king. Washington and Franklin could never do anything but what was imputed to pure disinterested patriotism. I never could do anything but what was ascribed to sinister motives.

4. I agree with you in sentiment that religion and virtue are the only foundations not only of republicanism and of all free government but of social felicity under all governments and in all the combinations of human society. But if I should inculcate this doctrine in my will, I should be charged with hypocrisy and a desire to conciliate the good will of the clergy towards my family—as I was charged by Dr. Priestley and his friend Cooper[19] and by Quakers, Baptists, and I know not how many other sects, for instituting a national fast, for even common civility to the clergy, and for being a churchgoing animal.

19. Thomas Cooper (1759–1840), an English-born lawyer and scientist who came to the United States in the 1790's, made a bitter attack on John Adams in 1799 and was punished with imprisonment and a heavy fine.

5. If I should inculcate those "national, social, domestic, and religious virtues" you recommend, I should be suspected and charged with an hypocritical, Machiavellian, Jesuitical, Pharisaical attempt to promote a national establishment of Presbyterianism in America, whereas I would as soon establish the Episcopal Church, and almost as soon the Catholic Church.

6. If I should inculcate fidelity to the marriage bed, it would be said that it proceeded from resentment to General Hamilton and a malicious desire to hold up to posterity his libertinism.

7. Others would say that it is only a vainglorious ostentation of my own continence. For among all the errors, follies, failings, vices, and crimes which have been so plentifully imputed to me, I cannot recollect a single insinuation against me of any amorous intrigue or irregular or immoral connection with woman, single or married, myself a bachelor or a married man.

8. If I should recommend the sanctification of the Sabbath, like a divine, or even only a regular attendance on public worship as a means of moral instruction and social improvement, like a philosopher or statesman, I should be charged with vain ostentation again and a selfish desire to revive the remembrance of my own punctuality in this respect; for it is notorious enough that I have been a churchgoing animal for seventy-six years, i.e., from the cradle. And this has been alleged as one proof of my hypocrisy.

9. Fifty-three years ago I was fired with a zeal amounting to enthusiasm against ardent spirits, the multiplication of taverns, retailers, dram shops, and tippling houses; grieved to the heart to see the number of idlers, thieves, sots, and consumptive patients made for the physicians in those infamous seminaries. . . .

Sermons, moral discourses, philosophical dissertations, medical advice are all lost upon this subject. Nothing but making the commodity scarce and dear will have any effect. And your Republican friend, and I had almost said mine, Jefferson, would not permit rum or whiskey to be taxed.

If I should then in my will, my dying legacy, my posthumous exhortation, call it what you will, recommend heavy prohibitory taxes upon spirituous liquors, which I believe to be the only remedy against their deleterious qualities in society, every one of your brother Republicans and nine tenths of the Federalists would say that I was a canting Puritan, a profound hypocrite, setting up standards of morality, frugality, economy, temperance, simplicity, and sobriety that I knew the age was incapable of.

10. Funds and banks. I never approved or was satisfied with our funding system. It was founded on no consistent principle. It was contrived to enrich particular individuals at the public expense. Our whole banking system I ever abhorred, I continue to abhor, and shall die abhorring. But I am not an enemy to funding systems. They are absolutely and indispensably necessary in the present state of the world. An attempt to annihilate or prevent them would be as romantic an adventure as any in *Don Quixote* or in *Oberon*. . . .

Now sir, if I should talk in this strain after I am dead, you know the people of America would pronounce that I had died mad.

11. My opinion is that a circulating medium of gold and silver only ought to be introduced and established, that a national bank of deposit only, with a branch in each state, should be allowed; that every bank in the union ought to be annihilated, and every bank of discount prohibited to all eternity. Not one farthing of profit should ever be allowed on any money deposited in the bank. . . .

Franklin, Washington, Hamilton, and all our disinterested patriots and heroes, it will be said, have sanctioned paper money and banks, and who is this pedant and bigot of a John Adams who from the ground sounds the toxin against all our best men, when everybody knows he never had anything in view but his private interest, from his birth to his death.

12. Free schools and all schools, colleges, academies, and seminaries of learning I can recommend from my heart; but I dare not say that "suffrage should never be permitted to a man who cannot read and write." What would become of the Republic of France if the lives, fortunes, characters of twenty-four millions and an half of men who can neither read nor write should be at the absolute disposal of five hundred thousand who can read?

13. I am not qualified to write such an address. The style should be pure, elegant, eloquent, and pathetic in the highest degree. It should be revised, corrected, obliterated, interpolated, amended, transcribed twenty times, polished, refined, varnished, burnished. To all these employments and exercises I am a total stranger. To my sorrow I have never copied nor

corrected nor embellished. I understand it not. I never could write declamations, orations, or popular addresses.

14. If I could persuade my Friend Rush, or my Friend Jay, or my Friend Trumbull,[20] or my Friend Humphreys, or, perhaps, my Friend Jefferson to write such a thing for me, I know not why I might not transcribe it, as Washington did so often. Borrowed eloquence, if it contains as good stuff, is as good as own eloquence.

15. The example you recollect of Caesar's will is an awful warning. Posthumous addresses may be left by Caesar as well as Cato, Brutus, or Cicero and will oftener, perhaps, be applauded and make deeper impressions, establish empires easier, than restore republics, promote tyranny sooner than liberty.

Your advice, my friend, flows from the piety, benevolence, and patriotism of your heart. I know of no man better qualified to write such an address than yourself. If you will try your hand at it and send me the result, I will consider it maturely. I will not promise to adopt it as my own; but I may make a better use of it than of anything I could write. . . .

John Adams . . .

To ADAMS

September 4, 1811

MY DEAR FRIEND,

. . . I am not satisfied with any one of your objections to my proposal of a posthumous address from you to the citizens of the United States. The "good that men do lives after them"; the evil they have done, or the evil that has been unjustly imputed to them, generally descends into the grave with them. I have lately met with a most furious attack upon the character of the celebrated Mr. Baxter written too immediately after his death.[21] This libel has died a natural death without affecting the real character of Mr. Baxter

---

20. John Trumbull (1750–1831), literary leader of the "Hartford Wits," was a one-time law student of Adams and a well-known legislator and judge.
21. Richard Baxter (1615–91) was a distinguished Nonconformist minister.

with posterity. He is justly considered as one of the greatest and best men England ever produced. . . . A library might be composed of the books written against Luther, Calvin, Whitefield, and Wesley.[22] Where are those books *now?* And who presumes at this day to call in question the integrity or the great achievements of those men in reforming and benefiting the world? . . .

No hand but your own must compose your voice from the tomb. Your style is bold, original, occasionally brilliant, and at all times full of nerve. There is not a redundant word in it. . . . It is the artillery of language. . . .

Had the scribblers who now fill the Boston prints with abusive publications against you known you in 1774, 1775, and 1776; had they heard you unfold the secret causes and the certain consequences of the American Revolution, and particularly *one* of its causes, viz., the monopoly of commerce and the future empire of the ocean by Great Britain; had they heard your uniform testimony in favor of republican forms of government, and that long before your letter to Mr. Wythe was published;[23] . . . had they heard your bold and eloquent speeches in favor of independence; and did they trace all their present liberty, their superb city houses, their splendid villas, and their bank and insurance stock in part to those exploits of your wisdom and patriotism, they would blush at their ingratitude and implore your forgiveness before you were removed forever from their sight. . . .

Benjn: Rush

To RUSH

December 4, 1811

DEAR SIR,

Shall I congratulate or condole with you on the appointment of your son to be Comptroller of the Treasury? You will lose the delightful comfort of

22. John Wesley (1703–91) and George Whitefield (1714–70) were founders of Methodism and noted evangelists.

23. Adams' *Thoughts on Government: Applicable to the Present State of the American Colonies* (Philadelphia, 1776) was a favorite essay, which he frequently referred to as his letter to George Wythe. See Adams to Rush, June 25, 1807, *Old Family Letters,* pp. 143–144.

his daily society and that of his lady and their prattling little ones, which I know by experience to be in old age among the sweetest enjoyments of life, provided always that it be not indulged to excess.

I should have thought, too, that his office of Attorney General and his practice at the bar would have not only given him better profits but opened to him better prospects. I should have thought, too, that he had too much genius, imagination, and taste to be able to reconcile himself to a life of such painful drudgery as casting accounts, examining vouchers, &c.

I presume, nevertheless, that he can reconcile himself to it; and there are many advantages in being near the fountain. Mr. Gallatin has been so long in that laborious situation that he probably will not be content to hold it many years.[24] I wish Mr. Rush may be his successor. . . .

We have seen advertised in the *Aurora* and several other southern papers Dr. Franklin's works and especially his journal in France; and although these advertisements have been continued and repeated for years, no man here has ever seen or heard of the book.[25] Pray tell me what this means?

I am told, too, that Colonel Duane has announced his intention to take me in hand for what I have published concerning Dr. Franklin. He is welcome. I have published my proofs as well as complaints. Let the world judge. I have not been such a disinterested patriot as to have five hundred and thirty thousand dollars to assist me in my defense. . . .

John Adams

To ADAMS

December 9, 1811

DEAR SIR,

You have touched me in a sore place in your letter of the 4th instant. My son Richard has accepted the office of comptroller general and is about to

24. Richard Rush became Comptroller of the Treasury in November 1811, in recognition of his opposition to the rechartering of the United States Bank. In 1814 President Madison offered him the position of Secretary of the Treasury or that of Attorney General, and he chose the latter.

25. William Duane began publishing Franklin's *Works* in 1808 and had brought out five of the six volumes by 1809.

remove with his family to Washington in the course of this month. . . . I pointed out the vexations, dangers, and poverty of political and official life, and mentioned the distress and obscurity in which many old patriots and servants of the public were now ending their days in many parts of our country. . . . Lastly I implored him by my affection for him, by my age, by my gray hairs, by the prospect of my death, which must according to the course of nature take place in a few years, and of the importance of his presence and patronage to his mother and to my young children when I shall be called from them. But alas! All these arguments and importunities were employed to no purpose. There was one insurmountable objection to them. His wife's connections live near Washington, and *her wishes* were to be near them. There are two classes of female tyrants—termagants and sirens. My son's wife belongs to the latter class. . . .

My son James, the young doctor to whom I shall now transfer the rank and privileges of primogeniture, is an excellent young man, well informed upon most subjects as well as in medicine, and will, I have no doubt, shine in his profession. But how little patronage does this "mute art" (as Ovid calls it when he speaks of Apollo being condemned to exercise it) [26] afford to a young family compared with the profession of law, especially when it is exercised by splendid talents and accompanied with a fair character?

You have nothing to fear from Duane's threat. Long before this time he has forgotten it. This is the manner of the man. . . .

Benjn: Rush . . .

To RUSH

December 19, 1811

DEAR SIR,

. . . By your own showing it was Richard's duty to be overruled or ruled over by his wife; and by my showing I shall make it appear to be his interest.

26. Rush probably intended to cite Virgil, *Aeneid* XII.396–397.

He will soon be Secretary of the Treasury, or he may be a judge of the Supreme Court, or an ambassador abroad when he pleases, or perhaps Vice-President or President.[27] Pennsylvania has not had her share, and Virginia a fourfold proportion of American honors. . . . The reason why Pennsylvania had not her share in the first twelve years was that Pennsylvania appeared, according to Farmer's *Daemonology*,[28] to be seized by the spirit which entered into the swine and rushed down steep into the sea. Mifflin, McKean, Dallas, all of you indeed, seemed to have adopted what The Great Randolph calls "the infernal principles of French fraternization." They were for going to war with England and forming a closer alliance with Robespierre and his forerunners and afterfollowers. I thought this project no better than making a league with the Devil. I have wondered that Jefferson did not promote Pennsylvanians. I am glad Madison begins to think of it.

I know how it is. It is so sweet, fatigued at night with study and business, to sit down and chat with consort and daughters and son Richard and his fascinating wife that you cannot bear to think of losing any part of the entertainment. Just so have I fretted several times when they have taken away from me my comfort. But NON NOBIS, NON NOBIS SOLIS NATI SUMUS.[29]

. . . The winds begin to rustle, the clouds gather, it grows dark; will these airy forces rear up the ocean to a foaming fury? A spirit seems to be rising; a spirit of contrition and shame at our long apathy and lethargy; a spirit of resentment of injuries, a spirit of indignation at insolence; and what to me is very remarkable, a spirit of greater unanimity than I have ever witnessed in this country for fifty years. What say you to your friend?

John Adams

27. Richard Rush served as United States minister to Great Britain, 1817–25, Secretary of the Treasury, 1825–29, and United States minister to France, 1847–51. For a time in 1817 he was Secretary of State pending the arrival of John Quincy Adams.

28. Hugh Farmer, *An Essay on the Demoniacs of the New Testament* (London, 1775).

29. "Not for ourselves, not for ourselves alone were we born." Cf. Cicero, *De Officiis* I.vii.22. Adams may have combined Cicero's thought with the phrasing of Psalms 115:1 in the Latin Vulgate Bible, "Non nobis Domine, non nobis: sed nomine tuo da gloriam."

To ADAMS

December 16, 1811

MY DEAR OLD FRIEND,

Mr. Jefferson and I exchanged letters once in six, nine, or twelve months. This day I received a few lines from him in which he introduces your name in the following words.[30] After mentioning the visit paid to you by his two neighbors the Messrs. Coles[31] last summer, he adds, "Among other things he [Mr. Adams][32] adverted to the unprincipled licentiousness of the press against myself," adding, *"I always loved Jefferson and still love him.* This is enough for me. I only needed this knowledge to revive towards him all the affections of the most cordial moments of our lives. It is known to those who have heard me speak of Mr. Adams that I have ever done him justice myself and defended him when assailed by others with the single exception as to his political opinions, but with a man possessing so many estimable qualities, why should we be separated by mere differences of opinion in politics, religion, philosophy, or anything else? His opinions are as honestly formed as my own. Our different views of the same subjects are the results of the difference in our organization and experience. I have never withdrawn from any man upon that account. Although many have done it from me, much less should I do it from one with whom I had gone through, with hand and heart, so many trying scenes. I wish therefore for an apposite occasion to express to Mr. Adams my *unchanged affection* for him. There is an awkwardness which hangs over the resuming a correspondence so long discontinued unless something should arise which should call for a letter. Time and chance may perhaps generate such an occasion, of which I shall not be wanting in promptitude to avail myself."

30. Though Rush was discreet in holding back some of Jefferson's comments, Jefferson was generally kind in his remarks and estimations. See Jefferson to Rush, Dec. 5, 1811, *The Writings of Thomas Jefferson,* ed. Paul Leicester Ford (New York, 1892–99), IX, 299–301n.

31. The Coles brothers, John and Edward, visited Adams for two days in 1811, and years later (1857) Edward gave an account of the visit to Henry S. Randall, who reproduced it in his *Life of Thomas Jefferson* (New York, 1858), III, 639–640.

32. MS has brackets.

And now, my dear friend, permit me again to suggest to you to receive the olive branch which has thus been offered to you by the hand of a man who still loves you. Fellow laborers in erecting the great fabric of American independence! —fellow sufferers in the calumnies and falsehoods of party rage! —fellow heirs of the gratitude and affection of posterity! —and fellow passengers in a stage that must shortly convey you both into the presence of a Judge with whom the forgiveness and love of enemies is the condition of acceptance! —embrace—embrace each other! Bedew your letters of reconciliation with tears of affection and joy. Bury in silence all the causes of your separation. Recollect that explanations may be proper between lovers but are *never* so between divided friends. Were I near to you, I would put a pen into your hand and guide it while it composed the following short address to Mr. Jefferson:

"Friend and fellow laborer in the cause of the liberty and independence of our common country, I salute you with the most cordial good wishes for your health and happiness.

John Adams."

Excuse the liberty I have taken, and be assured of the respect, affection, and gratitude of yours truly,

Benjn: Rush

To RUSH

December 25, 1811

[MY DEAR FRIEND,]

I never was so much at a loss how to answer a letter as yours of the 16th. Shall I assume a sober face and write a grave essay on religion, philosophy, laws, or government? Shall I laugh, like Bacchus among his grapes, wine vats, and bottles? Shall I assume the man of the world, the fine gentleman, the courtier, and bow and scrape, with a smooth, smiling face, soft words, many compliments and apologies; think myself highly honored, bound in gratitude, &c., &c.?

I perceive plainly enough, Rush, that you have been teasing Jefferson to write to me, as you did me some time ago to write to him. You gravely advise me "to receive the olive branch," as if there had been war; but there has never been any hostility on my part, nor that I know, on his. When there has been no war, there can be no room for negotiations of peace.

Mr. Jefferson speaks of my political opinions; but I know of no difference between him and myself relative to the Constitution or to forms of government in general. In measures of administration, we have differed in opinion. I have never approved the repeal of the judicial law, the repeal of the taxes, the neglect of the navy; and I have always believed that his system of gunboats for a national defense was defective. To make it complete, he ought to have taken a hint from Molière's *Femmes précieuses,* or his learned ladies, and appointed three or four brigades of horse, with a major general and three or four brigadiers, to serve on board his galleys of Malta. I have never approved his nonembargo or any nonintercourse or nonimportation laws.

But I have raised no clamors nor made any opposition to any of these measures. The nation approved them; and what is my judgment against that of the nation? On the contrary, he disapproved of the alien law and sedition law, which I believe to have been constitutional and salutary, if not necessary.

He disapproved of the eight per cent loan, and with good reason. For I hated it as much as any man, and the army, too, which occasioned it. He disapproved, perhaps, of the partial war with France, which I believed, as far as it proceeded, to be a holy war. He disapproved of taxes, and perhaps the whole scheme of my administration, &c., and so perhaps did the nation. . . .

We differed in opinion about the French Revolution. He thought it wise and good, and that it would end in the establishment of a free republic. I saw through it, to the end of it, before it broke out, and was sure it could end only in a restoration of the Bourbons, or a military despotism, after deluging France and Europe in blood. In this opinion I differed from you as much as from Jefferson; but all this made me no more of an enemy to you than to him, nor to him than to you. I believe you both to mean well to mankind and your country. I might suspect you both to sacrifice a little to the infernal gods, and perhaps unconsciously to suffer your judgments to be a little swayed by a love of popularity and possibly by a little spice of ambition.

In point of republicanism, all the differences I ever knew or could discover between you and me, or between Jefferson and me, consisted:

1. In the difference between speeches and messages. I was a monarchist because I thought a speech more manly, more respectful to Congress and the nation. Jefferson and Rush preferred messages.

2. I held levees once a week, that all my time might not be wasted by idle visits. Jefferson's whole eight years was a levee.

3. I dined a large company once or twice a week. Jefferson dined a dozen every day.

4. Jefferson and Rush were for liberty and straight hair. I thought curled hair was as republican as straight.

In these, and a few other points of equal importance, all miserable frivolities, that Jefferson and Rush ought to blush that they ever laid any stress upon them, I might differ; but I never knew any points of more consequence, on which there was any variation between us.

You exhort me to "forgiveness and love of enemies," as if I considered or had ever considered Jefferson as my enemy. This is not so; I have always loved him as a friend. If I ever received or suspected any injury from him, I have forgiven it long and long ago, and have no more resentment against him than against you. . . .

You often put me in mind that I am soon to die; I know it and shall not forget it. Stepping into my kitchen one day, I found two of my poor neighbors, as good sort of men as two drunkards could be. One had sotted himself into a consumption. His cough and his paleness and weakness showed him near the last stage. Tom, who was not so far gone as yet, though he soon followed, said to John, "You have not long for this world." John answered very quickly: "I know it, Tom, as well as you do; but why do you tell me of it? I had rather you should strike me." This was one of those touches of nature which Shakespeare or Cervantes would have noted in his ivory book.

But why do you make so much ado about nothing? Of what use can it be for Jefferson and me to exchange letters? I have nothing to say to him but to wish him an easy journey to heaven when he goes, which I wish may be delayed as long as life shall be agreeable to him. And he can have nothing to say to me but to bid me make haste and be ready. Time and chance, however, or possibly design, may produce ere long a letter between us.

John Adams

To ADAMS

December 26, 1811

MY DEAR OLD FRIEND,

During the time Cobbett was abusing me in his newspaper, to the great joy of a number of our tory citizens, I met Hamilton Rowan.[33] . . . He took me by the hand in the most cordial manner. "Our situation," said I, "Mr. Rowan, is a good deal alike in Philadelphia. We are both in an *enemy's* country." "No, sir," said he, "I am in a *foreign* country only," alluding to the avidity with which the scandal published against me had been devoured by the class of citizens above mentioned. It is true the papers no longer pour forth weekly and daily calumnies against me, but I am still in an *enemy's* country. My patients and my pupils (with a few exceptions) are my only friends out of my own family. Do you wonder then at my complaining of my son Richard for deserting me? Independently of his affection and kindness to me, his office kept libelers of my reputation in awe.

But what have you done to render your fellow citizens so hostile to you? I answer, my *first* offense was keeping company with the Messrs. Adams and John Hancock in the year 1774 and afterwards subscribing the Declaration of Independence. My *second* offense (of far less magnitude than the first) was opposing the wheelbarrow Constitution of Pennsylvania in 1776 and the men who supported it, particularly Joseph Reed, which acts are still remembered with resentment by some of our old Constitutional, now Democratic, citizens. My *third* offense was writing down the old sanguinary criminal law of our state, by which I made many Old Testament divines and saints my enemies. My *fourth* offense was writing against monkish learning,

33. Archibald Hamilton Rowan (1751–1834), an Irish revolutionary, had escaped to America and lived principally in Delaware from 1795 to 1800.

commonly called the Latin and Greek languages, by which I produced a confederacy of pedagogues against me. My *fifth* and last offense was teaching a new system of medicine, part of which consisted in the use of remedies that did violence to the feelings and common sense of our citizens, and in inculcating a belief that our yellow fever was of domestic origin. . . .

While I thus open my heart to my dear old friend in complaints against many of my fellow citizens, do not suppose that my life has been made completely miserable by them. The good I have enjoyed in Philadelphia since the year 1774 has far, very far, exceeded the evil I have suffered. I have been blessed with an excellent wife and affectionate as well as intelligent and worthy children. I have had the constant and faithful attachment and support of half a dozen powerful and popular citizens (several of whom are of the old school in politics) against the malice of my medical brethren. One of them opened his purse to me at the time when the publications against my practice reduced the income from my business £400 below the expenses of my family. In addition to these sources of enjoyment and comfort, I have derived from my studies and professional duties a large share of intellectual and moral pleasure. The midnight cry of "past twelve o'clock" has often found me insensible to the cold of winter and the heat of summer while I have been engaged with ineffable delight in forming a new arrangement of facts in order to derive from them new principles and new modes of treating diseases. For these and all God's other mercies to me, I desire to be truly, sincerely, and forever thankful. . . .

I do not consider my son as having been called upon to share in the honors of the general government, nor do I believe the office to which he has been appointed will satisfy the claims or appease the jealousy of Pennsylvania as you have supposed. You will say, perhaps, what can she mean by asking for a larger representation in the honors of the general government? Is not Mr. Gallatin a Pennsylvanian?[34] I once heard a servant girl who quarreled with a mulatto fellow servant and called him "a no nation son of b——h." Many of our citizens who would blush to apply such a low and

34. Albert Gallatin, a native of Switzerland, immigrated to New England in the 1780's and later moved to the Pennsylvania frontier.

indelicate language to any man do not hesitate to say Mr. Gallatin is "a *no state* man" and that he belongs as much to the Union as to Pennsylvania. . . .

Benjn: Rush . . .

To RUSH

January 8, 1812

MY WORTHY FRIEND,

. . . You mention Cobbett. . . . Now I assure you upon my honor and the faith of the friendship between us that I never saw the face of that Cobbett; that I should not know him if I met him in my porridge dish; that I never wrote one word in his paper and had no more connection with him than with Philip Freneau or Colonel Duane. . . .

Another thing, Dr. Rush! You know it was circulated and believed throughout the city of Philadelphia that I had set up and established John Fenno and his *United States Gazette,* to introduce monarchy. I say you know it, because you told me so yourself, and at the same time said that Freneau's *National Gazette* was set up to oppose the Vice-President and his *United States Gazette.*

Now I declare to you I never knew anything of Fenno till I found him established at New York and his paper established, that I never contributed a farthing to his establishment or support, and that I never wrote a line in his paper but the *Discourses on Davila.*[35]

You know, too, the time when there was not a Quaker or Proprietary partisan in Pennsylvania who would not gladly have seen my neck in a halter and me kicking in the air as Col. Harrison's imagination represented himself and Mr. Gerry; and that long before the Declaration of Independence and merely because I was suspected of having independence in view as a last resort. . . . Such are the terms upon which an honest man and real friend to his country must live in times such as those we have been destined to witness. And what is worse than all, we must leave these prejudices and enmi-

---

35. *Discourses on Davila* (Boston, 1805) consisted of essays written in 1790.

ties to our children as their inheritance. From the year 1761, now more than fifty years, I have constantly lived in an enemy's country. And that without having one personal enemy in the world that I know of. I do not consider little flirts and spats and miffs and piques forgotten by me in a moment as enmities, tho' others may have remembered them longer.

Now I hope I have prepared the way in some measure for giving you my opinion of your enemy's country, and I humbly hope in some, tho' a less degree I fear, of my own. In my opinion there is not in Philadelphia a single citizen more universally esteemed and beloved by his fellow citizens than Dr. Benjamin Rush.[36] There is not a man in Pennsylvania more esteemed by the whole state. I know not a man in America more esteemed by the nation. There is not a citizen of this Union more esteemed throughout the literary, scientifical, and moral world in Europe, Asia, and Africa. . . .

There is, nevertheless, not a tory and scarcely a whig in America but talks about Dr. Rush and will tell twenty absurd and ridiculous stories about him as well as John Adams. I will give you one example in perfect confidence. Let the secret be as close as the grave. A gentleman told me lately "that General Washington was a hypocrite!" A hypocrite! What do you mean? "He was a hypocrite"—and mentioned several things, but "one instance alone was sufficient proof of his hypocrisy." What is that? "He appointed Dr. Rush to a lucrative and respectable office, that of Treasurer of the Mint." And what proof of hypocrisy was that? "Why, I know that he thought Dr. Rush a villain; and believing him to be so, it was hypocrisy to appoint him to such an office of trust." And how do you know that he thought so ill of Dr. Rush? Such a gentleman, whom he named but I will not, "the most intimate friend of Gen. Washington, told me that he had heard him say *that he had been a good deal in the world and seen many bad men, but Dr. Rush was the most black-hearted scoundrel he had ever known."*

This is horrid, said I. . . . It was myself who appointed Rush Treasurer of the Mint, and so far from repenting of it or thinking it a proof of hypocrisy, I thought Dr. Rush one of the best men in the world and his appoint-

---

36. Adams' estimate is generally accepted by Lyman H. Butterfield. See *Letters of Benjamin Rush,* I, lxi.

ment one of the best that had been made. He acknowledged, if this was so, that he had been mistaken in the author of Rush's appointment but he was not so in the account he had given of Washington's speech to his friend.

Your posterity and mine, I doubt not, my friend, will be teased and vexed with a million of such stories concerning us when we shall be no more. . . . Rejoice in the promotion of your son. . . . He is in the road of honor and power and will do a great deal of good. . . .

John Adams

To ADAMS

February 12, 1812

DEAR SIR,

I did not require the anecdote you have communicated to me in your letter of last month to know that I had incurred the hatred of General Washington. It was violent and descended with him to the grave. For its not being perpetuated in the history of his life, I am indebted to the worthy and amiable Judge [Bushrod] Washington. I will give you a history of its cause in as short a compass as possible.[37]

During the session of Congress in Philadelphia in the year 1774 I met Mr. Washington at the coffeehouse at the time he was generally spoken of as commander in chief of the American army, and informed him that his appointment would give universal satisfaction to the citizens of Pennsylvania and hoped he would not decline it. I had reason to believe that he considered this opinion ever afterwards as an expression of attachment to his military character never to be canceled, and that a subsequent change of that opinion was an evidence of insincerity. The sequel of this letter will show that I was not singular in this respect.

In the summer of 1775 or thereabouts I dined in company with General, then Colonel, Stephen[38] on his way from Virginia to the camp. I sat next

37. Rush was deeply affected by Adams' remarks on this episode, and this letter was revised several times over some weeks before it was sent. See *Letters,* II, 1124–25n.

38. Adam Stephen (d. 1791) studied medicine in Edinburgh before he immigrated to America. Because of military experience in the Seven Years' War, he rose quickly to the rank

to him. In a low tone of voice he asked me who constituted General Washington's military family. I told him Colonel J. Reed and Major Thomas Mifflin. "Are they men of talents?" said he. "Yes," said I. "I am glad to hear it," said the General, "for General Washington will require such men about him. He is a *weak man.* I know him well. I served with him during the last French war."

After the defeats and retreats of our army in the year 1776, I went out as a volunteer physician to General Cadwalader's corps of Philadelphia militia.[39] During this excursion I rode with Colonel J. Reed from Bristol to headquarters on the Delaware nearly opposite to Trenton.[40] On our way he mentioned many instances of General Washington's want of military skill and ascribed most of the calamities of the campaign to it. He concluded by saying "he was only fit to command a regiment." General Gates informed me in March 1777 that Patrick Henry of Virginia had said the same thing of him when he was appointed commander in chief.

A little later than this time, General Mifflin told me "he was totally unfit for his situation, that he was fit only to be the head clerk of a London countinghouse," and as a proof of his assertion mentioned the time he wasted with his pen, and particularly noticed his having once transcribed a letter to Congress of three sheets of paper only because there were two or three erasures in the original.

The brilliant affair at Trenton in January 1777 dissipated all the impressions which those opinions and anecdotes of General Washington had excited in my mind. . . .

In April or May 1777 I accepted of the appointment of physician general of the military hospitals of the United States under the direction of Dr. Shippen.[41] Here I saw scenes of distress shocking to humanity and dis-

of brigadier general in the Revolutionary armies, but fell as quickly when a charge of drunkenness was proved at his court-martial. See Adam Stephen, "The Ohio Expedition of 1754," in *Pennsylvania Magazine of History and Biography,* XVIII (1894), 43–50.

39. Rush served under General John Cadwalader (1742–86) during the defense of Philadelphia and the operations around Trenton.

40. Joseph Reed was adjutant general of the American army.

41. Lyman H. Butterfield describes these relations between Rush and Washington, and the strain caused by Rush's indictment of Shippen, in *Letters of Benjamin Rush,* II, 1197–1208.

graceful to a civilized country. I can never forget them. I still see the sons of our yeomanry brought up in the law of plenty and domestic comforts of all kinds, shivering with cold upon bare floors without a blanket to cover them, calling for fire, for water, for suitable food, and for medicines—and calling in vain. . . . While hundreds of the flower of the youth of our country were thus perishing under the most accumulated sufferings, Dr. Shippen, the director general of the hospitals, whose business it was to provide all the articles necessary for their comfort, was feasting with the general officers at the camp or bargaining with tavernkeepers in Jersey or Pennsylvania for the sale of madeira wine from our hospital stores, bought by him for the use of the sick. Nor was this all. No officer was ever sent by General W. to command or preserve discipline in our hospitals (*a practice universal in European armies*), in consequence of which many of our soldiers sold their blankets, muskets, and even clothing for the necessaries of life or for ardent spirits.

In this situation of our hospitals, I addressed two letters to General W.—the one complaining of the above abuses and pointing out their remedies, the other impeaching Dr. Shippen of malpractices.[42] I expected a court-martial would be ordered to inquire into Dr. Shippen's conduct in consequence of my second letter. In this I was disappointed. Both my letters were sent to Congress, and a committee was appointed by them to hear my charges against the Director General. On my way to Yorktown, where the Congress then sat, I passed through the army at Valley Forge, where I saw similar marks of filth, waste of public property, and want of discipline which I had recently witnessed in the hospitals.[43] General Sullivan (at whose quarters I breakfasted) said to me, "Sir, this is not an army—it is a mob." Here a new source of distress was awakened in my mind. I now felt for the safety and independence of my country as well as for the sufferings of the sick under my care. All that I had heard from General Stephen,

42. Randolph G. Adams in his "Benjamin Rush, the Doctor in Politics," *Journal of the Michigan Medical Society*, XXIX (1930), 806, concludes that medical services in the Revolution were poorly managed and Washington did not know the facts.

43. Rush was undoubtedly referring to his impressions of camp conditions that he had noted in 1777. See "Historical Notes of Dr. Benjamin Rush, 1777," contributed by S. Weir Mitchell, *Pennsylvania Magazine of History and Biography*, XXVII (1903), 147–148.

Colonel Reed, Mr. Mifflin, and some others was now revived in my mind. At Yorktown I found alarm and discontent among many members of Congress. While there I wrote a short account of the state of our hospitals and of the army to Patrick Henry, and concluded my letter by quoting a speech of General [Thomas] Conway's unfriendly to the talents of the Commander in Chief. This letter Patrick Henry transmitted to General W——, and hence the *cause* and *only* cause of his hostility to me.

My charges against Dr. Shippen were soon dismissed by the Committee of Congress, in consequence of which I resigned my commission of physician general.

In the year 1779 [1780] Dr. Morgan dragged Dr. Shippen before a court-martial at Morristown, agreeably to an order of Congress, where I was summoned as a witness. During the trial several members of the court were changed—a thing I believe never done in such courts, nor in juries except in cases of sickness and death. The Doctor was acquitted but *without* honor, and by a majority of but *one* vote. Soon after this cold and bare acquittal, he resigned. General W. afterwards gave him a certificate approving of his conduct while director general of the hospitals, which the Doctor published in one of our newspapers about the year 1780. . . .

Feeling no unkindness to G. Washington during the years of the war after 1777 and after the peace, I cordially joined in all the marks of gratitude and respect showed to him from time to time by the citizens of Philadelphia. I *first* pointed the public attention to him as the future President of the United States in several of our newspapers while the Convention was sitting which framed the Constitution, at the same time that I mentioned your name as Vice-President. These acts were the effects of a belief that the counsels of Steuben, Greene,[44] and Hamilton, aided by his own experience, had qualified him for his station, and of a conviction that he always acted honestly and faithfully to promote the first interest of his country. In addi-

---

44. Both Friedrich von Steuben (1730–94) and Nathanael Greene (1742–86) were great military leaders in the American Revolution. Baron von Steuben trained and drilled American soldiers and advised on military strategy. Greene was the skillful general of American forces in the southern states during 1780–82.

tion to my uniting in public acts of respect to him, I entertained him while he presided in the Convention, and treated him with the utmost respect while he was President of the United States. At no time after the year 1777, however, did I believe him to be the "first in war" in our country. In addition to the testimonies of Stephen, Reed, and Mifflin, I had *directly* or *indirectly* the testimonies of Greene, Hamilton, Colonel Tilghman,[45] your son-in-law, and of many other of the most intelligent officers who served under him to the contrary. Nor have I ever dared to join in the profane and impious incense which has been offered to his patriotism and moral qualities by many of our citizens. Were I to mention all that I have heard of his "heart," and from some of his friends too, it would appear that he was not possessed of all the divine attributes that have been ascribed to him. But enough of this hateful subject! . . .

The venerable Charles Thomson,[46] now above 80 years of age, now and then calls to see me. I once suggested to him to write secret memoirs of the American Revolution. "No, no," said he, "I will not. I could not tell the truth without giving great offense. Let the world admire our patriots and heroes. Their supposed talents and virtues (where they were so) by commanding imitation will serve the cause of patriotism and of our country." I concur in this sentiment, and therefore I *earnestly request* that you will destroy this letter as soon as you read it. I do not even wish it to be known that General W. was deficient in that mark of true greatness which so preeminently characterized Julius Caesar, Henry the 4th of France, and Frederick the 2nd of Prussia—*the talent to forgive.*

Brutus said near the close of his life, "I early devoted myself to my country, and I have ever since lived a life of liberty and glory." Your correspondent early devoted himself to the cause of humanity. He has lived in a constant succession of contests with ignorance, prejudice, and vice, in all which his only objects were to lessen the miseries and promote the happiness of his fellow men, and yet he has lived a life constantly exposed to malice and

45. Lieutenant Colonel Tench Tilghman (1744–86), a merchant in Philadelphia before the Revolution, was Washington's aide-de-camp from 1776 to the war's end.
46. Charles Thomson (1729–1824), secretary of Congress, was a good friend of the Rushes.

persecution. "Blessed are they who are persecuted for righteousness' sake." I have derived great comfort and support from this passage of Scripture, for I believe it applies to all those persons who suffer from their zeal (whether successful or not) in the cause of truth, humanity, and justice in the present world. . . .

When Calvin heard that Luther had called him "a child of the devil," he coolly replied, "Luther is a servant of the most high God." In answer to the epithet which G. Washington has applied to me, I will as coolly reply, "He was the highly favored instrument whose patriotism and name contributed greatly to the establishment of the independence of the United States."

Adieu! my dear friend. I repeat again, or rather I entreat again, that you will destroy this letter as soon as you have read it. . . .

Benjn: Rush

P.S. March 9th. In your letters to me which are to follow the receipt of this, make no notices of anything that is contained in it beyond an expression of your satisfaction or dissatisfaction with my defense of my conduct in the above affair. This must be done without mentioning names. My reason for this request is, all my family have descended with the multitude down the stream created by the homage paid to G. W., and I have taken no pains to bring them back again. He is welcome to their praises and admiration. They know only that I am not one of his idolaters, and that I ascribe the success of our Revolution to an illustrious band of statesmen, philosophers, patriots, and heroes. They know likewise from your history of G. W.'s ten talents in one of your letters that we agree in ascribing honor to all to whom honor is due, and not to any one citizen soldier of the United States.

I hope the chain which now connects Quincy with Monticello continues to brighten by every post.[47]

---

47. In another letter to Adams, Feb. 17, 1812, Rush expresses happiness on the resumption of correspondence between Adams and Jefferson: "I rejoice in the correspondence which has taken place between you and your old friend Mr. Jefferson. I consider you and him as the North and South Poles of the American Revolution. Some talked, some wrote, and some fought to promote and establish it, but you and Mr. Jefferson *thought* for us all" (*Letters,* II, 1127).

To RUSH

March 19, 1812

DEAR SIR,

The greatest part of the history in your last letter was well known to me, and I could write you six sheets for your three, full of anecdotes of a similar complexion. I wanted no satisfaction. If I had, your letter would have given it.

The great character [Washington] was *a Character of Convention*. His first appointment was a magnanimous sacrifice of the north to the south, to the base jealousy, sordid envy, and ignorant prejudices of the southern and middle states against New England. I know what I say, and I will not tremble like your old friend at the danger of "giving offense." . . .

I mention a *Character of Convention*. There was a time when northern, middle, and southern statesmen and northern, middle, and southern officers of the army expressly agreed to blow the trumpet of panegyric in concert, to cover and dissemble all faults and errors, to represent every defeat as a victory and every retreat as an advancement, to make that Character popular and fashionable with all parties in all places and with all persons, as a center of union, as the central stone in the geometrical arch.

There you have the revelation of the whole mystery. Something of the same kind has occurred in France and has produced a Napoleon and his empire. And, my friend, something hereafter may produce similar conventions to cry up a Burr, a Hamilton, an Arnold, or a Caesar, Julius or Borgia. And on such foundations have been erected Mahomet, Genghis Khan, Tamerlane, Kublai Khan, Alexander, and all the other great conquerors this world has produced.

Pray have you not often heard the Honorable Timothy Pickering[48] speak

---

48. Before the Revolution Timothy Pickering (1745–1829) was a Massachusetts lawyer and politician. Upon the opening of hostilities he did active service in the army, becoming adjutant general and quartermaster general. After 1783 he entered business in Philadelphia and participated in the development of the Wyoming Valley of Pennsylvania. He held vari-

of The Great Character? I have. And at various periods of time from 1791, when I lived in Mrs. Keppele's house at the corner of Arch Street and Fourth Street, to 1797, after I was chosen President. . . .

April 22, 1812

Colonel Pickering made me a visit [in 1791] and, finding me alone, spent a long evening with me. We had a multitude of conversation. I had then lately purchased Mathew Carey's *American Museum,*[49] the ninth volume of which then lay upon my table. Colonel Pickering, observing the book, said he was acquainted with the work and particularly with that volume of it; and there was a letter in it that he was extremely sorry to see there. I asked what letter is that? Col. Pickering answered, "It is a letter from General Washington." . . . You, my Friend Rush, by looking into the 282nd page of that 9th volume, will find a letter from George Washington dated Mount Vernon, July 31st, 1788.[50]

Col. Pickering said he was extremely sorry to see that letter in print. I asked him why? What do you see amiss in it? What harm will it do? Col. Pickering said, "It will injure General Washington's character." How will it injure him? Stratagems are lawful in war. Colonel Pickering answered me, "It will hurt his moral character. He has been generally thought to be honest and I own I thought his morals were good, but that letter is false, and I know it to be so. I knew him to be vain and weak and ignorant, but I thought he was well meaning; but that letter is a lie, and I know it to be so." I objected and queried.

Pickering explained and descended to particulars. He said it was false in Washington to pretend that he had meditated beforehand to deceive the enemy and to that end to deceive the officers and soldiers of his own army; that he had seriously meditated an attack upon New York for near a twelve-

---

ous high administrative posts, serving for a time as Secretary of State under both Washington and Adams.

49. Mathew Carey (1760–1839), an Irish-born newspaper writer and editor, published *The American Museum* (1787–92) at Philadelphia.

50. Washington [to Noah Webster], July 31, 1788, *The American Museum,* IX (1791), 282–283.

month and had made preparations at an immense expense for that purpose. Washington never had a thought of marching to the southward, till the Count de Grasse's fleet appeared upon the coast. He knew it, and Washington knew it; consequently that letter was a great disgrace.

As I had never before heard Washington's veracity assailed, I was uneasy and argued and queried with him. But Pickering persisted, repeated, and urged facts and orders which I knew nothing of and could not answer. But he dwelt with most delight on Washington's ignorance, weakness, and vanity. He was so ignorant that he had never read anything, not even on military affairs; he could not write a sentence of grammar, nor spell his words, &c., &c., &c. To this I objected. I had been in Congress with Washington in 1774 and in May and part of June 1775 and had heard and read all his letters to Congress in 1775, 1776, 1777 and had formed a very different opinion of his literary talent. His letters were well written and well spelled. Pickering replied, "He did not write them, he only copied them." Who did write them? "His secretaries and aides," and I think he mentioned Reed, Harrison, and Tilghman.

Pickering had come from Wyoming [in Pennsylvania] to solicit employment, as I supposed. He obtained the Post Office, the Secretaryship of War and of State under Washington. . . .

Till 1797 when I was chosen President of U.S. I had never had much intercourse with any of the secretaries of departments; but now it became my duty to look into them. Washington had appointed them, and I knew it would turn the world upside down if I removed any one of them. I had then no particular objection against any of them. I called at the Treasury and conversed with Wolcott. I called at the office of State and conversed with Pickering. I was now elected and Washington upon the point of his departure from Philadelphia. Pickering, to my utter astonishment, began to talk about Washington in the same strain as in Mrs. Keppele's house six or seven years before. He said, "Washington was so extremely illiterate! He could not write a sentence without misspelling some word, nor three paragraphs without false grammar."

I was displeased at this ill nature and astonished that after so many years' service under Washington he should have retained the same malevolence and contempt which he had indulged so foolishly in my presence six or seven years before. I took no other notice of his indiscretion, however, than to say, with the utmost mildness, "Col. Pickering, you seem to me to be too much prejudiced. Washington certainly was not so extremely illiterate as you represent him; his letters and public performances show him quite otherwise." Pickering replied very sharply, "He did not write them." I asked who did? He answered, "His aides and secretaries." . . . I said from all the conversations I had held with him from the year 1774 he appeared to me to have a good deal of information. "Information?" said Pickering, "he had never read anything; not even on the military art; he told me he had never read anything but (I forgot what, probably Simes's *Military Guide*). He never had read Muller."[51]

This is the Colonel Pickering who is now holding himself up as the Friend and Admirer and Lover of Washington; a member of the Washington benevolent societies, affiliated with societies under the same appellation and for the same purposes in Canada.

This is the same Colonel Pickering who has opened his tiger jaws upon me in the newspapers and represented me to the universe as having sacrificed him to a corrupt bargain with Samuel and Robert Smith.[52]

I do not stand on equal ground with Mr. Pickering. A President of U.S. cannot vindicate himself without setting a dangerous example. I have written, however, to the Smiths and enclose the correspondence. Give me your advice. Shall I meet this rancorous caitiff in the newspapers? Return to me the correspondence with the Smiths by the post. . . .

John Adams

---

51. John Muller (1699–1784) was a German-born professor at the Royal Military Academy, Woolwich; he was an authority on fortifications and wrote a treatise on the artillery.

52. Although Robert (1757–1842) and Samuel (1752–1839) Smith were Republicans and supporters of the Madison administration, they were critics of the President's commercial and financial policies. Robert was Secretary of State from 1809 to 1811, when he published the famous *Address to the People of the United States.* Samuel was United States senator from Maryland, 1803–15. Pickering accused Adams of making a corrupt bargain with the Smiths to turn him out of office as Secretary of State; see Adams, *Works,* X, 4–9.

To ADAMS

May 5, 1812

MY DEAR OLD FRIEND OF 1774,

I return you the copies of your letters to the Messrs. Smith and their answer, with my advice (as you have done me the honor to ask it) *by no means to publish them.* "Scandal," Dr. Witherspoon used to say, "will die sooner than you can kill it." I can subscribe to the truth of this assertion of our old Scotch sachem from my own experience. Not a paragraph or even a line did I ever publish in reply to the volumes of scandal and falsehoods that filled our papers against me for more than three months in the year 1797. They have all perished, and I am still permitted to live with as much or more reputation than I deserve in the very city in which those publications were devoured like hot rolls every morning and evening by thousands of my fellow citizens. . . .

The tide of the passions of our nation for war has nearly spent itself. In Pennsylvania it is daily becoming more and more unpopular. I well recollect in opposing Mr. Dickinson's proposal for deferring the Declaration of Independence until we were more numerous and more powerful than we were in 1776, you said to me that time by increasing our numbers and wealth would increase our ties to Great Britain. Late events show that this is the case. The tories have increased four or fivefold by ordinary population, and an immense accession has been made to them of British emigrants and apostate whigs who have become wealthy by successful speculations in certificates and banks.

A declaration of war against France as well as against England would probably unite us and fill the treasury of the United States. It would do more: it would render a war wholly defensive, it would make both nations feel our importance, and it would produce such a reaction in domestic manufactures and internal commerce as would soon make us a great and independent nation. But why have I suffered my pen to run away with me? I know nothing of the subject which, alas! now so generally agitates and divides our country. I shall, however, venture to risk one question before I finish my letter. Do you think if the declaration of war against England had been made last fall, and the public mind thereby been instantly excited and inflamed to the *war point,* that so much clamor would have existed at this time against embargoes, loans, and taxes? . . .

Benjn: Rush

To RUSH

May 14, 1812

FRIEND OF '74,

Say what you will, that man is in a poor case who is reduced to the necessity of looking to posterity for justice or charity; and he who is obliged to fly to Newgate and to Cobbett for consolation is in a more forlorn situation still. . . .

Witherspoon had *Wutt* [wit] and sense and taste, but his maxim is not universally infallible. Scandal may be sometimes killed much sooner than it would die a natural death. You may be as wise as the old Scot, with his mitten-muffled tongue, by saying that scandal is the Devil, the author of all the evil in the universe, the cause of all the wars, dissensions and revolutions, duels, suicides, murders, massacres on this earth. You will soon see the fruits of scandal in the votes of Massachusetts and New York. . . . I would subscribe 100 guineas for a complete edition of all the scandal against me from 1789 to 1801, contained in the circular letters of the members of Congress from all the southern and middle states. . . .

If you can publish a complete treatise of madness, you will instruct mankind in a complete system of religion, morals, philosophy, and policy from the expulsion of Adam and Eve from Paradise to the last embargo and the last vote against an American navy.

By the way, I ought to say one word more about scandal. I know of no remedy against it but *puffing.* Lord Mansfield[53] took a fancy to our

---

53. William Murray, 1st Earl of Mansfield (1705–93), was chief justice of the King's Bench, 1756–88.

Copley.[54] He sat to him for his picture in every stage and station of his life, even to that of Minister Plenipotentiary, in which he had been employed to negotiate some trifling thing in the diplomatic way. He loved to chat with Copley and said to him one day, "Copley, your reputation and your employments and profits are not in proportion to your merits." "My Lord," said Copley, "I do not complain. I am not dissatisfied with my success." "Copley," said his Lordship, "you have not learned your art. You have derived no reputation from the puffers. You must find out and employ the puffers."

These puffers, Rush, are the only killers of scandal. Washington, Franklin—I will go no farther at present—killed all scandal by puffers. You and I have never employed them, and therefore scandal has prevailed against us. . . .

My son-in-law, whom you mention, I assure you never spoke in my hearing one disrespectful word of my man of ten or fifteen or twenty talents. I have never conversed with any officer who uniformly mentioned his general with more affection and respect. Steuben told Smith that Washington once said to him, "Steuben, that Smith was a stiff-backed young man." And this anecdote Smith told me.[55] But not one word did he ever utter in my presence of resentment and disrespect to Washington living or to his memory since his death. . . .

Farewell, friend [of] 1774, for the present.

John Adams

54. John Singleton Copley (1738–1815), the Boston-born portrait painter, came to London in 1774 when Mansfield was already far advanced in his career. Copley painted John Adams' portrait in 1783 and John Quincy Adams' in 1795.

55. Adams' son-in-law, William Stephens Smith (1755–1816), was aide-de-camp to Lafayette and Washington in the Revolution, secretary of the London legation under Adams, and surveyor of the port of New York for a time in 1800. He was a Federalist member of Congress from 1813 to 1815.

CHAPTER 10

The Blackest Cloud

"WITH YOU, I think the present war with Great Britain just and necessary; and with you, I am determined to stand or fall with the national government."[1] Still we may all be ruined, Adams cautioned, if the war continues without leadership, courage, and determination in the state and national government. Uncertainty divides the country, a rebellion troubles New England, and party spirit breeds hypocrisy. Black clouds are indeed forming, but we should not despair: "I say we do not make more mistakes now than we did in 1774.... It was patched and piebald policy then, as it is now, ever was, and ever will be, world without end."

Rush was less sanguine, wondering whether the nation was corrupted too much by selfishness, ignorance, and party bickering, whether the country was worth saving by waging war, whether it would be better to advertise in the newspapers of Europe—"For sale to the highest bidder, The United States of America." He asked Adams to contrast the Revolutionary ardor of 1776 with the crass materialism of 1812 and note how the present ruling groups derived power from military commissions, appointments, banks, funding systems, etc. "We are indeed a bebanked, a bewhiskied, and a bedollared nation."

---

1. Adams to Rush, July 18, 1812, *Old Family Letters*, p. 405. Madison sent his war message to Congress on June 1, 1812, but the bill was not ready for signature until June 18.

To RUSH

May 14, 1812

FRIEND OF 1774,

When I sat down to write to you yesterday, I really intended to write a sober letter; but fell insensibly into my habitual playful strain. I will now try the experiment whether I can write a serious letter to you without anything sportive or extravagant in it.

I cannot see with you that "a declaration of war against France as well as England would probably unite us." On the contrary, it appears to me it would divide us, essentially and fundamentally divide us, and end in a short time in a final separation of the states and a civil war. Instead of filling the loan, it would put a stop to it. Instead of either nation's feeling our importance, it would convince both that they can do without us. It would alienate our navigation and seamen and make them all British ships and British subjects. In such a case we could trade with no part of the world. Our navigation and commerce would be annihilated, which would drive the whole continent, but especially the northern half of the nation, to desperation. For they cannot, they will not, and they ought not to bear it or submit to it. We want no "reaction in domestic manufactures or internal commerce" to "make us a great and independent people." We are both already and want nothing to make it appear to all the world but common sense and common courage. We deceive ourselves if we imagine that our people will become sedentary and turn manufacturers. Where lands are so plenty and so cheap, mankind will never confine themselves to close rooms, hot fires, and damp cellars to through a shuttle or swing a hammer. Besides, if you once stop the exportation of corn and flour, there would be so little raised that we should often suffer a famine for bread. . . .

My confidence in the integrity of Mr. Jefferson and Mr. Madison, in their love of their country and the sincerity of their desires to serve its interests and promote its prosperity, is still entire. Of their genius, talents, learning, industry I am fully convinced, as all the rest of the world is. But either they are shallow statesmen or I am a natural fool. There is no other alternative or dilemma. Mr. Madison has more correct ideas; but as he has been borne up under the wing of Mr. Jefferson, he has been always shackled with Mr. Jefferson's visions and prejudices. But, my friend, as this is a serious letter, I must soberly tell you that the tories of New York and Boston are now retaliating upon Mr. Jefferson and Mr. Madison their own policy. I appeal to your conscience, and I say that you know that Mr. Jefferson, Mr. Madison, John Taylor, John Langdon, Frederick and Peter Muhlenberg, Tench Coxe, Pierce Butler, Thomas McKean, and others . . . set themselves deliberately to spread discontent among the people. . . . This was effected by such a series of libels as never appeared in America before.

The tories of New York and Boston for twelve years past have been retaliating upon them their own policy. An uninterrupted series of libels for eleven years, to be sure, have been poured from the press against Jefferson and Madison, and at last rebellion or quasi rebellion has been produced. An uninterrupted series of libels in like manner had been vomited forth against Washington and Adams during the first twelve years of the national government and produced riots, routs, unlawful assemblies, seditions, and quasi rebellions, if not real rebellions, against them. Compare in old times Freneau, Church, Brown, Bache, Duane, Paine, Callender, &c., &c., with the Boston *Gazette, Repertory, Centinel, Palladium,* Coleman's paper at New York &c., &c., &c., and say whether the motives and the means have not been equally honest or equally diabolical on both sides.[2] I look upon Cabot [and] Parsons, Chew and Willing, Jefferson and Madison, Hutchinson, Oliver, and Sewall in the same light, equally honest, equally able, equally ambitious, and equally hurried away by their passions and prejudices.[3]

2. William Coleman's papers were the *New-York Evening Post* (1801——) and the *New-York Herald* (1802——).

3. Adams was grouping his political figures—New Englanders, Pennsylvanians, and Virginians, and then the three Tories of Massachusetts. George Cabot was a Federalist who had served in the United States Senate (1791–96) and in state offices; he would be a delegate to the Hartford Convention in 1814. Theophilus Parsons (1750–1813) had an influential law practice, and in 1806 he became chief justice of the Superior Court of Massachusetts. Benjamin Chew (1722–1810) was judge and president of the High Court of Errors and Appeals of Pennsylvania from 1791 to its abolition in 1808. Thomas Willing (1732–1821) was president of the United States Bank to 1807. Peter Oliver (1713–91) was chief justice of the Superior Court of Massachusetts at the time of the Revolution.

The Republican party are now split into four or five factions, exactly as the Federal party was in 1799 and by the same causes and the same means. The dissatisfaction is universal, as it was then. I know you have never read my *Defence* and my *Davila*. If you had, you would see that it is always so. When a party grows strong and feels its power, it becomes intoxicated, grows presumptuous and extravagant, and breaks to pieces. There is not now one man upon the continent satisfied with the conduct of public affairs, nor was there one in 1799. What will set us agoing again for twelve years to come? (For it seems it must be a game of leapfrog. Once in twelve years the opposition must skip over the back of the administration.) Will it be fate? Will it be chance? No: neither. But it must be Providence, for there is no man, no party, capable of it.

Who will be President? Mr. Madison? Mr. Jay? Mr. Marshall? Chancellor Livingston? C. C. Pinckney? Mr. [Henry] Clay? or who?

Mr. Madison, I believe, upon the whole, but if he does not repeal his Embargo and Nonimportations, he will have an angry, stormy time, and if he does not set in earnest about raising a navy, he will not live out half of his four years in office.

This is a sober letter, by which an honest man may conscientiously die. Witness,

John Adams

To ADAMS

May 19, 1812

MY DEAR FRIEND OF 1774 AND 1812,

. . . I do not wish to see any of the men you have named in Mr. M[adison]'s place. . . . All Jersey is becoming disaffected. A change will certainly take place in the elections in our state next fall, but how far it will extend I know not. The Embargo is the chief cause of the dissatisfaction in the country, the Nonintercourse Law in our city. . . . There are at present not less than 1,000 houses empty in Philadelphia.

Nations seem to be created as necessarily subject to war as individuals come into the world predisposed to the smallpox and measles. No plans of a general peace, no embargoes, no negotiations, no *Wasps,* nor *Hornets,* nor Pinkneys, nor Barlows, nor appeals to the tribunal of reason, ever have or ever will prevent them while man is *man.*[4] Peace has its evils and its sufferings as well as war, but from the greater share the passions have in enabling us to support the latter, they are borne with more patience and fortitude than the former.

I admit your reasonings upon the subject of a war with France as well as England. I mentioned it as the only consistent measure of the present *Chinese* system of resisting foreign aggression.

You are mistaken in supposing I have not read your *Defence.* The first American edition of the 1st volume of it was printed by my advice in Philadelphia. The facts contained in it may be considered indeed as the history of the present times in the United States.

I write in great haste. Expect a sequel to this scrawl in a few days. . . .

Benjn: Rush . . .

To RUSH

May 26, 1812

FRIEND OF 1774 AND 1812,

I am such a miser that I cannot suffer a letter of yours to remain a day unanswered because my answer procures me an interest of eight per cent a month. I should have said such a *shaver,* for that is now the technical term and signifies more than *miser.* . . .

Men are at war with each other and against all living creatures. Beasts, birds, fishes, and insects are at war with each other and with all other species. . . . All animals take more pleasure in fighting than in eating. The pleasures of existence are not diminished by it. Since it is the destiny of our globe and our rank in the universe, why should a philosopher repine? Storms, earthquakes, famines, pestilences, Georges, Napoleons are but light afflictions and only for a moment. There is philosophy for you! And the

4. The *Wasp* and the *Hornet* were American warships. William Pinkney was minister to Britain, and Joel Barlow was then serving as a commissioner to France.

only philosophy that can make men happy or can keep them so. *Nil admirari prope res est una, Numici, solaque quae possit facere et servare beatum.*[5] There's philosophical poetry for you, which every schoolboy knows and believes as much as you or I. . . .

John Adams

To ADAMS

June 4, 1812

MY DEAR FRIEND,

In spite of the speech made by my wife a few days ago, "that you and I corresponded like two young girls about their sweethearts," I will not be outdone by you in the number and promptness of my letters.

The General Assembly of the Presbyterian Church have just finished a long and interesting session. Among other things done by them, they have addressed a petition to Congress praying that the post offices may not be opened on the Sabbath day. A vote was lost in the Assembly for petitioning the President to appoint a national fast. It was objected to only because a majority believed it would not be attended with success. Are we not the only nation in the world, France excepted, whether Christian, Mohammedan, pagan, or savage, that has ever dared to go to war without imploring supernatural aid, either by prayers, or sacrifices, or auspices, or libations of some kind? How few men know that man is naturally a "go-to-meeting animal," to use your definition of a New Englandman, or in other words that he is as naturally a *praying* as he is a breathing animal. Sailors, soldiers, Indians, nay more, Deists and Atheists, all pray by an unsubdued instinct of nature when in great danger or distress. How differently did the Congresses of 1774, 1775, and 1776 begin and conduct the war with Great Britain that ended in the establishment of the liberties and independence of our coun-

---

5. "Not to form an impassioned attachment for anything—that is perhaps the one and only thing, Numicius, that can make a man happy and keep him so." Horace, *Epistles* I.vi.1–2.

try! They appealed to the God of armies and nations for support, and he blessed both their councils and their arms. Do you recollect the rebuke you gave Mr. Jefferson in Congress upon this subject?

Our papers teem with publications against the *horrors* of war. They remind me of an amendment which Mr. Samuel Adams told me he had moved in a proclamation by the first convention that sat in Boston.[6] It was to strike out the word "horrors" and to substitute in its room the "calamities" of a civil war. The latter word, he said, would alarm less than the former; and war he believed at that time to be both inevitable and necessary for the safety of his country.

It is curious to observe how exactly the sentiments and language of a certain class of citizens upon the subject of a war with Great Britain accord with the sentiments and language of their ancestors in politics in the years 1773 and 1774. There is nothing new under the sun in the feelings, opinions, and conduct of parties, whether in or out of power. Your view of them in your *Defence of the American Constitutions* might pass for a history of the whigs and tories and of the Federalists and Democrats of the United States.

I believe with you that all men who affect to despise public slander are hypocrites. Sir Thomas Browne, a learned and pious physician of the 17th century, says in his *Religio Medici* that "he would rather be exposed to the stroke of a fiery basilisk than of an angry pen,"[7] and yet anger and malice had nothing to feed upon in his excellent character. General Washington, I have heard, felt public abuse in the most sensible manner. Mr. Jefferson told me he once saw him throw the *Aurora* hastily upon the floor with a "damn" of the author, who had charged him with the crime of being a slaveholder. It is even said that paper induced him to retire from the President's chair of the United States.

Physiologists teach us that sensations originally painful sometimes become pleasurable from repetition. In this way only can scandal give pleasure to an innocent mind. From experience I can say this to be the case. I review

6. The Convention of September 1768.
7. Pt. II, Sec. 3: "I had rather stand the shock of a Basilisco, than the fury of a mercilesse Pen."

the volumes of calumnies published against me by my brethren with more than pleasure. They are permanent memorials that the opinions and modes of practice which I introduced, and which my enemies have since adopted, were correct, and that thousands have owed their lives to them. . . .

Benjn: Rush

To RUSH

June 12, 1812

DEAR SIR,

. . . I agree with you, there is a germ of religion in human nature so strong that whenever an order of men can persuade the people by flattery or terror that they have salvation at their disposal, there can be no end to fraud, violence, or usurpation. Ecumenical councils produce ecumenical bishops, and both, subservient armies, emperors, and kings.

The national fast recommended by me turned me out of office. It was connected with the General Assembly of the Presbyterian Church which I had no concern in. That Assembly has alarmed and alienated Quakers, Anabaptists, Mennonites, Moravians, Swedenborgians, Methodists, Catholics, Protestant Episcopalians, Arians, Socinians, Arminians, &c., ... A general suspicion prevailed that the Presbyterian Church was ambitious and aimed at an establishment as a national church. I was represented as a Presbyterian and at the head of this political and ecclesiastical project. The secret whisper ran through all the sects, "Let us have Jefferson, Madison, Burr, anybody, whether they be philosophers, Deists, or even atheists, rather than a Presbyterian President." This principle is at the bottom of the unpopularity of national fasts and thanksgivings. Nothing is more dreaded than the national government meddling with religion. This wild letter, I very much fear, contains seeds of an ecclesiastical history of the U.S. for a century to come.

I recollect a little sparring between Jefferson and me on some religious subject, not ill-natured, however, but have forgotten the time and the particular subject. I wish you would give me the circumstances of the whole anecdote.

The similitude between 1773 and 1774 and 1811 and 1812 is obvious. It is now said by the tories that we were unanimous in 1774. Nothing can be farther from the truth. We were more divided in '74 than we are now. The majorities in Congress in '74 on all the essential points and principles of the Declaration of Rights were only one, two, or three. Indeed, all the great critical questions about men and measures from 1774 to 1778 were decided by the vote of a single state, and that vote was often decided by a single individual. . . . The history of the world is nothing else but a narration of such divisions. The Stuarts abdicated or were turned out and William came in by one or two votes. I was turned out by the votes of South Carolina, not fairly obtained. Jefferson came in by one vote, after 37 trials between him and Burr.[8] Our expedition against Cape Breton and consequent conquest of Louisburg in 1745, which gave peace to the world, was carried in our House of Representatives of Massachusetts by one single vote. . . . What is more awful than all. The Trinity was carried in a general council by one vote against a quaternity; the Virgin Mary lost an equality with the Father, Son, and Spirit only by a single suffrage.

All the great affairs of the world, temporal and spiritual, as far as men are concerned in the discussion and decision of them, are determined by small majorities. The repulsion in human nature is stronger than the attraction. Division, separation are inevitable. . . .

When I hear a man boast of his indifference to public censure, I think of Henry the 4th. A braggadocio in his army solicited advancement and command, and to enforce his pretensions, he extolled and exalted his own courage. "Sire, I know not what fear is, I never felt fear in my life." "I presume then, Sir," said the good-natured monarch, "you never attempted to snuff a candle with your thumb and finger."

Let Mrs. Rush laugh at my girlish folly as she will (which I cannot in

8. The electoral college of South Carolina gave Jefferson a one-vote edge over Adams; when the votes of Georgia and Tennessee came in, Jefferson and Burr tied for the presidency. The tie was broken on the 36th ballot in the House of Representatives, making Jefferson President by a vote of ten to four—only the New England states remaining loyal to Burr. See Noble E. Cunningham, Jr., *The Jeffersonian Republicans: The Formation of Party Organization, 1789–1801* (Chapel Hill, 1957), pp. 244–245.

honor or conscience deny). I will confess and insist upon it that your gentle emollients feel more comfortable to my skin than the blisters of Paine, Hamilton, and Callender.

I have heard much of Washington's impatience under the lash of scribblers, some of it from his own mouth. Mr. Lear related to me one morning the General's ripping and rascalling Philip Freneau for sending him his papers full of abuse.[9]

Many causes concurred to induce the General's resignation.

1. His ministers plagued him as they did me afterwards.

2. He could not get ministers such as he wanted, to serve with Hamilton. Several refused, and he was compelled to take such as he did not like, particularly Pickering and McHenry.[10] . . .

3. He knew there was to be an opposition to him at the next election, and he feared he should not come in unanimously.

4. The times were critical, the labor fatiguing, many circumstances disgusting, and he felt weary and longed for retirement; though he soon found solitude more fatiguing, more disgusting, and longed to return to public bustle again. Besides, my popularity was growing too splendid, and the millions of addresses to me from all quarters piqued his jealousy. The great eulogium "First in war, first in peace, and first in the affections of his country" was suspected by him and all his friends to be in some danger.[11]

5. I believe he expected to be called in again after a four years' respite, as he certainly would have been had he lived. . . . I was then convinced we must have him or Jefferson, and I thought him then the least visionary of the two. Considering his connection with Hamilton, I am now not so clear I was then right.

I must come to an end of my letter, though I shall never find an end of

9. Tobias Lear (1762–1816) was Washington's private secretary from 1785 to 1793 and holder of diplomatic assignments under Jefferson.

10. In the crisis of 1798 Washington told Hamilton that he had long known James McHenry to be "unequal to great exertions." *The Writings of George Washington,* ed. John C. Fitzpatrick (Washington, D.C., 1931–44), XXXVI, 394.

11. The famous eulogy is part of a resolution offered by John Marshall and his committee on Dec. 19, 1799, after Washington's death.

my regards to Mrs. Rush or her husband notwithstanding her just admonition to the incurable, incorrigible scribbler.

John Adams

To ADAMS

June 27, 1812

MY DEAR FRIEND,

. . . The anecdote I allude to respecting the fast day is as follows. Upon a motion for such a day, Mr. Jefferson not only opposed it but treated it with ridicule and hinted some objections to the Christian religion. You rose and defended the motion, and in reply to Mr. Jefferson's objections to Christianity you said you were sorry to hear such sentiments from a gentleman whom you so highly respected and with whom you agreed upon so many subjects, and that it was the only instance you had ever known of a man of sound sense and real genius that was an enemy to Christianity. You suspected, you told me, that you had offended him, but that he soon convinced you to the contrary by crossing the room and taking a seat in the next chair to you. . . .

The declaration of war has produced a suspension of political hostilities in our city, but no change has been induced in the minds of the persons who were opposed to it. They look forward to the next election for new rulers who shall restore peace and trade with Great Britain and make war upon France. Perhaps the increase of the power and influence of the ruling party from military commissions and appointments connected with them may disappoint them. Alas! what dead weights are banks, whiskey distilleries, and the funding system in the opposite scale to that which contains the patriotism, the justice, and the honor of our country! We are indeed a bebanked, a bewhiskied, and a bedollared nation.

Our wise men and women look back to the administration of Washington as the golden age of our country, without recollecting that the seeds of all the disputes which now divide our citizens, and of the controversy with France, were sown in it. I say the controversy with France, for this began in consequence of the offense given to her by the British treaty. But not only the seeds of political disputes but of our vices were sown during the same administration, by the funding system and the passion for banks which was created by the profits of scrip and of the immense interest of the Bank of the United States.

The capital now vested in banks in the city of New York is seventeen millions five hundred thousand dollars. There are twelve hundred whiskey distilleries in Lancaster County *only* in Pennsylvania. There have been 300 bankruptcies in our city since last April, and 700 more are expected, all of which have been produced chiefly by the two evils that have been mentioned, viz., banks and distilleries. . . .

Benjn: Rush

To RUSH

July 3, 1812

DEAR SIR,

. . . What are we to think of history? What dependence can we have on tradition? It lay as a confused recollection in my head that the little flirt between Jefferson and me (the only one that ever happened during our lives) was occasioned by a motion for Congress to sit on Sunday. If your memory and mine differ in so recent a transaction, what are we to think of the traditions of the Roman Church? What of the traditions of the North American Indians? The latter I believe are the least fraudulent. . . .

Never were three words better coined or applied than your "bebanked, bewhiskied, and bedollared" nation. The profits of our banks to the advantage of the few, at the loss of the many, are such an enormous fraud and oppression as no other nation ever invented or endured. Who can compute the amount of the sums taken out of the pockets of the simple and hoarded in the purses of the cunning, in the course of every year? Yet where is the remedy? The Republicans are as deep in this absurdity and this guilt as the Federalists.

If rumor speaks the truth, Boston has and will emulate Philadelphia in her proportion of bankruptcies; and West India and New England rum is as plenty and as precious as whiskey.

I have read nothing from Congress with so much pleasure or profit as the motion to raise annually a revenue of six millions of dollars on four and twenty millions of gallons of whiskey.[12] . . .

July 7, 1812

I believe with you that wars are the natural and unavoidable effects of the constitution of human nature and the fabric of the globe it is destined to inhabit and to rule. I believe further that wars, at times, are as necessary for the preservation and perfection, the prosperity, liberty, happiness, virtue, and independence of nations as gales of wind to the salubrity of the atmosphere, or the agitations of the ocean to prevent its stagnation and putrefaction. As I believe this to be the constitution of God Almighty and the constant order of his Providence, I must esteem all the speculations of divines and philosophers about universal and perpetual peace as shortsighted, frivolous romances. . . .

Our Massachusetts and Connecticut are a little out of humor and are retaliating upon Virginia and Pennsylvania . . . somewhat grossly, but the little eddy in the atmosphere will dissipate and whirl away. A vote to build a few frigates would blow it off at once. . . .

John Adams

To ADAMS

July 8, 1812

MY DEAR FRIEND,

. . . We are much alarmed at the news our papers daily contain of the opposition to the general government in our state. Massachusetts has long and

---

12. The fight over taxation was not decided until 1813. New York congressmen tried to defeat Gallatin's plan for a direct tax on land by providing for a tax on whiskey by the gallon. Henry Clay, by means of a caucus, persuasion, and breaking a tie with his own vote, killed the measure.

justly been considered as the right arm of the Union. Your physical force equals that of our state, but in *mental* force you tower much above us, nor will the physical force of Pennsylvania be brought into full operation upon the present occasion. Alas! our poor country! Even the powers delegated to carry on the war are divided. This has been seen during the whole of the last session of Congress, and lately in the refusal of Congress to comply with Mr. Madison's request to increase the number of general officers. . . .

Among the national sins of our country that have provoked the wrath of Heaven to afflict us with a war, I ought to have mentioned in my last letter the idolatrous worship paid to the name of General Washington by all classes and *nearly* all parties of our citizens, manifested in the impious application of names and epithets to him which are ascribed in Scripture only to God and to Jesus Christ. The following is a part of them: "our Saviour," "our Redeemer," "our cloud by day and our pillar of fire by night," "our star in the east," "to us a Son is born," and "our guide on earth, our advocate in Heaven." [13] With the sin of these epithets is connected two other sins: 1st, ingratitude to all other Revolutionary servants of the public in the cabinet or the field, Alexander Hamilton only excepted; and 2ly, a total unbelief in the divine talents and virtues ascribed to him by most of his companions in arms and contemporaries in the Revolution. . . . What an ocean of political turpitude has been wiped away by the ten letters that compose his name! . . .

Many calculations are made daily of the comparative wickedness of France and Britain and of the comparative injuries each has done us. I resolve the questions thus in *my own family*. France has thrown off all the restraints of religion, natural law, and national justice and professes to be governed only by convenience and self-interest. Britain professes to be a *Christian* nation and the defender of the religion, liberty, and even civilization of the world. Their crimes are the same, but in which of them are they most aggravated? Again France takes and burns our property *only;* Britain robs us of our citizens on the high seas, murders our women and children

13. The use of these phrases in honor of Washington parodies the litany.

on our frontiers, as well as robs us of our property. Which of them has done us the most injury? All this is between ourselves. I *think aloud* only in my own house and when I write to you.

With all the clamors against war with England *only,* and the destruction it is to bring upon our country, how will the minority in the Senate justify their voting for war with both England and France? Its evils must have been double if not fourfold. Alas! the *madness* of party spirit! Where—where is my tranquilizer? . . .

One of the most necessary ingredients in the apparatus of war is still wanting in our country. I mean *war passions.* No person appears to feel them as we felt them in 1774, 1775, and 1776. Even the friends to war talk of it with apathy. Without an *inflammation in our passions,* nothing effective can be done in the mighty contest before us. Reason cannot be substituted for it, "for what did Reason ever do that was great in human affairs?" says Frederick the 2nd of Prussia. He must have meant chiefly in military affairs. . . .

Benjn: Rush

To RUSH

July 10, 1812

MY DEAR FRIEND,

. . . There is an alliance between our Essex Junto and our New England theologians—Unitarians and Athanasians, Hopkintonians and Freewillers and all. *Bos, fur, sus, atque sacerdos,*[14] with a few bright exceptions.

If a Gallatin's Rebellion or a Fries's Rebellion should be excited by this coalition, I will not call it strange. Madison will have nothing to do but imitate my example (proud and impudent as it is in me to say it); he need not put the nation to the expense nor make the ostentatious parade of Washington to suppress it. . . .

The object of all this spiritual and temporal bluster is to get Madison

14. "Ox, thief, pig, and priest."

out. But who to get in? . . . I am the less anxious on this point because I know that, bring in who they will, he cannot essentially or materially depart from Madison's present system. Madison and Madisonians, however, should consider that whoever succeeds him will cherish a naval defense. And if he is rejected, it will be because he has not sufficiently advocated, as I was turned out because I too explicitly recommended, it.

There are several members of the House who have attracted my attention and convinced me that our country abounds with intelligence and talent— a Calhoun, a Lowndes, a Cheves, a Clay, a Porter.[15] These appear to me to be sensible men and honest—Grundy and Harper, too. John Randolph appears to be so tormented by his conscience in recollecting his own conduct in the 18th century that he is nearly fit for your chair.

I know not whether you have read the Address to the People of the State by our House of Representatives, or that of the minority in the House of Representatives in Congress to the People of the Union.[16] I wish my eyes would suffer me to write commentaries on these two studied compositions. . . . I am really grieved; I am ashamed; I am confounded to read such sophistry, such insincerity, such want of candor or want of information in such bodies of American citizens. If Jugurtha should see this to be the general character of American citizens, what would he say?[17] . . . Both parties in the United States have exhibited strong symptoms, made bold and daring advances beyond the boundaries of morality into the regions of ambition, selfishness, and rapacity. And who or what shall stop them in their careers? The lawgivers of antiquity—Solon, Lycurgus, Numa, Zeleucus—

15. Adams mentions prominent War Hawks, or the war party, who have brought the nation into the War of 1812: John C. Calhoun (1782–1850); William Lowndes (1782–1822); Langdon Cheves (1776–1857); Peter Porter (1773–1844). Felix Grundy (1777–1840) was a member of the foreign affairs committee, and John Adams Harper (1779–1816) of New Hampshire was elected as a War Democrat in 1810.

16. *The Debates and Proceedings in the Congress of the United States,* 12th Cong., 1st Sess. (Washington, D.C., 1853), pp. 2195–2222. Thirty-four members of the House of Representatives questioned the desirability of war with Great Britain when firesides and altars were safe and when commercial advantage was connected with British friendship. War instead invited invasion and commercial disaster.

17. Another reference to Jugurtha's famous speech: "O City soon to perish if you find a buyer."

legislated for single cities. But who can legislate for 18, 20, or 30 states, each of which is greater than all Greece or Rome at those times? No human mind, I believe, certainly none that has yet appeared in America, is equal to it. . . .

Mr. Calhoun speaks as I think. I will not charge Jefferson or Madison with cowardice. I believe it of neither. I will not call it weakness, for they are strong men. But I say this country ought to have been better prepared for war, especially by sea. This egregious defect was want of judgment and foresight at least. . . .

John Adams

P.S. Do you recollect the outrageous insolence of Tom Paine, Callender, Duane, and John Randolph, after their triumph in 1800. . . . If such was the triumph of the Democracy by one vote in 1800 and such its insolence and impudence, what would be the triumph of Aristocracy in 1813, if it should effect a change of administration in the midst of war? Our executive is made a mere *testa di legno.* A mere head of wood. A mere football, kicked and tossed by Frenchmen, Englishmen, or rather Scotchmen, and ignorant, mischievous boys. And yet you and Jefferson think our executive too strong.

To ADAMS

July 18, 1812

MY DEAR FRIEND,

During the Revolutionary War I kept notes and preserved pamphlets with a view to write memoirs of it. From the immense difference in my facts and opinions from those that were current and popular, I was sure if I had published them they would not have been believed and would moreover have exposed me and my posterity to persecution. I therefore burnt all my notes (the characters of the gentlemen who subscribed the Declaration of Independence excepted) and gave my pamphlets to my son Richard, who has carried them with him to Washington. . . . Were I compelled to write a history of any of the human race, it should be of my lunatic patients in the Hospital. There I should find *folly* only, for most of them are innocent and some of them amiable. There is not a French Jacobin, nor a visionary Democrat, nor an Essex Junto man, nor a priest deranged with Federalism or Democracy, nor a governor compounding praying and fasting with party politics, among them all.

Wars I believe are not only inevitable and necessary, but sometimes *obligatory* upon nations. "Nil dei mortalibus sine" (not only "labore") but "sine bello." [18] We rise in society and we preserve our property, our names, and our standing in it, nay more, our lives, by means of war. The weapons employed in this war are lawsuits, doors, and locks and bolts. To neglect to employ these weapons is to forfeit those blessings. Nations in like manner can exist with all the prerogatives of nations only by war. It is the condition by which they navigate the ocean and preserve their territory from incursion. To neglect to contend for both by arms is to forfeit their right to them. The ocean has been called the highroad of nations. It might be called God's gift to all nations. Not to maintain the exercise and enjoyment of this gift is (I hope I do not say too much when I add) ingratitude and disobedience to him that gave it. To expect perpetual peace therefore among beings constituted as we are is as absurd as to expect to discover perpetual motion. I have read no other state paper upon the subject of our war but Mr. Madison's message to Congress recommending a declaration of war, but from my knowledge of the authors and subscribers of the addresses you allude to, I am prepared to believe all you say of them. Some of them or of their leaders I know cursed Mr. Jefferson some years ago for his cowardice for not doing exactly what Mr. Madison has done.

I blush for the selfishness, ignorance, and party spirit of our citizens, and in thinking of them have often applied to them the words of Jugurtha. . . . Is our nation *worth* a war? Would it not have been more correct, and more in unison with our habits and principles, had Congress instead of declaring war sent an advertisement to be published in all the newspapers in Europe drawn up in some such form as the following?

18. "The gods have given nothing to mortals without (not only labor but) war." Adapted from Horace, *Satires* I.ix.59–60.

"For *Sale*
to the highest bidder.
The United States of America. . . ."

You are mistaken in supposing that I think our executive too strong. I wish it were wholly independent of the Senate in all its appointments. I wish further that the President should be chosen for 7, 9, or 11 years, and afterward become ineligible to that or any other station or office, with a salary of 2 or 3 thousand dollars a year to compensate for that disability and to enable him to support the expenses to which his having filled the office of President would expose him in subsequent life. This would give him an independence as the first magistrate of the nation that would obviate one half the evils of our government. . . .

July 20, 1812

Our old friend Samuel Adams used to say "nations were as free as they deserved to be" and that "even enslaved nations were free when they preferred slavery to liberty, inasmuch as freedom consisted in possessing the objects of our predilection." Alas! For what have you thought and read and wrote and spoke and negotiated? They have taken away my gods, they have taken away the profits of our banks and whiskey distilleries and reduced the price of our grain. What! what! have we left?—Yes, the last has been taken away for a *time* only, that you may enjoy a high price for it forever. Happy would it be for our country if the two former were taken away forever.

Benjn: Rush

<hr/>

To RUSH

August 1, 1812

DOCTOR RUSH,

. . . You and I have both been to blame. You, for destroying your notes of the Revolution; I, for keeping none and making very few. You have much merit in preserving the pamphlets you have given to the oratorical controller. . . . I am much to blame for preserving no pamphlets. I have been overwhelmed with such multitudes of them in America, France, Holland, and England that if I had attempted to preserve them, I must have said as the Evangelist said in his time of the spurious Gospels, Acts, and Epistles, "the world could not contain them."[19] You was better employed in the service of your fellow men, women, and children. I was fully employed, whether better or worse I know not. I was very safe in bidding high for a true history of the Revolution because I knew, as you know, that no true history of it ever can be written. My premium, therefore, never could have been awarded. . . .

In the investigation of principles and the search of springs, you have gone through as much labor, ran as many risks, and suffered as much hardship as Bruce did in pursuit of the sources of the Nile.[20] But you have done more lasting good to your species by those means than he did. Your writings are worth much more than his, and your life has been much more useful.

I would agree to every part of your amendment of the Constitution. . . .

Sam Adams' liberty was like the liberty of Parson Burr of Worcester, an ancestor of Aaron. The liberty of a man chained hand and foot in a dungeon: that is, a perfect liberty to stay there. The liberty of Sterne's Starling to flutter in his cage when he could not get out.[21] The liberty of the patient in your tranquilizing chair. Sam's doctrine, however, is true and has a good tendency to excite vigilance and energy in defense of freedom. The observation, however, was not original. It was not uncommon before he was born.

One is always in danger of adopting an opinion that human nature was not made to be free. No nation has long enjoyed that partial and im-

19. John 21:25.

20. The heroic attachment that James Bruce (1730–94) had for exploration led him to devote his life to an examination of the Nile River valley. His important book, *Travels to Discover the Source of the Nile* (Edinburgh, 1790), was reprinted in 1805 and 1813.

21. "In my return back through the passage, I heard the same words repeated twice over; and looking up, I saw it was a starling hung in a little cage—'I can't get out—I can't get out,' said the starling. . . . God help thee! said I—but I'll let thee out, cost what it will. . . . I fear, poor creature! said I, I cannot set thee at liberty—'No,' said the starling—'I can't get out—I can't get out.'" Laurence Sterne, *A Sentimental Journey through France and Italy,* ed. Wilbur L. Cross (New York, 1904), p. 241.

perfect emancipation that we call a free government. Banks, whiskey, *panis et circenses,* or some other frivolities, whims, caprices and, above all, idolatries and military glories, luxuries, arts, sciences, taste, mausoleums, statues, pictures, adulatory histories and panegyrical orations, lies, slanders, calumnies, persecutions have sooner or later undermined all principles, corrupted all morals, prostituted all religion; and where then is liberty? . . .

John Adams . . .

To ADAMS

July 13, 1812

MY DEAR FRIEND,

Will you bear to read a letter that has nothing in it about politics or war?—I will, without waiting for an answer to this question, trespass upon your patience by writing you one upon another subject.

I was called on Saturday last to visit a patient about nine miles from Philadelphia. Being a holiday, I took my youngest son with me to drive me instead of my black servant. After visiting my patient, I recollected that I was within three or four miles of the farm upon which I was born and where my ancestors for several generations had lived and died. The day being cool and pleasant, I directed my son to continue our course to it. In approaching it I was agitated in a manner I did not expect. The access to the house was altered, but everything around it was nearly the same as in the days of my boyhood, at which time I left it. I introduced myself to the family that occupied it by telling them at once who I was and my motives for intruding upon them. They received me kindly, and every branch of the family discovered a disposition to satisfy my curiosity and gratify my feelings. I asked permission to conduct my son upstairs to see the room in which I drew my first breath and made my first *unwelcome* noise in the world. My request was readily granted, and my little son seemed to enjoy the spot. I next asked for a large cedar tree which stood before the door, that had been planted by my father's hand. Our kind host told me it had been cut down 17 years ago, and then pointed to a piazza in front of the house, the pillars of which he said were made of it. I stepped up to one of those pillars and embraced it. . . .

The house, which is of stone, bore marks of age and decay. On one of the stones near the front door I discerned with difficulty the letters J. R. Before the house flows a small but deep creek abounding with pan fish. The farm contains 90 acres, all in a highly cultivated state. I knew the owner of it to be in such easy circumstances that I did not ask him his price for it, but requested, if he should ever incline to sell it, to make me or my surviving sons the offer of it, which he promised to do. While I sat in his common room, I looked at its walls and reflected how often they had been made responsive by my ancestors to conversations about wolves and bears and snakes in the first settlement of the farm—afterwards about cows and calves and colts and lambs, and the comparative exploits of reapers and mowers and threshers, and at all times with prayers and praises and chapters read audibly from the Bible, for all who had inhabited it of my family were pious people and chiefly of the sects of Quakers and Baptists.

On my way home I stopped to view a small family graveyard in which were buried three and part of four successive generations, all of whom were descended from Captain John Rush, who with six sons and three daughters followed William Penn to Pennsylvania in 1683 in the 60th year of his age and died in 1702. He commanded a troop of horse under Oliver Cromwell, and family tradition says he was personally known to him and much esteemed by him as an active, enterprising officer. When a young man, I was sometimes visited by one of his grandsons, a man of 85 years of age who had lived many years with him when a boy and often detailed anecdotes from him of the battles in which he had fought under Cromwell, and once mentioned an encomium upon his character by Cromwell when he supposed he had been killed. . . . As the successor to the eldest sons of the family, I have been permitted to possess his sword and watch. In walking over the graveyard I met with a headstone with the following inscription:

In memory of
James Rush
Who departed this life March 16th, 1727
aged 48 years.
I've tried the strength of death,

And here lie under ground,
But I shall rise above the skies,
When the last trump shall sound.

This James Rush was my grandfather. My son the physician was named after him. I have often heard him spoken of as a strongminded man and uncommonly ingenious in his business, which was that of a gunsmith. The farm still retains the marks of his boring machine. My father inherited both his trade and his farm.

While standing near his grave and recollecting how much of my kindred dust surrounded it, my thoughts became confused, and it was some time before I could arrange them. Had any or all my ancestors and kinsmen risen from their graves and surrounded me in their homespun and working dresses (for they were all farmers or mechanics), they would probably have looked at each other with some surprise and said, "What means that *gentleman* by thus intruding upon us?"—"Dear and venerable friends! Be not offended at me. I inherit your blood, and I bear the name of most of you. I come to claim affinity with you and do homage to your Christian and rural virtues. It is true my dress indicates that I move in a different sphere from that in which you passed through life, but I have acquired and received nothing from the world which I prize so highly as the religious principles I inherited from you, and I possess nothing that I value so much as the innocence and purity of your characters." . . .

Mr. Pope says there are seldom more than two or three persons in the world who are sincerely affected at hearing of the death of any man, beyond the limits of his own family. It is, I believe, equally true that there are seldom more than two or three persons in the world who are interested in anything a man says of himself beyond the circle of his own table or fireside. I have flattered myself that you are one of those two or three persons to whom the simple narrative and reflections contained in this letter will not be unacceptable from, my dear and much respected friend, yours very affectionately,

Benjn: Rush

To RUSH

July 19, 1812

DEAR SIR,

. . . Retaliation, the old Jewish doctrine of an eye for an eye and a tooth for a tooth, has revived and taken possession of the world for a time. I shall take advantage of the fashion so far as to retaliate upon you, your family history. I would give more money than the circumstances of my family could afford for such a family history of my friend Jay. Such families are for a time the salt of the earth, and in their course become its poison and its curse. . . .

Henry Adams, a Congregational dissenter from the Church of England, persecuted by the intolerant spirit of Archbishop Laud, came over to this country with eight sons in the reign of King Charles the First. One of the eight returned to England; seven remained in America and left families, who by intermarriages and natural generation have multiplied like the sands on the seashore or the stars in the milky way, to such a degree that I know not who there is in America to whom I am not related. My family, I believe, have cut down more trees in America than any other name! What a family distinction! Have I not a right to glory in it? There are, however, no parchments to prove it, and the fact may be disputed. I do not therefore insist upon it.

This Henry and his son Joseph became original proprietors of the town of Braintree, incorporated in the year one thousand six hundred and thirty-nine, having previously settled near the foot of Mount Wollaston, which was then incorporated with twenty-seven thousand acres of land in the new township. This Henry and his son Joseph, my great-grandfather, and his grandson Joseph, my grandfather, whom I knew, tho' he died in 1739, and John, my father, who died in 1761, all lie buried in the Congregational churchyard in Quincy, half a mile from my house. These were all possessed of landed estates and all tradesmen. They wrought on their farms in summer and at their trades in winter. All reared families of eight, ten, or a dozen children except my father, who had but three. All these children were married and had numerous families; and such was the effect of industry, frugality, regularity, and religion, that death was rarer among them than men and women of 70, 80, 90, and 96 years of age.

You may suppose that we have as steady habits as the pious folk of Connecticut when I tell you that of all the land that was ever owned by any one of the breed is now owned by some one of the name and blood, excepting about ten acres of miserable, barren, stony land which my father was compelled to take for a debt, and which he sold to defray part of the expense of my education at college.

The second house that was built by my ancestor on the original spot was taken down two or three years ago at the age of one hundred and forty years. The land remains in two men, direct descendents, of the same name. I would give twice the value of it; but I should as soon think of asking them to sell me two pounds of their flesh like Shylock. On their first settlement they erected a malthouse *pro more Anglicano,* which converted barley into beer for the whole town and neighborhood. Many a time when I was a little boy have I carried barley for my father to be malted by my great-uncle, captain and deacon Peter Adams, who used to pat my cheeks and pinch my ears and laugh and play and sport with me as if I were one of his younger schoolmates.

In the month of March last I was called to the house in another part of the town which was built by my father, in which he lived and died and from which I buried him; and in the chamber in which I was born I could not forbear to weep over the remains of a beautiful child of my son Thomas that died of the whooping cough. Why was I preserved ¼ of a century, and that rose cropped in the bud? I, almost dead at top and in all my limbs and wholly useless to myself and the world? Great Teacher, tell me.

What has preserved this race of Adamses in all their ramifications, in such numbers, health, peace, comfort, and mediocrity? I believe it is religion, without which they would have been rakes, fops, sots, gamblers, starved with hunger, frozen with cold, scalped by Indians, &c., &c., &c., been melted away and disappeared. . . .

John Adams

To ADAMS

August 8, 1812

DEAR FRIEND,

The paternal farm which I visited on the 11th of last month lies *two miles* further from Philadelphia than the cottage where you once did me and my brother the honor to take a family dinner with my dear and venerable mother. She purchased and retired to it after she gave up business in Philadelphia. I had seen my native place but once since I was six years old, and that but for a few minutes on a winter's day five-and-thirty years ago, a time when war and news and politics occupied my mind so entirely as to exclude all moral and domestic reflections. The impressions made by my visit to that beloved and venerated spot have not passed out of my mind. I hope to revisit it and shall try by every honest effort to purchase it from its present owner.

Many anecdotes of the American progenitor of our family have been reviewed in my memory by association since the day I stood upon his dust. I shall mention two of them which will give you an insight into his character. In one of his reconnoitering excursions during Cromwell's wars, he came to a farmhouse where he was kindly received and waited upon by a pretty young girl of 17 years of age. The whole family were Roundheads. When he left the house, he thanked the family for their civilities to him, and particularly the young woman who had been so attentive to him, and in parting with her said, "When the war is over I will come back again and court this pretty little maiden." This he did, according to his extempore and perhaps unmeaning promise, and married her. She was the mother of all his children and accompanied him to Pennsylvania, where she survived him several years. There is a record of her baptism in the books of a Baptist church in the neighborhood of the place where she lived after she was 80. She had been before that time a Quaker.

When the Old Trooper left England, one of his relations entreated him to leave one of his grandchildren behind him. "No—no," said he, "I won't. I won't leave even a *hoof* of my family behind me." He had been persecuted for his religious principles and left his native country in a fit of indignation at its then intolerant government. His name is mentioned in Fox's *Journal.*[22]

The "retaliation" as you have called it, or the history of your ancestors, has given great pleasure to my family. They were men of whom England was not worthy. How much greater the achievement to subdue a wilderness such as you say they found at Braintree, than to conquer a province! You are indeed "well born," for all men are so who are descended from a long line of pious ancestors. I agree with you that the pleasure we derive from the respect and homage we pay to our forefathers, and from visiting the spots where they worked or walked or prayed, is a proof of *disinterested* benevolence, and I agree further with you that it shows the principle you allude to in all nations and individuals to be a natural one, and to be implanted in us for wise purposes. I possess Butler's *Sermons,* also his *Analogy,*[23] and have read them over and over and marked and selected passages from each of them. They are monuments of the strength of the human understanding. I feel in reading them as if I were in company with a visitor from another planet, alike elevated above ours in size and in the intellect of its inhabitants.

Here I would willingly lay down my pen, but I cannot take leave of you without heaving a sigh over our beloved country. "A blacker cloud" (to use the words of the Bishop of St. Asaph[24] in speaking of the probable issue of the Boston port bill) "never hung over our nation." *Black* from the disaffection of New England to the war, *black* from the *time* (too *late* or too *soon*) in which it was declared, and *blackest* of all from the manner in which it *has been, is,* and *will be* conducted. It has been called a "reelection war," also "a dramatic war." Alas! it has none of the properties of the war of 1775.

You have misapprehended me in supposing that I believe the govern-

22. Rush was reciting family tradition. The John Rush mentioned in the *Journal* died in Warwick jail. *The Journal of George Fox,* ed. Norman Penney (Cambridge, Eng., 1911), I, 199, n. 2.
23. Joseph Butler published his *Fifteen Sermons* in 1726 and his *Analogy of Religion* in 1736.
24. The Bishop of St. Asaph, Jonathan Shipley (1714–88), was a liberal clergyman, friend of Franklin and America, who voted against penalties for Massachusetts in 1774. These quotations are not taken from the bishop's written address, *A Speech Intended to Have Been Spoken on the Bill for Altering the Charters of Massachusett's Bay* (London, 1774).

ment of France to be more profligate than that of England. On the contrary, considering the high pretensions of Britain to piety and morality, I believe her conduct to be more criminal towards the whole world than that of France, for she adds to her wickedness the crime of hypocrisy. . . .

Benjn: Rush

To RUSH

August 17, 1812

[MY DEAR FRIEND,]

I object to your black cloud. An infinitely blacker cloud hung over us in 1774; and an infinitely blacker cloud hung over us in 1797 when I mounted my Rocinante.[25] Nay, a blacker cloud hung over us in Shays's insurrection, in Gallatin's insurrection, in Fries's insurrection than these flying, heat-lightning clouds that the western winds have brought over us.[26] The wind is now northwest as it should be. We may have a thunder gust and a shower; but fair weather must and will follow it. . . .

I acknowledge all the blunders you have hinted at, and a thousand more. But I say we do not make more mistakes now than we did in 1774, '5, '6, '7, '8, '9, '80, '81, '82, '83. It was patched and piebald policy then, as it is now, ever was, and ever will be, world without end. The essential stamina remain and will remain. Health will be restored. The main pillars are founded on a rock. Winds and floods will not shake them.[27] As I said to my wife 37 years ago in an intercepted letter, you and I may rue. But what are you and I to 8 millions of people? What are you and I to the family of man? Great Brit-

25. Don Quixote's famous horse. A polite reference by Adams to Rush's fondness for *Don Quixote.*

26. These revolts were regional disturbances. Shays's Rebellion (1786–87) broke out in central and western Massachusetts as a result of economic conditions which had brought debtor's imprisonment on many who could not pay their taxes. Gallatin's Rebellion, more commonly known as the Whiskey Rebellion (1794), was a protest by western Pennsylvanians against Hamilton's Excise Act of 1791 and the Washington administration's practice of bringing offenders to trial in eastern Pennsylvania. Fries's Rebellion (1799) occurred in Bucks and Northampton counties, Pennsylvania, and was a protest against federal taxation on land and buildings.

27. Matthew 7:24–25.

ain demands of us treason against human nature. She demands of us the repeal and surrender of the law of nations. We project everything, we conduct
everything, as well now as we did in our war, and we are now better united
than we were then. Do you remember the conduct of our war in Canada?
We lost it there by the eternal opposition to it and embarrassment thrown
in the way of it in Congress, and if we lose it now, it will be by the same
means and will be nothing new. . . .

The approaching election is the blackest cloud that I see. I never could
and cannot yet calculate the eclipses of New York and Pennsylvania, their
conjunctions and oppositions; but one thing I know, that New England
must not much longer be despised, trampled on, and trodden under foot.
Commerce must be protected. Naval force for that purpose must be provided. Or—fill up the blank with as many clouds, storms, pestilences,
earthquakes as you will. Your inventive genius, your creative imagination
can suggest nothing too horrible. . . .

John Adams

To ADAMS

August 21, 1812

MY DEAR FRIEND,

. . . Our country is divided into two great parties called Federalists and
Democrats. The former are subdivided into *British* Federalists, *tory* Federalists, and *American* Federalists. The latter are divided into *French* Democrats, *Irish* Democrats, and *American* Democrats. They all hold different
speculative opinions in government and different views of the proper mode
of conducting public affairs. Suppose a ship to be manned by sailors of six
different nations, and suppose no one of them to understand the language
of the other. Suppose the ship to be overtaken by a storm, and the captain
and mates to be able to speak the language of but one class of the sailors.
What do you suppose would be the fate of that ship? Is not this the exact
situation of our country? Can Captain Madison and his cabinet mates under such circumstances bring her into port?

It is one of the laws of epidemic diseases that when two or three of them appear at the same time, the most powerful one chases away the weaker ones or compels them to do homage to it by partaking of some of its symptoms. British and tory Federalism have had that effect upon *American* Federalism. It wears their livery everywhere—that is, it adopts a part of their principles. French Democracy has had the same effect upon American Democracy, so that we rarely see a pure unsophisticated American Federalist or American Democrat. We are not *all* Federalists and *all* Republicans. We are nearly all British Federalists or French Democrats. The former are more numerous and powerful than the latter. Our ancient habits, our commerce, our language, and even our family connections favor this preponderance in our country. . . .

Benjn: Rush . . .

To RUSH

September 4, 1812

MY DEAR FRIEND,

Little can be added to your distinctions of principles and delineation of parties. . . . Permit me, however, to intimate one idea. The pious and virtuous Hamilton, in 1790, began to teach our nation Christianity and to commission his followers to cry down Jefferson and Madison as atheists in league with the French nation, who were all atheists. Your "British Federalists" and your "Tory Federalists" instantly joined in the clamor. Their newspapers and their pulpits, at least in New England, have resounded with these denunciations for many years.

At the same time Great Britain has been represented as the bulwark of civil liberty and the Protestant religion. All the pious souls in the world are in England and America. Napoleon is Antichrist. The millennium is near. You would be utterly astonished to attend one of our Federal churches on a fast or thanksgiving day. Calvinists, Athanasians, Hopkintonians, Arians, [etc.] . . . all most harmoniously agree in representing England as standing in the breach in defense of religion and liberty, and Napoleon and the French as despots, oppressors, tyrants, destroyers of religion and liberty, as sharks, tigers . . . and serpents.

These things have affected and intimidated numbers of your "American Federalists."

At the same time how shall we vindicate our friends Jefferson and Madison? You and I know that they very early read and studied Furneaux' controversy with Blackstone[28] and Priestley's controversy with Blackstone, on the subject of ecclesiastical establishments. They read also Blackburne's *Confessional.*[29] From these and Locke and Price, &c., they adopted a system which they had influence enough to introduce into Virginia. They abolished the whole establishment. This was enough to procure them the characters of atheists all over the world. I mean among the fanatical advocates for establishments, and these have been almost universally the fashionable advocates till very lately all over the Christian world.

But how shall we defend their political administration? For my part I give it up. In everything for twelve years it has been diametrically wrong. Their friends (and I am one of them) will plead in their favor popular opinion, general sense, national sense, and public opinion. If by all this is meant the opinion of a majority of numbers throughout the seventeen or twenty states and territories, it will not be denied. But as such considerations never have been allowed by me to justify myself or reconcile measures to my own conscience or honor, I cannot admit them in favor of Jefferson and Madison any more than in favor of your British Tory or Essex Junto's.

As if heaven spoke in revelation to Jefferson and Madison in condemnation of their systems, this week has brought us the story of the *two Hulls.* Rodgers[30] has shown the universe that an American squadron can traverse the ocean in spite of the omnipotence, omniscience, and omnipresence of

---

28. Philip Furneaux (1726–83) challenged the theories of Sir William Blackstone (1723–80), the great jurist who had pronounced nonconformity a crime in his famous *Commentaries on the Laws of England.* Furneaux denied that religious truths could be morally enforced by civil penalties. Priestley also objected to Blackstone's theories and drew a reply.

29. Francis Blackburne (1705–87) published *The Confessional: Or, A Full and Free Inquiry into the Right, Utility, Edification, and Success, of Establishing Systematical Confessions of Faith and Doctrine in Protestant Churches* (London, 1766) as an answer for those advocating conformity. The Bible was the only necessary test for Protestants.

30. John Rodgers (1773–1838), the hero of the 1811 engagement of his *President* against the *Little Belt,* took the fleet into combat immediately after the declaration of war, chased the *Belvidera* from American waters, and captured many merchantmen.

the British navy. He has shown that American seamen can manage and maneuver great ships as well as small ones. . . .

The war I justify, but the conduct of it I abhor. Not a word should have been said about Canada. The whole resources of the nation should have been sent to sea. If Canada must be invaded, not a foot should have been set on that shore till we had a decided superiority of naval force upon all the Lakes. Trains of field artillery and of heavy cannon and mortars. No rotten carriages. Powder in abundance. Disgrace after disgrace. Disaster on the heels of disaster, ruin upon ruin will be the course. . . . Is Dearborn, is Hull, is Van Rensselaer, is Wade Hampton qualified for the vast system of war and policy they are called to plan and execute?[31] Could not you have selected greater statesmen and greater commanders? . . .

John Adams

31. Henry Dearborn (1751–1829), a veteran of the Revolution and senior major general in the United States army, was highly regarded at the opening of the War of 1812 and was put in charge of the northwest front against the British army in Canada. William Hull was in command of the American forces in Michigan. Military reverses already were causing Americans to question the abilities of Dearborn and Hull. Stephen Van Rensselaer (1764–1839) was then major general of New York's militia. A politician, officeholder, and wealthy landowner, he was an amateur soldier who soon proved his inexperience. Wade Hampton (ca. 1751–1835) had seen service in the Louisiana military district and was then in charge of fortifications at Norfolk, Virginia.

CHAPTER II

Sons Will Blush

"THE NATION," Adams noted, "is greatly and justly alarmed at the imbecility of the last twelve years. But those who brought us into this confusion are the best qualified to bring us out of it." "[I have often been asked] what course I would have pursued had I been continued President. . . . I said that must have depended upon Congress. . . . I would not have repealed the taxes. . . . I would have fortified the frontiers. . . . I would have gradually increased the navy. . . . I would have declared war against Great Britain five or six years ago. . . . I would not have said a word about Canada . . . till we had a decided supremacy of naval power upon all the lakes." In response, Rush first marveled over the vigor of Adams at seventy-seven. "You . . . have united the durable luster of [Dr.] Johnson with the versatility of mind of Bolingbroke at an advanced stage of life in a degree which I have seldom met with in the histories of public men."[1] These comments undoubtedly reflected Rush's own thoughts on his age and health, but he turned quickly to Adams' invitation to comment on the war: "The finger of heaven points to the ocean as the theater on which America must again contend for her independence."

To RUSH

September 6, 1812

DEAR SIR,

Will your tranquilizing chair exorcise demonics? Will it cure the hydrophobia? I am sure our country is possessed—I am almost prone to say, of

1. Rush to Adams, Jan. 8, 1813, *Letters,* II, 1175.

the devil—but Hugh Farmer, my quondam friend, reinforced by Dr. Mead and his great ancestor, the friend and correspondent of Dr. Twisse—convince me that I ought to say only—of a demon.[2]

If your chair can cast out demons, or if it can cure the hydrophobia, I wish every man, woman, and child in the United States were set in it long enough to heal these diseases.

That the nation has one or both these distempers is most certain from their abhorrence of a navy and from their beginning the war upon land or sea before they had army or navy or money, and before they possessed enough of the confidence and affection of each other to be able to procure either. . . .

John Adams

To ADAMS

September 11, 1812

MY DEAR FRIEND,

I will say of the wine which you have done me the favor to accept what you said to me when I called to thank you for the appointment you gave me at the Mint: "You have not more pleasure in receiving it than I had in giving it to a faithful old Revolutionary whig." I hope the wine is of a good quality and that it will assist the influence of the present times in invigorating your body and mind so as to prolong life for many years to come.

I convene in all the sentiments contained in your letters of September 4th and 6th. The thoughts upon a navy I had anticipated and written them to my son. Captain Hull's success[3] strongly points out to us that the ocean,

2. Hugh Farmer (1714–87), English Nonconformist minister and antagonist of Joseph Priestley, wrote *An Essay on the Demoniacs of the New Testament* and other books of a similar kind. Richard Mead (1673–1754) was a distinguished physician who did experimental work on snake poison and its effect upon human beings. Joseph Mead (1586–1638) joined William Twisse (ca. 1578–1646) in publishing a book; their fifteen letters were published in Richard Mead's work.

3. Captain Isaac Hull in the *Constitution* successfully attacked the *Guerrière* on Aug. 19, 1812.

not Canada, should be the theater of our war. The Chinese system, so dear to philosophers and so repugnant to our habits, to good sense, and apparently to the will of heaven, I fear will ruin our country. I shall not wonder nor even complain of a *Northern* Confederacy if a change in measures should not take place after the next election. Our state, it is said, will support Madison and Gerry. Had the proposed taxes and a nonexportation of flour followed the declaration of war (as they honestly ought to have done), there would have been a total change in the representation from Pennsylvania.

The *English* and *Tory* Federalists who deny that we have any cause of war, and who justify all the aggressions of Great Britain, form a bond of union to the Democrats. Did they condemn the conduct of Britain and object only to the manner in which the war has been and is likely to be conducted, they would carry a great body of the Democrats with them at the next election. . . .

I have not broken my head unnecessarily by meddling with the controversy about madness being a demoniacal disease in my work now in the press. Sir John Pringle[4] and Shakespeare thought very differently from your friend Farmer upon that subject. . . .

Benjn: Rush

To RUSH

September 18, 1812

MY DEAR FRIEND,

In the good old English phrase, I give you ten thousand thanks for the muscat wine of Samos, which is now in my cellar, in good order and of good quality. You did not foresee one effect of it. It will increase my love of Greek and Latin more than my patriotism. Oh! How I heard a circle of ladies of the first quality, old and middle-aged, and young, praise it last evening! If indeed there is any such thing as quality in our country.

4. Sir John Pringle (1707–82), physician general of the British Army, was the author of *Observations on the Diseases of the Army* (London, 1752), a medical classic which was edited by Rush in 1810.

When you thanked me, in strict propriety you was in error. You did wrong. I gave you nothing. I was trustee for our country. Had I known a man more fit, more deserving, you would not have been selected. You have given me your own. I have accepted your own. I ought therefore to give you ten thousand, thousand thanks, and you ought to have given me none at all. You have a head metaphysical enough to discern and an heart susceptible enough to feel these nice distinctions and therefore to be convinced that I ought not always to lay under the weight of this great obligation. . . .

You have done wisely in avoiding controversy about the questions whether apostate angels, fallen angels, or in other words devils, possessed the demoniacs of the New Testament, or whether demons and Beelzebub, the prince of demons, possessed people in Judea. The great question whether demons and their prince are the same spirits as the Devil and his angels did not necessarily fall within the compass of your inquiry. . . .

For my part I am of opinion with mad Johnson that all mankind are a little mad. You cannot therefore describe all the species of this distemper nor cure them all. I believe none possessed either by devil or demon. It is all vice or distemper, moral or physical evil.

To be sober, I believe Mr. Madison will be again elected; and upon the whole, I wish it, because I see no man who will be likely to do better. The nation, it is true, is greatly and justly alarmed at the imbecility of the last twelve years. But those who brought us into this confusion are the best qualified to bring us out of it, if they can be made to attempt it in the right way. Madison's private opinions, and Jefferson's, too, are more correct than their public conduct has been, for that has been dictated by their party. . . .

I am perfectly of your opinion that the Federal[ist] denial of the justice of the war, by which they identify themselves with the tories and the English, is as great a blunder on their part as any that has been committed by their antagonists these twelve years. The Federalists are as apt to stumble as the Republicans and are no more to be trusted than they; yet as the latter are in possession of the fond affections of the people, they can do better, if they will, than the former. I speak with deference, however, having been so long out of the world. . . .

John Adams

To ADAMS

_____

November 4, 1812

MY DEAR FRIEND,

Herewith you will receive a copy of my *Medical Inquiries and Observations upon the Diseases of the Mind.* I shall wait with solicitude to receive your opinion of them. . . .

Pray furnish me with the details of the intrigues that led to the permanent establishment of Congress in Washington, and mention the circumstances that led H. to threaten W. with writing the history of his battles and campaigns.

The Democrats of our city begin at last to think that the ocean is the theater upon which the Americans must defend their independence. In the year 1778 I published several numbers under the signature of Leonidas in favor of a navy in Bradford's paper.[5] I have never for a moment changed my opinion upon the subject of its importance to our country. It is the *safest* defense of a nation. It is its *cheapest* defense. It can be managed only by men of *some education.* Illiterate men of all professions and occupations may make brave and popular colonels and majors of an army, but they can neither navigate or fight a ship of war. A navy upon this account will always command the *best resources* of our country in talents and character. It will become the depot of supernumerary sons of all the wealthy families in the United States. It is less destructive to *human life* by diseases than an army, and far less so *to morals.* There are no taverns nor brothels in ships of war. All this is *inter nos.* For I dread above all things having my name connected in any way with a political or military opinion of any kind. . . .

Benjn: Rush

P.S. From the great extent of our seacoast, from the immense number of bays, rivers, and deep creeks which intersect our country, all of which are covered for 8 months in the year with shallops and market or ferry boats,

_____

5. Rush's "Leonidas" articles appeared in the *Pennsylvania Journal* in 1782. His essay on the navy is reprinted in *Letters,* I, 273–277.

and from the heat of our climate disposing our boys to bathe and swim 6 months in the year, our citizens are a kind of amphibious animals, alike at home and in their element on water and land. . . .

To RUSH

November 14, 1812

MY DEAR FRIEND,

. . . You ask me for "details of the intrigues that led to the permanent establishment of Congress at Washington." I am not good at details. My patience has not enough of marble, steel, or adamant in it. Summaries, or rather hints, are better adapted to my capacity.

Congress was scarcely assembled and organized at New York in 1789 before motions were made in both houses to proceed to the designation of the Federal District, the territory of ten miles square, the National City. One proposition was to establish it at New York, another at Trenton, a third at Germantown or somewhere in the neighborhood of Philadelphia, a fourth at Lancaster, a fifth at Yorktown, a sixth at some place on the Susquehanna River, a seventh at Georgetown, an eighth at Alexandria. I know not whether Baltimore and Annapolis were not proposed publicly. They were certainly mentioned and talked about. But the present site was favorable to the fortunes of my friend Carroll of Carrollton[6] and to Washington and Custis, and their favorite as much as Fort Washington on Hudson River had been once before.

Rhode Island had not acceded to the union. Twelve states only were represented by 24 senators. The before-mentioned motions were all debated with great zeal and at great length. When the question was put, twelve senators were in the affirmative and twelve in the negative. The Vice-President must decide. I gave my opinion, in every instance promptly and decidedly in the negative, from the first question to the last inclusively of both. This

6. Charles Carroll (1737–1832) of Carrollton was a signer of the Declaration of Independence and a member of Maryland's legislature. He served as United States senator from 1789 until his resignation in 1792.

contest continued a long time from day to day. Never in my life was I more tortured and agitated. Such a responsibility was a serious thing. Hitherto I had heard all with close attention but said nothing but No, No, No, No, No, No. At last I arose and asked leave to explain my reasons for the constant and persevering votes I had given in the negative, to every plan and project. The speech was not short; but the points that I relied on were. The time was not arrived to define the ten-mile territory or determine the permanent seat of government. The geography of the country and the center of population was not yet sufficiently ascertained. The government was not settled; the people and the House were too much divided, as well as the Senate. No census was yet taken. I was for an adjournment of Congress to Philadelphia, and for leaving to time and more deliberate investigation and consideration to enlighten the legislature before they should decide upon the subject. Upon this, the question subsided and lay dormant for some weeks.

Robert Morris, who was then thought to be infinitely rich, though I never believed him to be worth a groat if his debts had been paid, was extremely impatient to get to Philadelphia. The advocates for the Columbian District and the Washington City entered into underhand negotiation with Morris and compromised ten years' residence in Philadelphia for the permanent seat at Potomac, and were thus boosted up on their hobby by a single vote in Senate. Then Washington, Jefferson, and L'Enfant proceeded to plan the City, the Capitol, and Palace.

Though I was strenuously opposed to the whole system in every grade of its progress, yet Tom Paine has transmitted me to the world and posterity as casting my eye over the great City, its cloud-capped towers and gorgeous temples and palaces, exultingly exclaiming, "Is not this great Babylon that I have builded!"[7] And I never had one friend in the world to contradict the

7. Adams was severely attacked by Paine in Letter II of the seven letters entitled "Thomas Paine to the Citizens of the United States" which appeared in *The National Intelligencer* during 1802 and 1803. "Knowing, as I do, the consummate vanity of John Adams, . . . I can easily picture to myself that when he arrived at the Federal City he was strutting in the pomp of his imagination before the presidential house . . . and exulting in the language of Nebuchadnezzar, 'Is not this great Babylon, that I have built for the honor of my Majesty!'" *The Life and Works of Thomas Paine,* ed. William M. Van der Weyde (New Rochelle, N.Y., 1925), X, III.

lying rascal, tho' hundreds were able to do it of their own knowledge. It was a great neglect and oversight in me not to hire puffers. . . .

John Adams

To ADAMS

November 17, 1812

MY DEAR FRIEND,

. . . A night or two after receiving your last letter, I fancied in a dream that I was elevated upon a bench in our Hospital yard surrounded by between 60 and 70 of my lunatic patients. Deeply impressed with the contents of your letter, I addressed them upon the subject of a navy. While I was speaking, one man came up to me and said, "I am Solon," a second said he was William Penn, a third said he was Numa Pompilius, and all of them asked me how I dared to attempt to instruct them upon the means of defending our country. A 4th spat in my face, a 5th hissed me, a 6th called me a fool, a 7th said I was crazy, an 8th took up a stone and threw it at me. In an effort to avoid it I awoke, satisfied that such would have been my treatment in the House of Representatives in Washington, had I addressed them upon the same subject and had they not been restrained by the habits of civilized life.

The American States consist of three districts, the Northern, Southern, and *Western,* all of which are divided by different interests, habits, manners, and principles. In the midst of them is a gas more powerful than steam in its repulsive nature. A despotic stopper might keep it from exploding, but kept together as those districts are by voluntary association, the gas must operate, and a separation of them must take place unless a conformity to mutual interests should speedily prevent it.

Canada is likely to become to us what Flanders and Hanover have been to England, the slaughterhouse of generations of our citizens, and for no one purpose but such as are of a selfish nature. Admit that we have conquered it. As a republic we cannot hold it as a vassal province; and as a member of the Union, what can be expected from a representation in Congress composed of Englishmen and Frenchmen? When the news of the surrender of Quebec [1759] and all its dependencies reached Philadelphia, Joseph Galloway, Joseph Fox, and a Dr. Evans rode out in great haste to Fairhill, the seat of Isaac Norris, then speaker of our assembly, and told him the news with great exultation.[8] "I am sorry to hear it," said the Quaker sachem. "Farewell now to the liberties of America."

The Stamp Act in 1765 showed the wisdom of this remark. Should the subjugation of Canada or her union with us in Congress take place, with equal propriety might we not say, "Farewell to the Union of the American republics"? A man's evil passions help to keep him alive no less than his good ones. Individual enemies help to make men wise, prudent, and successful in life. Britain and France have been made equally great in national character by their hereditary and perpetual hostility to each other. A circumambient pressure of England on the north and east, and of Spain, France, and Indians on the south and west, would probably have kept our states together for many centuries to come.

It is somewhat remarkable that in none of the works of the primitive fathers or reformers do we find plans for perpetual and universal peace. They knew too well what was in man to believe it possible in his *present weak* and *depraved* state. Such plans have been suggested chiefly by infidels and atheists, who ascribe all that is evil in man to religion and bad governments. The Quakers, it is true, are advocates for universal and perpetual peace. But examine their disposition to other sects. Do they breathe love or peace to any of them? Look at their conduct in politics. Are they more under the influence of Christian principles than other people? Let the immense proportion of Porcupine's subscribers to his paper when in Philadelphia answer this question. . . .

Benjn: Rush

8. Joseph Galloway (1731–1803), famous Pennsylvania Loyalist, served with Adams in the First Continental Congress. He fled to England in 1778. Joseph Fox (ca. 1709–79), Quaker landowner and merchant, was a member of the Pennsylvania assembly. Cadwalader Evans (d. 1773), a Quaker physician, was active in Pennsylvania business ventures. Isaac Norris (1701–66), Quaker merchant and politician, was speaker of the Pennsylvania assembly from 1750 to 1764.

P.S. I spent a few minutes in Mr. George Clymer's company this morning. He *feels* as we do for our country, and he *thinks* as we do of the necessity of its being defended by a navy. He remarked that every ship of war we built would call for two from Britain to watch it, and that in a few years we should draw a large portion of the British navy from her own coast and thus expose her to her European enemies.

To RUSH

November 29, 1812

DEAR SIR,

I have received your valuable volume on the diseases of the mind, which will run mankind still deeper into your debt. You apprehend "Attacks." I say, the more the better. I should like the sport so well that, if I could afford the expense, I would advertise a reward of a gold medal to the man of science who should write the best essay upon the question whether the writings of Dr. Franklin or Dr. Rush do the greatest honor to America or the greatest good to mankind. I have no doubt but such a point mooted would produce a salutary controversy. You would not have been so industrious nor so useful if you had not been persecuted. These afflictions are but for a moment, and they work out greater glory.

Dream for dream. When it was proposed to institute a democracy in France, I dreamed that I was mounted on a lofty scaffold in the center of a great plain in Versailles, surrounded by an innumerable congregation of five and twenty millions, at least, of the inhabitants of the royal menagerie. Such a multitude is not to be described or enumerated in detail. There were among them the elephant, [the] rhinoceros, the lion, the hyaena, the wolf, the bear, the fox, and the wildcat, the rat, the squirrel, as well as the calf, the lamb, and the hare. There were eagles, hawks and owls of all sorts, and storks and cormorants and crows, and ducks, geese, turkeys, partridges, quails, robins, doves, and sparrows. There were whales, sharks, dolphins as well as cod, mackerel, herrings, and even minims and shiners.

My design was to persuade them to associate under a free, sovereign, annimatical government, upon the unadulterated principles liberty, equality, and fraternity among all living creatures. I had studied a long speech, arranged it in exact method, with a beginning, a middle, and an end, with an exordium and a very pathetic peroration, according to the most orthodox rules of the most approved rhetoricians. Throwing my eyes round and gracefully bowing to my respectable audience, I began:

"My beloved brothers! We are all children of the same Father who feeds and clothes us all. Why should we not respect each other's rights and live in peace and mutual love!"

I had not pronounced all these words before the elephant pouted his proboscis at me in contempt, the lion roared, the wolf howled, the cats and dogs were by the ears, the eagles flew upon the turkeys, the hawks and owls upon the chickens and pigeons. The whale rolled to swallow twenty at a mouthful, and the shark turned on his side to snap the first he could reach with his adamantine teeth. In a word, such a scene of carnage ensued as no eye had ever seen and no pen or pencil ever described. Frightened out of my wits, I leaped from the stage and made my escape — not, however, without having all my clothes torn from my back and my skin lacerated from head to foot. The terror and the scratches awakened me and convinced me forever what a fool I had been.

The question concerning Canada is so great and complicated with so many considerations present and future that I do not like to form any settled opinion upon it. Knowing that the result must be uncertain, I leave it to the counsels of the nation, acquiescing in whatever they may determine. Of one thing I am certain, that a decided superiority of force upon the lakes will henceforward be indispensable for us, or a stipulation that neither nation shall have any. It was easy to foresee at the Peace of 1783 that as long as neither party should have any military power upon those waters, none would be necessary, but as soon as one should begin the other must follow. This necessity will now excite an emulation that will cost us as much to maintain, perhaps, as it will to conquer the province when no artillery will be wanted so far from the ocean.

The Christian religion was intended to give peace of mind to its disciples in all cases whatsoever but not to send civil or political peace upon earth but a sword, and a sword it has sent; and peace of mind, too, to millions by conquering death and taking away his sting.

Anecdote for anecdote. I recollect to have heard in 1774 the sagacious prediction of Isaac Norris of Fairhill; and I well remember another of another sachem of equal reflection and penetration.

Colonel James Otis, the sire of all the Otises you have ever seen or heard, told me that in 1758 in company with many members of our provincial legislature, when the conversation turned upon the expedition against Quebec, John Choate of Ipswich,[9] a colonel of militia and member of the House, said the army was gone against Quebec, but he hoped they would never take it. The whole company cried out in astonishment, "What do you mean? No man has been more active in forwarding every measure to promote the enterprise, and now not wish it success! What can have got into your head?" "It is true I have done everything to give a check to the French power; but as soon as the English conquer Canada, they will take hold of us and handle us worse than the French and Indians ever did or ever can." Two years had not passed before the British cabinet ordered Charles Paxton and his Subordinate, Cockle, to apply for Writs of Assistance to break open houses, cellars, ships, shops, and casks to search for uncustomed goods.[10]

Our English cousins by Adam and Eve may laugh at our uneducated sages and heroes; but what then? His forecast was as sure and his bravery as great and his education as classical, for anything that I know, as the Duke of Marlborough's.[11] He was one of our Massachusetts colonels who conquered Cape Breton in 1745. . . .

9. John Choate (d. 1765) was a member of the House of Representatives and the Council of Massachusetts. His military exploits are described in *The Pepperrell Papers,* Massachusetts Historical Society Collections, 6th Ser., X (Boston, 1899), 33–38, 43–48.

10. Adams is referring to the famous dispute over the Writs of Assistance that began with William Pitt's order of 1760 to enforce the trade laws. The issue of their legality arose when a renewal of authority was necessary in 1760 due to George II's death. The surveyor of customs at this time, Charles Paxton (1704–88), served many years in various posts that regulated trade at Boston. James Cockle was the collector of customs at Salem from 1760 to 1764.

11. Adams reaches hard to make a point. John Churchill, the Duke of Marlborough, commanded allied forces in Holland from 1701 to 1711. Choate was a colonel among colonels in the spring-summer engagement of 1745 against Louisburg.

I congratulate you upon the certain prospect of the reelection of Mr. Madison. I have nothing to say, because I know nothing, against Mr. Clinton. I read panegyrics upon him and philippics against him; but these are the common lot of all candidates. His election at this time would have produced such an unnatural confusion of administration and opposition as would have been very dangerous. I am grieved and ashamed at the apostasy of so many people in our northern states. But the French Revolution, its anarchy first and its military despotism at last, have frightened them out of their habitual cool good sense. . . .

John Adams

To ADAMS

December 14, 1812

MY VENERABLE AND DEAR OLD FRIEND,

You have so far outdreamed me in your last letter that I shall be afraid hereafter to let my imagination loose in that mode of exposing folly and vice. My whole family was delighted in contemplating you upon your rostrum in the garden of Versailles and in witnessing the effects of your speech upon your hairy, feathered, and scaly audience. Let it not be said, "De republica America fabula narratur." [12]

I thank you for your kind reception and favorable opinion of my book upon the diseases of the mind. It has been well received by many of my fellow citizens, . . . but not a single physician in our city (one young man excepted) has taken the least notice of it in any of my interviews with them since its publication. . . . It is a curious but not a singular fact that those of them who owe me most obligations are the most hostile to me.

In spite of their malice, aided by all the disadvantages to which my whig principles and conduct during the Revolutionary War have exposed me from the tories, it has pleased God to crown the labors of the evening of

12. "The story is told of the American republic." Rush is adapting for his purposes Horace, *Satires* I.i.69–70.

my life with such abundant success that I am now in easy circumstances. My excellent wife says, "We have enough," and urges me to retire to our little farm in the neighborhood of the city and leave our son James the inheritor of my business. We have now a competent and regular income, chiefly from well-situated real property, and we do not owe a dollar upon note, bond, or mortgage in the world. I would follow my wife's advice by retiring, did not the probable changes in the expenses of my family render it improper. My 2nd daughter and her two children are still with me, and should her husband fall in battle (which is, alas! not improbable, for he is now at Queenstown or in the neighborhood of it with his regiment, the 49th), his whole family would remain with me for life with but a scanty inheritance from him.

I am now visiting Mr. Clymer, who is indisposed. I read your dream to him yesterday. He was delighted with it. "What an imagination," said he, "the old gentleman possesses!"

Captain Decatur's victory has produced a navy ardor in our city such as I never witnessed before.[13] I wish it may excite equal enthusiasm for a navy in Washington. . . .

Benjn: Rush

To RUSH

December 8, 1812

DEAR SIR,

On horseback on my way to Weymouth on a visit to my friend Dr. Tufts, I met a man leading a horse, who asked if I wanted to buy a horse. . . . I found [the animal] . . . was a colt of three years old that month of November, his sucking teeth were not shed, he was 17 or 18 hands high, bones like massy timber, ribbed quite to his hips, every way broad, strong, and well filled in proportion, as tame, gentle, good-natured and good-humored as a

13. Stephen Decatur (1779–1820) defeated and captured the British frigate *Macedonian* on Oct. 25, 1812.

cosset lamb. Thinks I to myself, this noble creature is the exact emblem of my dear country. I will have him and call him my Hobby. He may carry me five and twenty or 30 years if I should live. I [will] ride him every day when the weather suits, but I should shudder if he should ever discover or feel his own power. By one vigorous exertion of his strength, he might shake me to the ground, on the right hand or the left, pitch me over his head, or throw me back over his rump.[14] . . .

One day after a long ride upon Hobby I came home well exercised, in good health and spirits, went to bed, to sleep, and dreamed.

An open theater was erected in the center of a vast plain in Virginia, where were assembled all the inhabitants of the U.S., eight millions of people, to see a new play, advertised as the most extraordinary that ever was represented on any stage, excelling Menander, Terence, Shakespeare, Corneille, and Molière.

I shall not give you the dramatic persons at length. . . . I shall only give you a hint of a part of one scene.

A distant view of the ocean was presented with Hull and his *Constitution* blazing away his horizontal volcano of a broadside at the *Guerrière,* which is soon seen to explode; after the explosion, the *Constitution* sails majestically but slowly along the whole length of the theater and comes to anchor, in full sight of the audience; then Jones with his *Frolic*[15] succeeded and anchored near the *Constitution,* and it was remarkable that the audience applauded him with as much enthusiasm as Hull. . . . After a pause for the spectators to gaze and admire, Mrs. Siddons was selected to address the audience.[16] Slowly and gracefully swimming over the stage, she approached

14. Adams' literary image was undoubtedly inspired by Laurence Sterne. See *The Life and Opinions of Tristram Shandy,* ed. Wilbur L. Cross (New York, 1904), I, 22–37 (Bk. I, Ch. viii–x): "The thing I had in view was to shew the temper of the world." The imaginary horse allowed one to go through life riding his own special hobbies.

15. Jacob Jones, commander of the *Wasp,* captured the British ship *Frolic.* New York City gave a celebration in the fall of 1812 for "Hull and the *Guerrière,*" "Decatur and the *Macedonian,*" and "Jones and the *Frolic.*" See Irvin Anthony, *Decatur* (New York, 1931), p. 195.

16. Sarah Siddons (1755–1831) was a well-known actress of the London stage, a woman of great beauty, grace, and dignity.

near enough to be heard by all, with all the advantages of her face, figure, gestures, and intonations, pointing with her hand to the glorious spectacle of the navy, in the words of Adam to Eve when she first saw her face in the clear stream, she only said,

"America! This, fair Creature, is thyself!" [17]
"Samson! There, is thy Lock of divine Power!"
"Hercules! Behold the emblem of thy Strength, [which] is to subdue
    Monsters and conquer Oppressors."
"David! Lo, thy sling, which is to bring Goliath to Reason!"

Observing that this overgrown colt of a nation had, after all this, no feeling of its strength nor any sense of its glory, any more than my Hobby, I obtained a speaking trumpet and made a motion, which was carried, that the play should be dismissed and the nation resolve itself into a committee of the whole house on the state of the nation, Dr. Rush in the chair. It was my intention to record the phizzes of the tories, about one third; the speeches of the deep Democrats, about another third, who abused me so much a dozen or fourteen years ago on account of my navy, which is now saving them from destruction.

The exultations of the remaining third, who had been always friendly to naval defense, which . . . amounted to little more than "Did we not always tell you so?"

The sensations and reflections of Jefferson, Madison, Giles, &c., as well as their orations, you may imagine. . . .

I shall give a sketch only of the speech of John Randolph, and that only on a separate piece of paper which I conjure you by our friendship to burn, the moment you have read it, for it is fit only to be seen by your eye. . . . The vote was called and a small majority heavily and languidly appeared for a few 74 and twenty frigates.

Oh! The wisdom! The foresight and the hindsight, the rightsight and the leftsight; the northsight and the southsight, the eastsight and the westsight,

---

17. Milton, *Paradise Lost*, I V.468: "What there thou seest, fair creature, is thyself."

that appeared in that august assembly! Many Quaker women, Dr. Dwight, and Dr. Osgood spoke, and had Joel [Barlow] been there, no doubt he would have delivered an epic poem.[18]

So much business could not be done in a short time. The sun now blazed through the windows upon my eyes and awoke me. . . .

John Adams

To ADAMS

December 19, 1812

MY DEAR FRIEND,

Better and better! Dream on, my venerable friend! In one of the King of Prussia's poetical letters to Voltaire written immediately after reading his *Henriade,* he tells him that he had dreamed that he had visited Elysium, where he saw Homer and Virgil walking with dejected countenances.[19] They were on their way, they said, upon asking them what was the matter, to Minos, to ask permission to return for a short time to the earth in order that they might burn their respective epic poems, now become obsolete and dishonored by the superior merit of the *Henriade.* Could I obtain permission from my patients and my pupils, I would visit Quincy and there search in your desk for all my dreams in order that I might burn them (if you have not in kindness to me done it already) to prevent their being disgraced by your speech in a dream in the garden of Versailles and your subsequent dream of events and scenes in Washington.

---

18. Timothy Dwight (1752–1817), president of Yale College from 1795 to 1817, was a member of the "Hartford Wits," poet, essayist, and preacher of prominence. David Osgood (1747–1822), a Congregational pastor at Medford, Mass., for fifty years, was a zealous Federalist and outspoken foe of the War of 1812. Barlow's popular poem, *The Columbiad* (Baltimore, 1807), was reprinted many times during these years.

19. Rush may have read Frederick II's account in some place other than in the letters to Voltaire. Frederick in a letter to Voltaire, Aug. 8, 1736 (*Posthumous Works of Frederic II, King of Prussia* [London, 1789], VI, 5), praises the Frenchman's poetry, saying: " . . . you ennoble the art." In a preface to the *Henriade,* Frederick writes of the poem and speaks of Henry IV's dreams (*Posthumous Works,* V, 332). Frederick has many comments on the *Henriade* (VI, 23–24, 207, 329, 462, 476, 499–531).

I recollect the last verse of a song which a British lieutenant with whom I crossed the ocean on my return from England in 1769 used to sing to the cabin passengers every Saturday night. It was composed in honor of Prince Ferdinand and the Marquis of Granby after the celebrated victory of Minden.[20] In describing the restraint imposed upon the valor of the Marquis, whom he compares to a lion, the chorus concludes with "While Sackville held him by the tail." Say, my friend, who is the Sackville that holds the patriotism and valor of our country by the tail? Who is it that has clipped the wings of the American eagle in order to prevent her spreading them upon the ocean? Who has broken her bill in order to prevent her picking out the eyes of the British lion?

But I hasten from this painful subject to pay my respects to Mr. Hobby. "Tread gently and safely, highly favored beast, while your master bestrides your back. Shake every blood vessel of his body, and gently agitate every portion of his brain. Keep up the circulation of his blood for years to come, and excite aphorisms and anecdotes and dreams for the instruction and amusement of his friends by the action of his brain upon his mind. Be assured, Mr. Hobby, your master will not be ungrateful to you for your services. He will not send you to vendue *and sell you for 75 dollars* after the painful and disinterested labors of your life are over.[21] . . . When you pay the debt of nature, he will not permit your carcass to furnish a repast for weeks to buzzards and other birds of prey, but decently inter you beneath the shade of one of the ancient and solitary oaks of his fields, and say of you as he turns his back upon your grave: 'Alas! my Hobby!—but you have done your DUTY, and this is more than can be said of most of the heroes and philosophers of ancient or modern times.'" . . .

Benjn: Rush

20. Prussian and British forces led by Prince Ferdinand of Brunswick and the Marquis of Granby won a victory over France at Minden. Complete destruction of the army was prevented, however, by the action of George Sackville (1716–85), who was later court-martialed and publicly disgraced for his failure to carry out orders.

21. Rush is referring to a current story about Washington. See his extended remarks in the letter of Jan. 8, 1813.

To RUSH

―――――――――――――――――

HONORED AND LEARNED SIR,

Be pleased to accept my humble duty for the notice you have conde-
scended to take of me. I will do my best to shake a little animation into my
master for a few days or months or possibly years. But what is the prospect
before him? What can he expect? or hope? or wish? He is 77 and more; three
and twenty years will make him 100; thirteen years will make him 90; three
years will bring him to four score. And what are three, thirteen, or three and
twenty years at any stage of life, in infancy, manhood, or old age? especially
in extreme old age? How many pains and aches, which I cannot shake away,
has he to endure? How much low spirits? How many gloomy, anxious
moments for the dangers, disgraces, disasters, degeneracy, vices, follies, ignorance, stupidity, and vanity of his country? How many wives, daughters,
sons, grandchildren, brothers, cousins may he lose in 23, 13, or 3 years? How
many of the few remaining public political friends must disappear? Even
Dr. Rush himself? Oh! If he were to read this, he would shed many tears.
Pray conceal it from him! But there are other things. How much ecclesiastical bigotry, superstition, and persecution may he have to bewail? How
much calumny, intrigue, party spirit, political fury, and civil war may he
have to deplore? I will leave the rest, Sir, to your profound reflections. I will
only compare the foregoing periods with some of his past life. Fifteen years
he spent at schools, male and female, grammar and A.B.C. When he played
truant, and when he did not, he spent all his mornings, noons, and nights
in making and sailing boats, in swimming, skating, flying kites, and shooting in marbles, ninepins, bat and ball, football, &c., &c., &c., quoits,
wrestling, and sometimes boxing &c., &c., &c., and what was no better,
running about to quiltings and huskings and frolics and dances among the
boys and girls!!! These 15 years went off like a fairy tale. Apply such a 15 years
to his present age and it will make 93.

He then spent 4 years at college. He had begun to love a book. Farewell,

288 · THE SPUR OF FAME

shooting, skating, swimming, and all the rest. Oh! the mathematics, the metaphysics, the logic, not forgetting classics! Seeking books and bookish boys, devouring books without advice and without judgment. The 4 years were gone like a tale that is told. Add such a 4 years to his present age and it will make him 81.

He then passed 3 years at Worcester, among black-letter French and Latin law, and kept a school to pay for the privilege. The 3 years were gone seemingly in the twinkling of an eye. Add such a three years to his present age and it will make him 80. He then removed to Braintree, County of Suffolk, in Massachusetts, where he spent 17 years at the bar, riding circuits, getting money and a wife and children. But the 17 years flew away like the morning cloud. Add 17 such years and you will make him 90. Four years were then spent in Congress, you know how. But they were gone like a dream. Add 4 such years to his present age, and you make him 81. Then he was ten years in Europe, on the mountain wave, over the hills and far away. But the 10 years were gone he scarcely knew how. Add 10 such and they will make him 87. He had then an interval of eight or nine months. Then he was 8 years Vice-President, a target for the archers, a constant object of the billingsgate, scurrility, misapprehensions, misconstructions, misrepresentations, lies, and libels of all parties. These 8 went away like a nauseous fog. Add such an 8 to his age, and you make him 85. He was then President for 4 years. A tale told by an idiot, full of sound and fury, signifying nothing. Vanity of vanities, all was vanity! Add such a four years and you would infallibly kill him long before he would be 81. Twelve years have passed in solitude, far the pleasantest of all; yet where are they? Gone like the dew, the blossoms, the flowers, and the leaves. Add such another 12 and you make him 89; withered, faded, wrinkled, tottering, trembling, stumbling, sighing, groaning, weeping! Oh! I have some scruples of conscience, whether I ought to preserve him; whether it would not be charity to stumble and relieve him from such a futurity. Add only 24 such years as have passed since his return from Europe to America and you make him 101, an object of wonder and of pity to a gaping, staring world!

And now, my venerable, learned, philosophical, religious, virtuous, excellent Sir, permit me to ask whether this address is not as monitory a moral essay as any in Johnson's *Rambler* or his *Prince of Abyssinia?* Remember, too, it is a Horse that asks the question, and that Horse is

Hobby[22]

To RUSH

December 27, 1812

DEAR SIR,

Letters! What shall I say of letters? Pliny's are too studied and too elegant. Cicero's are the only ones of perfect simplicity, confidence, and familiarity. Madame Sévigné has created a sweet, pretty little amusing world out of nothing.[23] Pascal's *Provincials* exceed everything ancient or modern; but these were labored with infinite art.[24] The letters of Swift and Pope are dull! Frederick's to Voltaire and D'Alembert are sickish and silly. His adulation of Voltaire is babyish. He knew nothing of Homer or Virgil. He was totally ignorant of the language of both. Have mercy on me, posterity, if you should ever see any of my letters.

But, *majora canamus!*[25] Last evening I dined with about twenty of our most learned, most scientific, most tasty, most opulent, and most fashionable gentlemen in Boston, at Mr. Peter Chardon Brooks's.[26] As I am incontestably the greatest man (you know) in this part of the world, I am always placed, of course, on the right hand of the lady or gentleman host. The

22. Note that Hobby's addition is sometimes inaccurate.

23. Marie de Rabutin-Chantal, Marquise de Sévigné (1626–96), studied the art of letter writing and carried on a long correspondence with her daughter, son, and many distinguished French personalities. Her letters to her daughter appeared in six volumes between 1734 and 1737; later editions gave a wider and better collection of her correspondence.

24. Blaise Pascal (1623–62), French religious philosopher, wrote eighteen letters—polished pieces of prose done with dramatic power, religious conviction, irony, humor, and eloquence—in defense of Antoine Arnauld, who was denied absolution by his parish priest for alleged Jansenist tendencies. See *Les Lettres provinciales de Blaise Pascal,* ed. Hugh F. Stewart (Manchester, Eng., 1920), xxxvii.

25. "Let us sing of higher things." Virgil, *Eclogues* IV.1.

26. Peter Chardon Brooks (1767–1849), successful merchant in the East India trade, was president of the New England Marine Insurance Company and a state senator from 1806 to 1814.

rich and honorable Mr. Thorndike, a very well-bred man, really very much of a gentleman, the great rival in wealth of my friend Gray, was by the master of ceremonies placed next to me.[27] When the most clamorous demands of appetite began to be a little appeased, Mr. Thorndike said to me, "Sir, . . . you have been so long and so invariably the friend and advocate of a navy that these late victories at sea must have given you peculiar pleasure." The most accomplished, the most finished courtier in Europe, you see, could not have more delicately touched the vein in my system the most susceptible of flattery. You will easily believe it gave a spur to my vanity, set my imagination on the wing, freshened and quickened my memory, and set my tongue a running with mighty volubility.

I assured Mr. Thorndike that our naval conquerors had given me the most complete satisfaction, that I contemplated them and their immortal victories with the highest delight. "I thought," said Mr. Thorndike, "it could not be otherwise; but is it not surprising that our navy should have been so long neglected by our government? . . . The experience we had of its utility, twelve or fourteen years ago, . . . and since, in the Mediterranean, and indeed in the Revolutionary War, one would have thought, should have been sufficient to convince the government." My surprise, Mr. Thorndike, is as great as yours, that it has not convinced the whole nation; but there seems to be a general disposition to forget everything that has been done at sea. "Why," said Mr. T., "I have a general notion that the little force we had in the Revolution was beneficial, but I was young and I wish we knew more about it; the public seems to have very little information of its history."

If an old man's garrulity, Mr. T., could be pardoned, I could give you a rough sketch. A Captain John Manley in 1775 offered General Washington to go out and take him some prizes.[28] Washington, dreading the responsi-

27. Both Israel Thorndike (1755–1832) and William Gray (1750–1825) were prosperous and wealthy owners of merchant vessels. Thorndike served thirteen terms (1788–1814) in the Massachusetts legislature, and Gray was lieutenant governor for two terms (1810–12).

28. Before the Revolution John Manley (ca. 1734–93) was commander of vessels trading with the West Indies. When the war broke out, Washington gave him command of the *Lee*, which made fortunate captures of enemy ships until 1777, when he was imprisoned by the British. Released and exchanged twice in the next four years, he ended his naval career as commander of the *Hague* in 1783, when he took the last valuable prize of the war.

bility and doubting his authority, wrote to Congress.[29] Silas Deane made a motion to commit the letter. I seconded the motion. But oh! the debate, the opposition, the terror of taking the bull by the horns. However, in spite of all the learning, eloquence, and pathos of opposition, we carried a vote of commitment by a majority, though very small. The committee were Silas Deane, John Langdon, and John Adams. We met and, unanimous, in an instant agreed and reported a resolution authorizing Washington to fit out a vessel. But oh! the opposition! Oh, the tedious debate!

At last we carried it by a majority of one or two. Manley was fitted out and took transports with soldiers, clothing, arms, ammunition, and the noble mortar which was called the *Congress* and drove the British army from Boston and navy from its harbor. "Oh!" said Mr. Thorndike, "I have seen Manley and remember the story of the mortar." The mortar is still in being (I continued) and this success made our little majority more valiant and enterprising. We moved for a committee to build, purchase, equip, officer, man, provision, &c. a number of ships of war. After an obstinate opposition and a tedious debate, we carried this resolution by our small majority. John Langdon, John Adams, Governor [Stephen] Hopkins, Richard Henry Lee, Christopher Gadsden were chosen the committee, Silas Deane having been turned out of Congress by his state.

We met every night and sat often till midnight, and in a few weeks had a fleet at sea under [Esek] Hopkins, who went and took the island of New Providence [in the Bahamas] and brought home all the cannon and public property. We were now able to carry a vote to grant letters of marque. But the opposition was still as eloquent, pathetic, and tedious as ever.

The privateers and public ships were soon so successful that Congress grew bolder. Some of the anti-navalists went out, and Robert Morris came in and proved a respectable reinforcement of our naval majority. Congress now appointed a committee of one for each state and ordered twelve new frigates to be built at one vote. "Astonishing," said Mr. Thorndike, "six and thirty years ago!" "Pray, considering the present population, wealth, extent of commerce, number of seamen, naval skill, &c., what naval force could

29. Washington's vigorous part in getting the Revolutionary navy started is described by William Bell Clark, *George Washington's Navy* (Baton Rouge, 1960), pp. 3–14.

this country now produce in proportion to what you had then?" Twenty ships of the line and forty frigates, Mr. Thorndike, could in my opinion be now provided and supported with less difficulty and be less burdensome to the nation than our flotilla was then. "I believe it," said Mr. T. "Why then does not our government exert itself in this way?" Why! Ah, why! said I, smiling. Why does not the town of Boston exert itself now as it did then? One thousand British ships were condemned as prizes in Judge Nathan Cushing's court of admiralty in Boston in that war.[30] "A thousand! You amaze me." Look into the record of that court and you will see a thousand and odd. Boston was then all alive. Privateering was in fashion. Now that rich and powerful city has not a ship that I have heard. Here the colloquy ended. I was called to the carriage to return with my family to Quincy.

You ask, "Who is the Sackville that holds the lion by the tail? that holds the patriotism and valor of our country by the tail? that has clipped the wings of the American eagle in order to prevent her spreading them upon the ocean?" . . . Shall I answer like my countrymen? Who has held France by the tail? Who has held Holland by the tail? Who would have held England by the tail, if she had been a continental power? The answer is the landed interest and its jealousy of the commercial interest. The great proprietors in France are never satisfied with armies. They would multiply them without end, but will never suffer much to be done for a navy. They love to serve by land but hate to go to sea. In Holland the four inland provinces would never vote for ships unless the three maritime provinces would vote for more troops. The consequence of their mutual jealousy has been the annihilation of their navy, army, and country, too. We are going the same way.

If this answer is not the point, let me add the southern and middle states held the lion by the tail the first 8 years of this century and the northern are now holding him. If this is not particular enough, I will be more personal. On the 16th January, 1804, I wrote to a correspondent, "I wish Jefferson no ill; I envy him not. I shudder at the calamities which I fear his conduct is preparing for his country, from a mean thirst of popularity, an inordinate ambition, and a want of sincerity."

30. Nathan Cushing was judge of the Plymouth district of the admiralty court. Clark lists some 55 seizures of vessels for 1775–77 (*George Washington's Navy*, Appendix B, pp. 229–236).

Madison was his pupil, held the tail of the noble animal too long, and I fear has not yet entirely let go his hold. Thus I have answered your question with more candor than prudence; and now you ought with the same sincerity to give me your sense of the question. . . .

December 29, 1812

I have not done with your letter of the 19th. . . . You must know that I have the honor to be president of the American Academy of Arts and Sciences, of the Massachusetts Society for Promoting Agriculture, and of the Board of Trustees of this Society and of the Board of Visitors of the Professorship of Natural History at the University. There are twelve of us of these boards. We meet once a month, on the last Saturday, at each other's houses at our own expense. Every one but myself is a staunch Anti-Jeffersonian and Anti-Madisonian. . . . These are all real gentlemen; all but me, very rich; have their city palaces and country seats, their fine gardens and greenhouses and hot houses, &c., &c., &c. Men of science, letters, and urbanity, even *Spartacus out of a newspaper or a pamphlet* is all this.[31]

On the last Saturday of October at Mr. Pomroy's of Brighton, the gentlemen were in good spirits and indulged in a little political conversation, the detail of which would be too long. I had not agreed to the selection of Mr. [De Witt] Clinton, though I should acquiesce if he were chosen.

Spartacus the Slave![32] Spartacus the Rebel! Spartacus the Rebel Slave! Spartacus the Rebel Leader of Rebel Slaves! asked me with an air of candor what course I would have pursued had I been continued President to this time? I said that must have depended upon Congress. The gentlemen expressed a wish to know my single opinion of the best plan. I said time would fail me to give details, but I could give in short hand a sketch of a few principal strokes. . . . I said I would not have repealed the taxes; no, not a shilling of them. With that revenue I would have fortified the frontiers on the lakes and rivers as well as on the ocean. I would have gradually increased the navy

31. Adams is undoubtedly referring to John Lowell, Jr. (1769–1840), known as the "Little Rebel" or "Boston Rebel" for his radical secessionist position during the War of 1812.

32. Spartacus led a successful revolt at Capua in 73 B.C. Other discontented peoples joined him until his army numbered 90,000 men. In 71 B.C. Crassus challenged him in Lucania and destroyed his forces. See Plutarch, *Lives*, "Crassus," VIII–XI.

by additional ships every year that we might be in a condition to meet the mighty mistress of the ocean on her own element and convince her that she is not all powerful there. I would have declared war against Great Britain five or six years ago when the King issued that most atrocious of all violations of the law of nations, his proclamation for impressing seamen from our ships. I would not have said a word about Canada; . . . I would not have invaded it till we had a decided supremacy of naval power upon all the lakes and waters from Michilimackinac to Montreal if not to Quebec; nor then till I had an army of 35 or 40 thousand men. With such an army in four divisions, a small one in Michilimackinac, a larger at Kennebec River, a larger at Detroit, and the largest of all at Niagara, I would have made short work with Canada and incorporated it into the union. "What a satire," said Spartacus, "upon our administration!" Here I was called to my carriage to come home, having a dozen miles to ride after dark, and consequently heard no more remarks.

Ever yours,

John Adams

December 30th. This moment the sun rising in the southeast and blazing with glorious effulgence on my eyes, through the window, reminds me of the glorious news in last night's paper, from Washington, of the law to build four 74 and six 44s. *Io triumphe!*[33] The sun now shines upon our country. A happy New Year!

John Adams again.

To ADAMS

January 8, 1813

MY DEAR FRIEND,

. . . I was much gratified with your account of your conversations at two late public dinners. But I was more struck with the wonderful health and

---

33. "Hail the triumph!" This was the shout of the Roman soldiers and crowd on the occasion of a triumphal procession.

spirits which you discover in being able at 77 to occupy a chair at a large convivial board, to take an active part in the subjects that are usually discussed in such companies, and afterwards to ride 12 miles in the dark or by moonlight to Quincy. It was said of Dr. Johnson after he published his *Lives of the Poets* that, "like *tin,* he was bright to the last." . . .

You have given the true reason for the hostility to a navy at Washington. Were the resources of our country which are now thrown away on the borders of Canada concentrated in a navy, very different would be the situation of the United States. The finger of heaven points to the ocean as the theater on which America must again contend for her independence. Your anecdotes of the laborious birth of our little navy in the beginning of the Revolutionary War are truly interesting. You may add to them what I once saw from the pen of Paul Jones and heard from the lips of Commodore Barry.[34] In the journal of the former are the following words: "My hands first hoisted the American flag."[35] The latter with equal exultation once said to me, "The British naval flag first struck to me," alluding to his having taken the first British sloop of war. . . .

Remember me most gratefully to my friend Hobby, and thank him for his admirable letter. Read my lecture to him on the veterinary art, and tell him of my regard for his whole species. I admire nothing more in the character of Howard than the provision he made for all his superannuated horses.[36] I was charmed in hearing of the affection of Burke for this noble animal. In walking through one of his fields at Beaconfield, he suddenly left his company and ran towards a horse which he embraced and kissed. "This horse," said he to his company when they came up to him, "was rode by my deceased son." A physician died in this city about 20 years ago and left a horse on which he had visited his patients for many years. His son declared he should never be rode nor worked again. He sent him to a farmer in the neighborhood of Philadelphia, where he was well fed and lived and died

34. John Barry (1745–1803) participated in many naval engagements during the Revolution as commander of the *Lexington* and the *Effingham.*

35. John Paul Jones (1747–92) began his naval career on the same day that the Continental Congress adopted the design of the United States flag.

36. John Howard (ca. 1726–90), the English prison reformer, was invited by Rush to visit the United States in 1789.

agreeably to the declaration of the heir of his master. After these facts, what shall we say of an officer of high rank in the American army who sold his charger, on which he had rode during the greatest part of the Revolutionary War, for 75 dollars? This officer, I was told, was a rich man. For the honor of our country we must conceal his name.

Our excellent Revolutionary friend Mr. Clymer is, I fear, in the last stage of a disease which too generally in old people resists the power of medicine. A great mass of genius, knowledge, and patriotism, without the least portion of party spirit, will descend with him to the grave. He is one of those few citizens of the United States who admits the outrages and dreads the power of *both* France and Britain. . . .

Benjn: Rush

To RUSH

January 15, 1812 [13]

DEAR SIR,

. . . I respect your science and humanity as a veterinarian; but is there not a little "disease of the mind" in your and Howard's and Burke's enthusiasm for old horses? The weakness is amiable; but I doubt the real rational humanity of it. The old farmer's maxim is founded in more judicious experience. "If you would have an old man or an old horse good for anything, you must keep him always going, always in use." This is conformable to all my experience of man and horse. Burke's affection was not for the horse but for his son whom, from a distemper of the mind, he adored, and to whom he had hoped to transmit that *peerage* which was the object of his invariable aim and pursuit, as really as a bishopric in England was that of Dr. Swift. Would not the expense of keeping old useless horses be more humanely employed in relieving prisoners, orphans, and widows?

The old white charger is a different story. I never heard of but one charger in America, nor of more than one banqueting room. Were not both these titles given from some little lurking disease of the mind?

Your book has made it very clear and very certain that we all labor under diseases of the mind. . . . The book is in so much request among my five inquisitive females that I could not keep it, and then my neighbor Dr. Vinton, one of your ardent admirers, must have it, and he has let others read it, and I cannot get it. But I have read enough to make me tremble. . . .

I mourn for our friend Clymer.[37] With him I admit the outrages of both France and England; but I dread the power of neither. I dread nothing but the disease of the mind in my own dear beloved nation. But that must and will be cured. So wishes, so prays, so hopes, and so undoubtingly believes the same, *semper idem,*

John Adams . . .

To ADAMS

January 22, 1813

MY DEAR FRIEND,

. . . Our excellent friend Mr. Clymer is still living, but a day or two, it is expected, will close the scenes of his useful life. In one of my visits to him in the early stages of his disease, he put a few lines of poetry into my hands, of which the following is a copy:

> At first the affair of *Chesapeake.*
> Hull sorely did our Yankees pique.
> For then the honor of the nation,
> Stood foremost in their estimation;
> Indeed so valued they that prize,
> E'en codfish to't they'd sacrifice.
> But as things often change about,
> And patriotism may wear out,
> So let them now put both in scale
> And see which of them would prevail.
> I dare to say, tho' strange it seem,
> *Codfish makes honor kick the beam.*

37. George Clymer died on Jan. 24, 1813.

... Captain William Jones, who succeeds P. Hamilton as secretary of the navy,[38] is up to the patriot of Quincy in his zeal to extend, protect, and properly employ a navy. He is a man of a bold and original mind, but well drilled for his office by a practical education as a naval officer in the Revolutionary War and as a sea captain and merchant ever since the war. A letter from you I am sure would animate him to carry his plans for rendering the United States a naval power into execution. ...

Benjn: Rush

To RUSH

January 29, 1813

DEAR SIR,

... Our brother Clymer is pretty severe upon us, but whose flour, tobacco, and cotton "makes honor kick the beam"? I hope the penitent saint will be forgiven his anti-Novanglianism! But that is a prejudice, a distemper of the mind, a contagious one, too, with which the Quakers, the Irish, and the Scotch and the whole body of Presbyterians have infected the souls of every man, woman, and child in Pennsylvania, your own pure, philosophical, and Christian soul not excepted. ...

But to return to sober sense. Your character of the Honorable William Jones, Esqr., the new Secretary of the Navy, gives me great and sincere pleasure. I shall probably have occasion to write to him on several occasions, for I am determined not to be bashful in recommending men of merit whom I know, but in whom I have no personal interest. ...

As to your book, you must give it and all your other writings, as Lord Bacon did, "to your country after a few generations are overpassed."[39] No early and active agent in the Revolution ever was or ever will be forgiven till

38. William Jones (1760–1831) succeeded Paul Hamilton (1762–1816) on Jan. 12, 1813, and served for nearly two years. In 1816 he became first president of the second United States Bank.

39. Adams may have taken his quotation from Bacon's last will: "I bequeath my soul and body into the hands of God. ... For my name and memory, I leave it to men's charitable speeches, and to foreign nations, and the next ages." *The Works of Francis Bacon,* ed. James Spedding et al. (London, 1857–74), XIV, 539.

all the early and active enemies of it and their children and disciples are dead, if then. I always knew it and expected it.

Our seamen continue to act like themselves; but I can never cease to lament the twelve years' neglect of them. . . .

John Adams

To ADAMS

February 8, 1813

MY DEAR SIR,

. . . You do me great injustice in supposing I possess a single Pennsylvania or anti-New England prejudice. I know my native state too well. It is a great exchange filled with men of all nations who feel no attachments to each other from the ties of birth, education, and religion, and who from that circumstance are incapable of a *state* character. From that small number of our citizens with whom ancient English blood and the principles of our ancestors *ought* to have united me, my whig principles and conduct have *wholly* separated me. Had it not been for what are called newcomers and strangers, I could not have retained my standing in Philadelphia. With a few exceptions they have been my most steady personal and professional friends.

Before the Revolution we had two aristocracies in our city—the Friends[40] and the officers of the proprietary government. For more than 60 years they were enemies to each other, but the Revolution united them. They are now all-powerful in all our monied institutions except one, in our Library, Hospital, and University, and possess universal professional, mercantile, maritime, and mechanical patronage. The principles which produced their union must necessarily lead them to expatriate a man who subscribed the Declaration of Independence. In the city of London or Constantinople I should not feel myself more a foreigner than I do in the city of Philadelphia. I do not mention these facts as matters of complaint, but

40. Rush generally uses the word "Quaker" instead of "Friends" when writing of the religious organization. Here he is obviously satirizing their political practices.

to convince you how little disposed I am to absolve my Pennsylvania fellow citizens from the charges you have made against them. There have been times when I have been ready to say of my native state what Dr. Swift said of Ireland, "I am not of this vile country." . . . But these times have been transient in their duration, and the hectic produced by them has soon passed away. . . .

Benjn: Rush

To RUSH

February 21, 1813

DEAR SIR,

I beg your pardon for hinting, tho' in jest, at any anti-Novanglian prejudice. I do believe you as free from it as you ought to be or as I am. Dearly as I love New England, I know it and its faults.

Your idea of Pennsylvania is perfect. In a few days you will see that I have been reviewing an old scene. In 1775, you will see how the Committee on Trade and on a Navy struggled. Debates, delays, embarrassments, perplexities. In 1774 and 1775 when Congress first met, the delegates from South Carolina were as patriotic, ardent, bold, and resolute as those of Massachusetts. Indeed, their constituents were so. But the moment they arrived in Philadelphia, they were besieged and surrounded with Quakers, Proprietarians, and Anglomanes. . . .

When armed ships came in question, you can hardly imagine the opposition. My zealous efforts to promote a naval force were the most decisive and obnoxious proof of my design at independence. We could carry votes but by small majorities. Consider who were there. Mr. Duane, Mr. Dickinson, Mr. Willing, Mr. William Livingston, &c., &c., &c., even my own colleagues, Mr. Paine, Mr. Cushing, were opposed to me. Mr. Hancock was president and was silent. After the business was established, he became ambitious of stealing the glory of it—of the naval armament! South Carolina were perverted by your Quakers and Proprietarians. Ned Rutledge was the most earnest, the most zealous, the most flippant and fluent of all the opposers.[41] . . . Gadsden, however, was faithful found, immovable as a rock, stable as the mountains. Such men are born for the public, not for themselves. But Rutledges, Middletons, and even Lynch flinched![42]

"They are now all powerful in all our monied institutions, except one, in our libraries, hospital, and university, and possess universal professional, mercantile, maritime, and mechanical patronage." These are your words applied to Philadelphia and Pennsylvania. You may apply the same words with the same truth to Boston and Massachusetts. . . .

I have no idolatry for politicians or warriors. Who would not prefer Hippocrates to Alexander or Demosthenes? Every discovery, invention, or improvement in science, especially medical science, is lasting. Political and military glories transient as the wind. Solon and Lycurgus have passed away, and what good have they done? It would be republican blasphemy to say that Pisistratus, the tyrant, did more good than both. Yet history would countenance a doubt.

Alas! Defeat after defeat. I hope these defeats will teach us the necessity of system, subordination, discipline, and obedience! That the entire prosperity of every state depends on the discipline of its armies! by sea and land. Our naval conquerors have proved this to the immortal glory of our nation. Boyd alone has behaved like a soldier, I mean at Tippecanoe![43] . . .

John Adams

41. Edward Rutledge (1749–1800) opposed, at first successfully, Adams' suggestion that American sea captains be turned loose to prey upon British shipping, but when Washington requested naval help Congress appointed a committee, composed of Langdon, Deane, and Adams, and its report eventually led to the establishment of the Revolutionary navy. See Page Smith, *John Adams* (Garden City, N.Y., 1962), I, 217–218.

42. Though a delegate from Rhode Island proposed the creation of a navy, Adams himself was enthusiastic about the idea from the beginning of congressional debate. His letter to James Warren, Oct. 19, 1775, clearly shows his feelings: "What Think you of an American Fleet? I don't Mean 100 ships of the Line, by a Fleet, but . . . any naval Force consisting of several Vessells. . . . The Expence would be very great—true. But the Expence might be born." *Warren-Adams Letters,* ed. Worthington Chauncey Ford, Vol. I, Massachusetts Historical Society Collections, Vol. LXXII (Boston, 1917), 145.

43. John Parker Boyd (1764–1830), Massachusetts-born soldier of fortune, fought for the East India Company and the Indian princes and then, upon his return to America, joined the 4th Infantry as colonel. He served with W. H. Harrison in the Battle of Tippecanoe in 1811 and held several commands along the Canadian frontier during the War of 1812.

To ADAMS

February 15, 1813

MY DEAR FRIEND,

I am now attending a daughter of Mr. Mathew Carey's. In one of my visits to her, I mentioned your opinions to him upon the subject of a navy and your documents upon the subject of its origin in the United States. He requested a sight and copies of your letters containing those opinions and documents for a publication which he expects shortly to issue from his press. I said I could not comply with his request without your consent. Should you yield to his wishes, I will take care to furnish him with nothing unconnected with the subject of the navy. Perhaps you would prefer dilating those subjects into a sheet or two of paper and addressing them to Mr. Carey from under your own hand. . . .

The defeat of General Winchester has produced, it is said, a great deal of sensation at Washington. "We must command the navigation and possess the dominion of the ocean," says Great Britain. "We must have no hostile nation contiguous to us," says Bonaparte, and "We must have the navigation and empire of the lakes, and tolerate no hostile province near to us," say the United States. One of the prophets speaks of the "nations being drunk."[44] Which of the above three nations exhibits the strongest signs of intoxication? . . .

Benjn: Rush

To RUSH

February 23, 1813

MY FRIEND,

I lose no time in answering your letter of the 15th that my confidence in your love to your country, the rectitude of your judgment as well as your intentions, and your personal friendship to me is so entire that you are at liberty to make what use you judge for the public good, of my name and my

44. Jeremiah 51:7.

letters. Personal and local and state reflections and allusions, in which I have indulged myself to you without reserve and almost without limits, you will of course suppress. . . .

There is no intoxication, my friend, in the foresight of the *tumble bug*. There is none in the foresight of the necessity of the dominion of the lakes. . . . They are of infinite importance to the middle and southern states. Without them there can be no security against the Indians, to say no more.

Winchester's defeat is a dreadful affair to Kentucky, Ohio, and all of us. But you and I and our contemporaries have no right to reproach the present government or the present generation. We blundered at Lexington, at Bunker's Hill, [etc.]. . . . Where, indeed, did we not blunder except Saratoga and York, where our triumphs redeemed all former disgraces? My heart bleeds for the frontiers and much more for the unfeeling insensibility which too much prevails in this quarter. ARE WE ONE NATION OR 18? Yours six times,

John Adams

To ADAMS

March 16, 1813

MY DEAR SIR,

. . . The documents you sent me relative to the origin of the American navy are now in the hands of Mr. Carey, who is heartily disposed to do ample justice to the early, uniform, and zealous advocate of that important part of the defense and honor of our nation.

I have spent 4 hours in the day since Thursday sennight in examinating candidates for degrees, and expect to spend the same number of hours in the same dull, mechanical, and fatiguing business for more than a week to come. This employment has reduced the hours I usually devoted to your instructing and delightful correspondence. Oh! worse and worst—*omnia in pejus ruunt.*[45] The blunders, disasters, and disgraces of 1774 and 1775 and 1776 are poor apologies for similar events in 1812 and 1813.

---

45. "Everything is rushing to deterioration"—an obvious play on Rush's name. Cf. Virgil, *Georgics* I.199–200.

Count Saxe says three things are requisite to make a general, viz., courage, genius, and *health*.[46] Three of our generals are above *sixty*, a time of life in which the employments inseparable from a camp and military duty seldom fail of deranging the body and mind. Each of those generals has been laid up with sickness since their appointment, and two of them nearly in sight of the enemy.

Alas! the abortive issue of the new loan! I possess notes of a speech you made in Baltimore upon the question of raising the interest to be given by Congress upon money from 4 to 6 per cent. Richard Henry Lee opposed it—you defended it. Your words were, "Unless, Mr. President, we accommodate our measures to the *interest* of the Tories as well as the feelings of the Whigs, we shall never be able to govern this country." I wish this aphorism were inscribed over the doors of both houses of the present legislature of the United States. Yours . . . ,

Benjn: Rush

To RUSH

March 23, 1813

MY DEAR FRIEND,

. . . For mercy's sake don't let Mr. Carey see my ribaldry about Mr. Tompson [Thorndike], nor my oath about the committee of Deane, Langdon, and Adams. Pray tell me what work Mr. Carey is about publishing. Do not let him see any of my nonsense. If you or he can find any sense, you are welcome to that.

Give yourself no concern to answer my letters. Your employments are better and more important. I cannot bear to hear that examination of candidates is a dull employment. The honor to your country and the everlasting benefit to this nation ought to render the fatigue itself sweet and delightful. Your pupils will transmit science to theirs, to the latest generation.

The tories are determined to destroy the country, as the Jacobins and to-

46. Count Hermann Maurice de Saxe (1696–1750), natural son of Augustus II of Saxony, was made marshal of France for his exploits in the War of the Austrian Succession. His *Mes Rêveries* (1757) is a classic discussion on the art of war.

ries, too, were in 1800, by stopping the wheels of government. If the good were not to be ruined with the evil, I would not much regret it. But no angel will warn Lot out of town. Indeed, where can he go? He must sink or swim with the government and nation with all the faults of both.

It is a lamentable thing that so little of the talent and experience in war which remains in the country has been called into service. Yours *ut supra,*

John Adams

To ADAMS

April 10, 1813

MY DEAR FRIEND,

I put the papers you sent me into the hands of Mr. Carey. Some of them will be published in an appendix to his history of the rise and progress of the American navy. . . .

I rejoice with you in the 5th naval victory of our country.[47] The year 1812 will, I hope, be immortal in the history of the world for having given the first check to the overgrown power and tyranny of Britain and France. Russia and the United States may now be hailed as the deliverers of the human race. . . .

Is the present a war for the liberty of the ocean between Britain and the United States, or for the power of the Union between the southern and eastern states? It is, alas! conducted and opposed as if this were the case.

My son Ben returned to us last week by the way of New York in good health and fine spirits, much pleased with his voyages and grateful for his escapes from the plague in Smyrna, from Algerine pirates and British cruisers, as well as from the dangers of the sea. His details of what he has seen and heard form every day the pleasantest part of the repast of our table.[48]

Adieu! my dear old friend. Yours truly,

Benjn: Rush

47. Rush is undoubtedly referring to the victory of the *Hornet* over the *Peacock* on Feb. 24, 1813.

48. Benjamin Rush, Jr. (1791–1824), tenth child and sixth son, was apprenticed to a Philadelphia merchant and traveled widely in conducting his employer's business.

P.S. Knowing that my time is short and that the night of imbecility of mind or of death is fast approaching, I have sat down to prepare two small tracts for the press which have long been called for by my pupils. One of them will contain the outlines or elements of my specific opinions in medicine as far as they relate to the nature of diseases. It will be accommodated to *all* classes of readers.

To RUSH

April 18, 1813

DEAR RUSH,

I thank you for the slip of a newspaper. On that subject my feelings are unutterable. The day of the safe return of my son and his family, if I should live to see it, will be the happiest day of my life. I almost envy you the joy on the return of your Benjamin. Thank him for my Samos muscat. Tell him my girls shall all drink his health in a bumper of it. I wish my sons and grandsons had been to Samos instead of losing their lives and labors as their father and grandfather did in diplomatic dullness, where knaves find fortunes and honest men ruin.

In Edes's *Gazette,* printed in Watertown, November 13, 1775, is a copy of "An act for encouraging the fixing out of armed vessels to defend the seacoast of America and for creating a court to try and condemn all vessels that shall be found infesting the same." [49] If Mr. Carey will print this law, . . . I will send him a copy of it, tho' made at the expense of my worn eyes and trembling fingers. . . .

I think it one of the most curious, interesting, and important documents in the history of the world. It is the first ray of Aurora. It is the commencement of an epoch in the history of mankind. It is the beginning of a system which is to produce a revolution on this globe. It is to destroy the despotism of Great Britain; the universal government of Great Britain; the

---

49. Benjamin Edes and John Gill took over the Boston *Gazette* in 1755 and changed its title to the *Boston-Gazette and Country Journal.* It became the newspaper of the Patriot faction and was published from Watertown when Boston was besieged. Except for the substitution of "creating" for "erecting," Adams' citation of the act's title is correct.

universal empire of Great Britain over the ocean and consequently over the globe. Not indeed to produce a revolution in the empire of the ocean in favor of America nor substitute one despotism in the place of another, but to annihilate all domination at sea and establish a universal and perpetual liberty for all nations, neutral and belligerent, on that element. . . .

Your time will be well applied in preparing your two tracts for the press. Posterity will do you justice.

"Sons will blush their fathers were your foes."[50]

So wishes and so believes, without a doubt, one who is and who was and who will be your friend.

John Adams

50. Alexander Pope, "An Essay on Man," Epistle IV, line 388.

CHAPTER 12

Posterity Pays Its Debt

DURING FEBRUARY, MARCH, AND APRIL, 1813, Benjamin Rush was thinking about the effect of climate, diet, and habit on the health of human beings and planning a treatise. He found time also to advise the trustees of the University of Pennsylvania about the need of required lectures on natural philosophy and midwifery. And he wrote Thomas Jefferson that the year 1812 would be memorable for witnessing the first checks to the power of France and Great Britain on land and sea. He again referred to Adams and the correspondence he was cultivating between the former Presidents. Until the very end he was busy with projects and correspondence. News of Rush's death on April 18, therefore, came as a shock to his friends.

To MRS. RUSH

April 24, 1813

DEAR MADAM,

Yesterday morning hoping to receive a letter from your husband, the messenger brought me a letter from Dr. Waterhouse with the melancholy, the afflicting account of his death. There is not a man out of my own family remaining in the world in whom I had so much confidence, for whom I had so tender an affection, and whose friendship was so essential to my happiness. My loss and my sensibility of it can bear no proportion, however, to yours. . . . Most sincerely do I sympathize with you and your family under this severe dispensation of Providence. The worth of this dear departed friend, his talents, his virtues, his services to his country and to mankind are

308

far beyond my powers to describe. They are fortunately recorded in his imperishable works.

For himself he had lived long enough. Not a doubt can be entertained for a moment of his present felicity. He has left you, Madam, for your consolation sons and daughters worthy of him and of you, ornaments to their family and their country. I pray you, Madam, to present to each of them my cordial condolence and best wishes for their prosperity.

The lot of humanity cannot be changed or avoided. Inevitable misfortunes must be borne and ought to be welcomed as the result of wisdom and benevolence intended for our ultimate benefit. So believes and so in this instance prays, Dear Madam, your sincere friend and obliged servant,

John Adams

To JAMES RUSH

April 28, 1813

MY DEAR SIR,

I received yesterday your obliging favor of the 21st and was sensibly affected by your early attention to me in communicating immediate intelligence of an event so deeply afflictive to you and your amiable family. . . . When I read again the last letter your father wrote to me and the last I wrote to him and remark the gravity of the former and the levity of the latter—I could not refrain from tears. Though he expressed a consciousness of his age, he had no apprehension of so sudden a termination of his life, for he proposes to prepare for the press a considerable medical work. This work, my young friend, I hope you will not suffer to be lost to mankind.

To me this loss is irreparable. I shall never find another correspondent in whom I can have the confidence inspired by eight and thirty years of unchangeable friendship. In such cases I know of no consolation but the philosophy and the religion which teach us that every adversity, every calamity, every affliction is a blessing intended for our good and demanding our gratitude instead of our complaints. My friend has left sons and daughters who inherit his talents and virtues, to every one of whom I can only say *Macte virtute patris.*[1]

John Adams

Adams announced Rush's death to Jefferson on May 29, and then, in a reply to Jefferson on June 11, he recovered sufficiently from his sorrow to write: "I lament with you the loss of Rush. I know of no Character living or dead, who has done more real good in America."[2]

For Rush, posterity now would fix his proper place in history. The sons would judge whether the autobiography, the letters, and the projected edition of his works would be published. Adams would occasionally write letters to the sons, but he turned primarily now to that correspondence with Jefferson encouraged so insistently by Rush. In the next decade the frequent letters of these former Presidents became a magnificent monument to Rush's foresight and patriotism, one of the unique correspondences of history.

Adams died on July 4, 1826, the same day Jefferson died. Their names were tied together in numerous funeral observances. Edward Everett, in *An Address Delivered at Charlestown* (Boston, 1826), noted that "contemporary and successive generations of men will disappear. . . , the Tribes of America, like those of Greece and Rome, may pass away. . . . The fabric of American Freedom, like all things human . . . may crumble into dust. But the cause in which these our Fathers shone is immortal." Timothy Ford, in his *Eulogy on John Adams* (Charleston, 1826), observed that the "desire for posthumous fame is an affection purely intellectual—standing in close connexion with the immortality of the soul."

At various times in life Adams accused Jefferson, Hancock, and Hamilton of stealing his right to fame. Adams feared that posterity would be permanently hoodwinked by the "puffers" and idolaters and would be unable to discern fact from fancy. His fears had been partly justified even before his death by the flood of literature immortalizing Washington. Biographies by

1. "Hail to your father's virtue."
2. Lester J. Cappon, *The Adams-Jefferson Letters* (Chapel Hill, 1959), II, 328.

Parson Weems and John Marshall were taking all the blood from Washington's veins and pulling him heavenward, and popular imagination was doing the rest. Rush hesitated to say anything about Washington's imperfections even in his own home and trembled over the possibility of the letters falling into hostile hands. Unlike Rush, Adams did not abandon hope that one day they would be given proper credit for what they did for the nation. He kept his letters and Rush's, too, and conducted correspondence with many people, offering interpretations of events and evaluating the characters of his associates. Admittedly he assumed a tremendous risk, because future generations would label his opinions as jealousy and the rantings of an old man, but he was certain that some day posterity would do them justice.

The families of both men saved their fathers' letters. The Adamses gave John a careful ten-volume selection of his letters and essays in the 1850's, and his son and grandson wrote a biography that was published as a volume of the papers. The biography, revised and corrected, was published in two volumes in 1871 and was the standard biography until Gilbert Chinard published his *Honest John Adams* in 1933. Over the years, of course, there were other studies and biographies, and Adams' name was always prominent among the founders of the republic. In contrast, however, the letters and works of Washington and Franklin were the subject of many editions. Washington in 1932 was honored by a national celebration of the two hundred years since his birth, and multivolume accounts of his life and an unprecedented publication of his letters marked the event. The anniversary of Adams' birth in 1935 passed almost unnoticed; even Chinard's excellent biography was overshadowed by a biography of Thomas Jefferson. Adams remained a figure obscured by time.

By the 1950's, however, new interest in Adams had arisen, stimulated partly by the penetrating studies of Zoltan Haraszti, Stephen G. Kurtz, and Bradford Perkins and partly by the opening of the Adams papers to scholars.[3] This vast collection of manuscripts, long closed to most researchers,

3. Haraszti, *John Adams & the Prophets of Progress* (Cambridge, Mass., 1952); Kurtz, *The Presidency of John Adams; the Collapse of Federalism, 1795–1800* (Philadelphia, 1957); Perkins, *The First Rapprochement: England and the United States 1795–1805* (Philadelphia, 1955).

was made available by means of microfilm, and the Adams Manuscript Trust announced plans to publish most of the papers. By the middle 1960's Adams' diaries and family letters had appeared, as well as a Pulitzer Prize-winning two-volume biography by Page Smith[4] and a provocative reanalysis of Adams' thought by Edward Handler entitled *America and Europe in the Political Thought of John Adams*.[5] It is not an exaggeration to say that in the past fifteen years more works on Adams have been produced and more interest created than in the preceding one hundred twenty-five years.

Like his friend Adams, Benjamin Rush was "discovered" recently by historians. In 1934 Nathan G. Goodman published the first full-length biography;[6] then John H. Powell, in his *Bring Out Your Dead* (Philadelphia, 1949), told the story of the yellow-fever epidemic of 1793 and Rush's part as a medical doctor; and finally George W. Corner edited Rush's *Autobiography* in 1948. It was left to Lyman H. Butterfield in 1951, however, to edit the first major collection of Rush's papers. Like Adams, Rush has grown in stature since 1951, his name and opinions appearing frequently in articles and books on the Revolution and the new nation.

If posterity has not yet done them justice, the approaching celebration of the two-hundredth anniversary of the American Revolution will afford an opportunity for the rediscovery of the importance of Adams and Rush as national heroes.

4. *John Adams* (Garden City, N.Y., 1962).
5. Cambridge, Mass., 1964.
6. *Benjamin Rush: Physician and Citizen, 1746–1813* (Philadelphia, 1934).

Index

classical languages and literature, 9, 180,
182, 183, 184–87, 191–94
Clay, Henry, 249
Clinton, George, 120, 281
Clymer, George, 131, 141, 278, 296, 297
Cobbett, William, 10, 15, 65, 181, 222
Cockle, James, 280
Colbert, Jean Baptiste, 100
Coleman, William, 239
Coles, Edward, 216
Coles, John, 216
Committee for Foreign Affairs, 41 n
Committee of Secret Correspondence, 39,
41
Common Sense (Paine), 12, 88, 96, 164
Condorcet, Marie Jean Caritat, Marquis de,
68, 70 n, 71
constitutions: American, 2, 60–61 n, 72,
117, 118, 119–20, 152 n; British, 2; democ-
racy and, 72; Massachusetts, 14, 152 n,
157–58; Pennsylvania, 220
Continental Congress: Adams in, 6 n, 11, 13;
Rush and, 12
Conway, Thomas, 227
Cooper, Thomas, 208
Copley, John Singleton, 236
Corner, George W., 312
Cowper, William, 57 n
Coxe, Tench, 116
Cranch, Richard, 96
Cumberland, Richard, 61
Curran, John Philpot, 183
currency, 50–51, 190, 197, 210
Cushing, Nathan, 292
Cushing, Thomas, 158, 182, 204
Cuthbert, Ross, 21 n

d'Alby, Antoine Sartine, Count, 159
Dana, Francis, 174
"Dangers of American Liberty, The"
(Ames), 189
Danton, Georges Jacques, 29
Davies, Samuel, 107
Dayton, Jonathan, 47
Deane, Silas, 291
Dearborn, Henry, 268
Decatur, Stephen, 282

Declaration of Independence: Adams on,
197, 198; Rush on, 198, 234; signing, 198
*Defence of the Constitutions of Government of
the United States of America* (Adams), 14–
15, 72 n, 152 n, 189, 241, 243
democracy: Adams on, 20, 26 n, 27, 55–56,
72; compared to an epidemic, 20; con-
stitutions and, 72; human nature and,
71–72
Democratic Party, 132, 265–66, 271
Dickenson, John, 234
Diderot, Denis, 67 n, 138
Diodati, Count, 155
"Discourses on Davila" (Adams), 8, 189, 222
disinterestedness, 100–105, 106, 208
Don Quixote, 22, 115, 154 n, 264 n
Dryden, John, 110
Duane, William, 40, 213, 214
Duer, William, 36
Dumouriez, Charles François du Perier, 126
Dwight, Timothy, 285

Early, Peter, 59
Eaton, William, 81
Eden, William, 140
Edes, Benjamin, 306
Edinburgh Review, The, 188
education: Adams on, 210; Bacon on, 17;
classics, 9, 180, 182, 183, 184–87, 191–94;
oration, 69; Rush on, 82 n, 104–5, 206
elections: of 1800, 16–17, 40, 147 n; of 1808,
122, 131; of 1812, 265; Burr, 245; Jefferson,
245; presidential, 245
eloquence, 211
Embargo Act of 1807, 112, 113, 116, 119, 121,
123, 124, 133, 135, 139, 145, 240
embassies, 150, 174
empires, 87–88, 96–97, 185–86
England: Adams in, 14–15; compared to
France, 250–51; despotism, 306–7; Embargo, 113, 139 n; government, 130, 264;
influence on U.S., 30, 121, 140; liberty,
266; Napoleon Bonaparte and, 126; naval
power, 109, 126, 167; religion, 266; South
America, 60; treaty of 1783, 14; war as
possibility, 234–35, 238
envy, 96

Smith, William Stephens, 35, 60, 204, 236
Snyder, Simon, 27, 138
Socrates, 129
Sons of Liberty, 156 n
South, Robert, 67
South America, 60, 65
Spartacus, 205, 293
Stamp Act, 11, 277
Stephen, Adam, 224
Sterne, Laurence, 256 n, 283
Steuben, Friedrich von, 227
Stockton, Hannah, 61 n
Stockton, Richard, 31
Stoics, 70
Strong, Caleb, 101 n
suffrage, 28, 206, 210
Sulley, Maximilien de Béthune, Duc de, 46, 83–84, 84 n, 96, 100
Sullivan, John, 226
Swift, Jonathan: on Ireland, 93; "Ladies Dressing Room, The," 123; leapfrog, 120; stolen words, 105; *Tale of a Tub,* 74 n, 75
Sydenham, Thomas, 20, 168

Tacitus, 120
Talleyrand-Périgord, Charles Maurice, 59–60
Tamerlane the Great (Timur Bec), 185
taxes, 77, 249, 264 n
Télémaque (Fénelon), 188
Thomson, Charles, 184, 228
Thorndike, Israel, 290
Thou, Jacques Auguste de (Thuanus), 64, 106 n, 165
Thoughts on Government: Applicable to the Present State of the American Colonies (Adams), 13, 157, 212 n
Tilghman, Tench, 228
Tippecanoe, 301
titles. *See* aristocracy/monarchy
Tories: Adams on, 304–5; of Boston, 196; funding system and, 33; Hamilton and, 33, 34–35; Jefferson and Madison and, 239; size of party, 234; Washington and, 33, 35
trade: Adams on, 77; Embargo Act of 1807, 112, 113, 116, 119, 121, 123, 124,

133, 135, 139, 145, 240; England, 139; France, 139; "Plan of 1776," 41 n; quarantine law, 32; shipping, 113, 115; War of 1812 and, 238
tranquilizers, 186
treasury, 9–10, 36, 43, 212
trial by jury, 154
Trumbull, Jonathan, 16
Twisse, William, 270
tyrants, 186–87, 189

United States: Adams' dream of, 282–85; Adams on War of 1812, 269–70; Adams speculating on fate of, 55; alliances between states, 147; arts and science transferred to, 96–97; "bebanked, bewhiskied, bedollared nation," 247, 248; compared to Adams' horse "Hobby," 283, 284, 286, 289; divided by different interests, 276; "for sale," 255; independence of western states, 81, 82–83, 84, 86; materialism, 114, 237; money *vs.* liberty, 114; national character, 32, 58, 59–60; patriotism, deserving of, 117; population growth, 87–88; power transferred to, 87–88, 96–97; Rome, compared to, 46; Rush on, 179, 247, 255, 277; strength of the union, 109, 277; wealth, 111, 117–19, 120–21
United States Gazette, 222

vanity, 96
Van Rensselaer, Stephen, 268
Vergennes, Charles Gravier, Count de, 159
Virginia, 110, 215
Voltaire, François Marie Arouet de, 136
voting, 28, 69, 206, 210, 245, 253

Walpole, Horace, 33 n
Walpole, Sir Robert, 33
war (*see also* American Revolution): Adams on, 40, 41, 122, 149–50; alternatives to, 78; civil war, 85–86; consequences, 76–77; crimes, 149; Embargo as substitute for, 139 n; human nature and, 240–42, 249, 254; Jefferson and, 72; liberty and, 249; as obligatory, 254; preparing for, 135;

This book is set in Adobe Garamond. Robert Slimbach modeled his design of Claude Garamond's type on sixteenth-century original manuscripts. The companion italic was drawn from the types of Robert Granjon, a contemporary of Garamond.

This book is printed on paper that is acid-free and meets the requirements of the American National Standard for Permanence of Paper for Printed Library Materials, z39.48-1992. ∞

Book design by Louise OFarrell,
Gainesville, Florida
Typography by G & S Typesetters, Inc.,
Austin, Texas
Printed and bound by Worzalla Publishing Company,
Stevens Point, Wisconsin